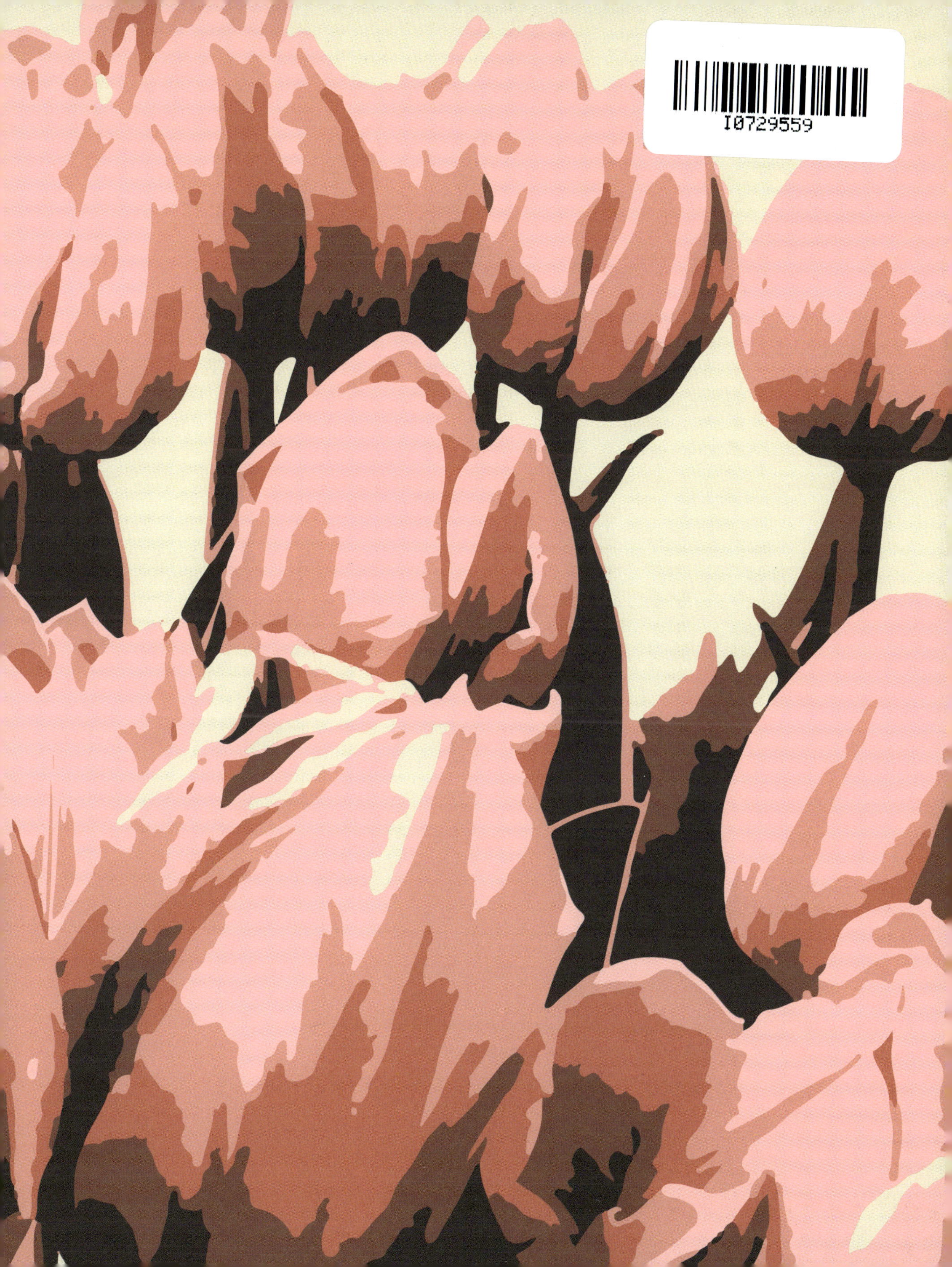
I0729559

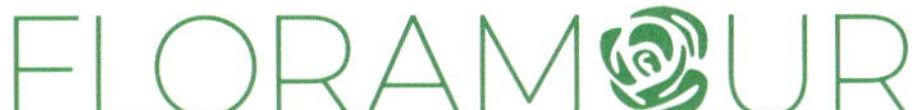

KARIN GREINER & SIMONE BRAUN

TULIPS
TULPEN

teNeues

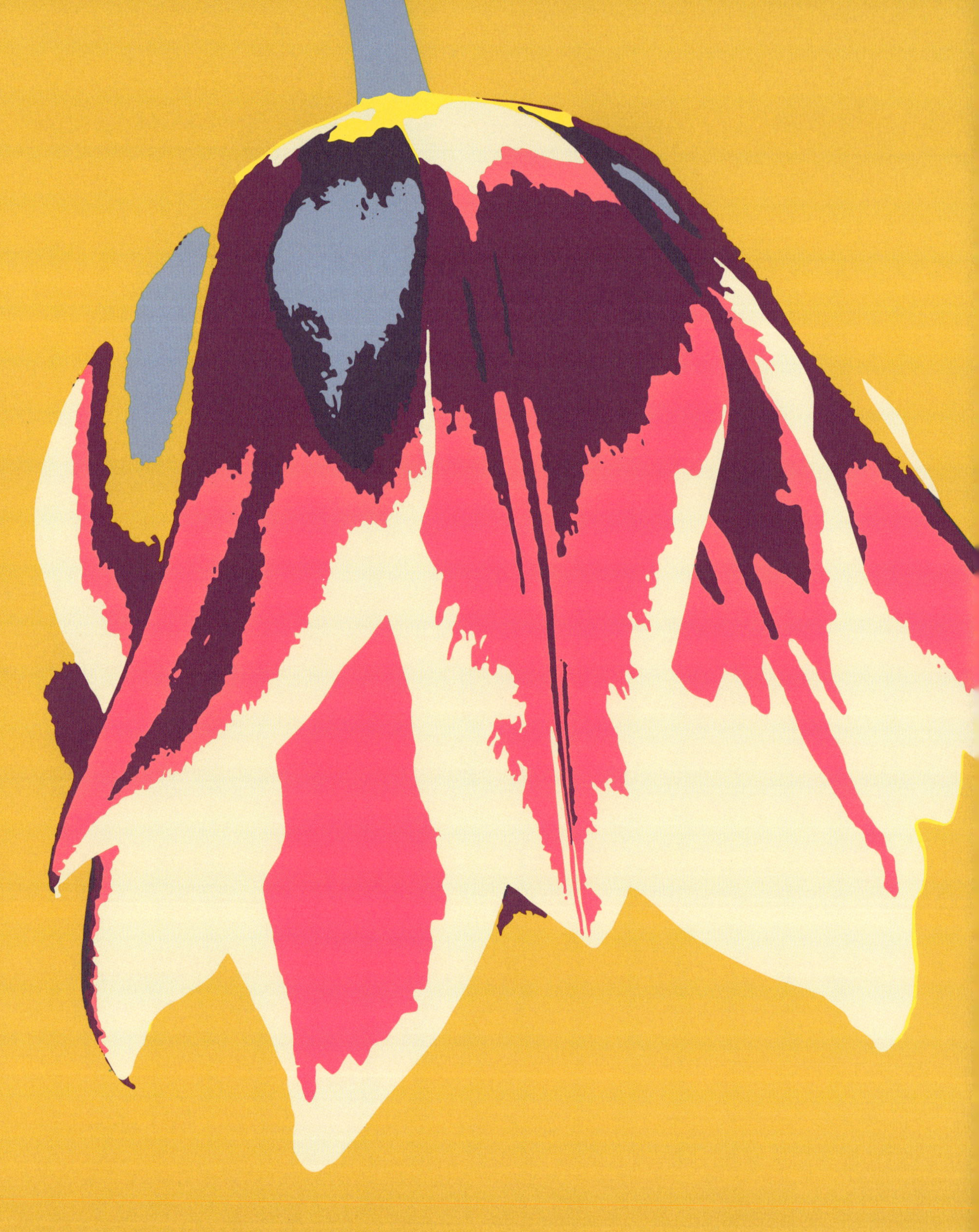

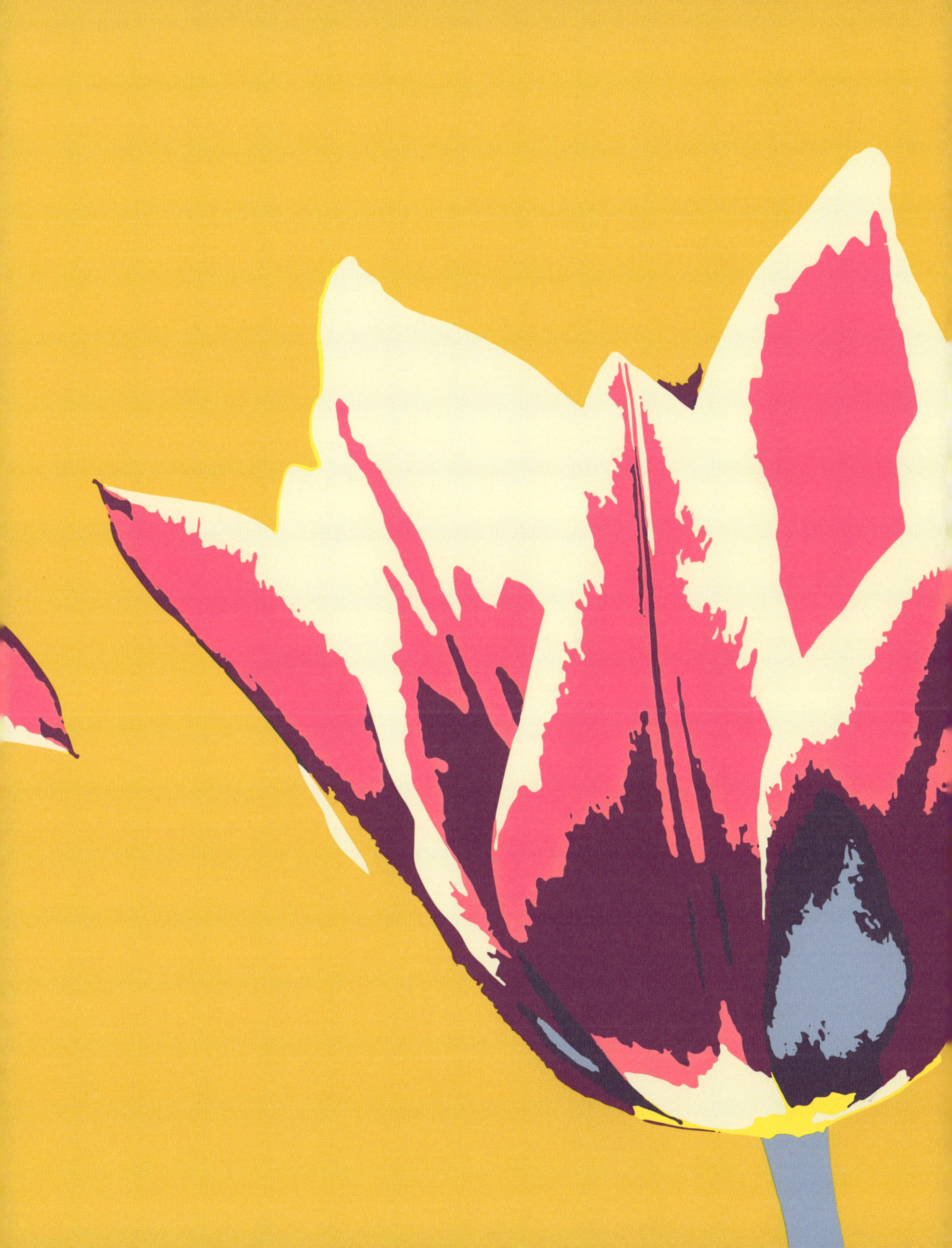

CONTENT
INHALT

CONTENT | INHALT

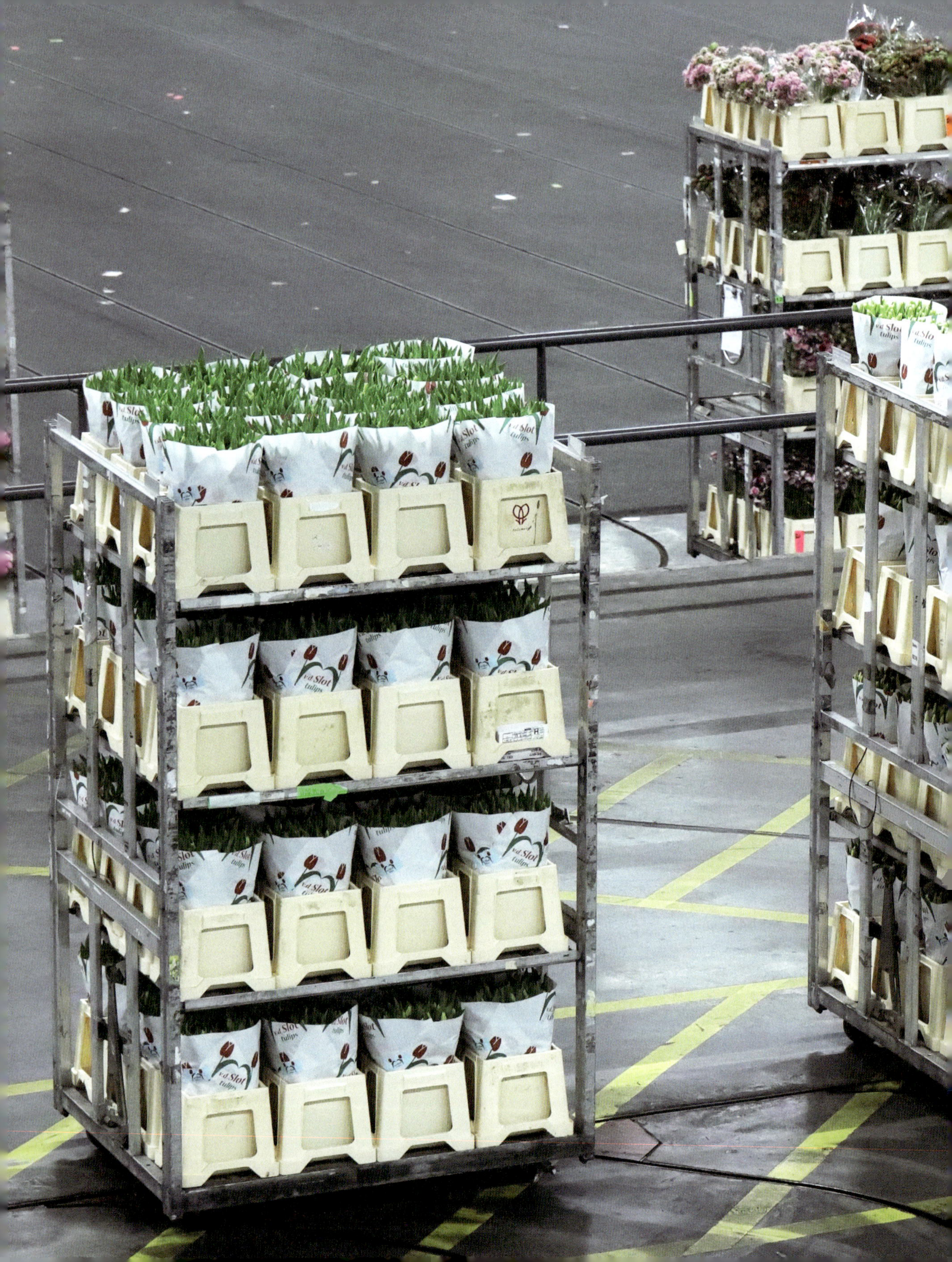

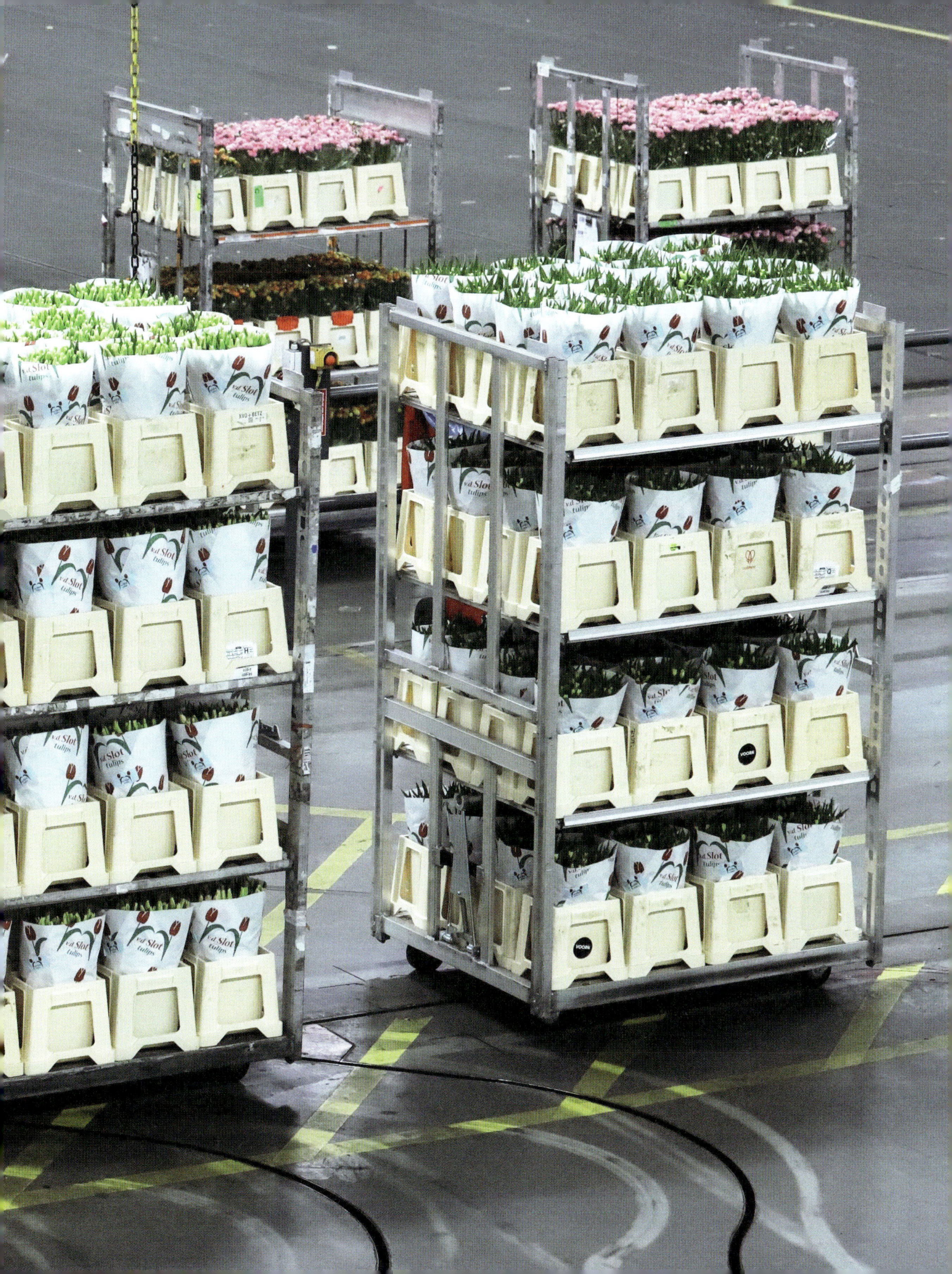

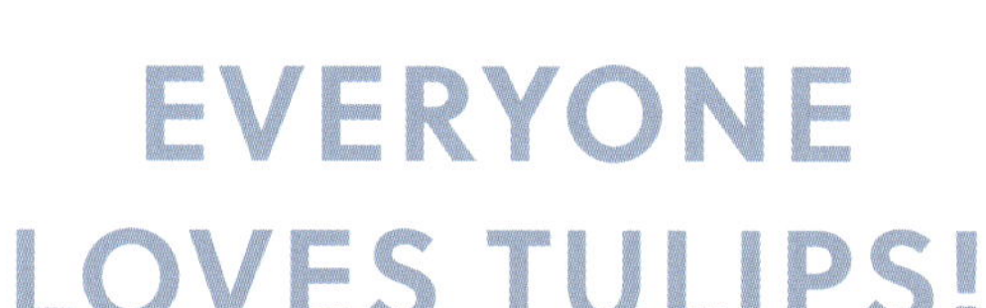

EVERYONE LOVES TULIPS!

The rose is considered the queen of flowers. What rank, then, shall we award the tulip? In the *Giardino di Primavera*, the Garden of Spring, tulips are clearly the ladies at court. Even though their fragrance is unremarkable and they only achieve any kind of notable effect in large groups, you cannot help but notice them as you pass. The secret to their dazzling appearance is their magnificent flower heads.

Yet has the tulip's beauty sealed its fate? Its spectacular bud, which takes on ever-new forms and colors, has made it a status symbol, the object of speculative trade, and a firm favorite among cut flowers. Its fame must be rooted in more than just a flowery spectacle; surely, the fact that all this beauty unfolds from an unremarkable bulb that lies hidden beneath the earth for the best part of the year must have contributed to its popularity.

"I love tulips better than any other spring flower; they are the embodiment of alert cheerfulness and tidy grace, and next to a hyacinth look like a wholesome, freshly tubbed young girl beside a stout lady whose every movement weighs down the air with patchouli." This passionate statement comes from the British writer and garden enthusiast Elizabeth von Arnim (1866–1941).

Now, allow yourself to be enchanted, too!

Karin Greiner and Simone Braun

ALLE LIEBEN TULPEN!

Rosen gelten als die Königinnen der Blumen. Welcher Rang gebührt dann den Tulpen? Ganz klar, die Rolle der wahren Ladys im *Giardino di Primavera*, dem Frühlingsgarten. Keiner kann achtlos an ihnen vorübergehen, obwohl sie nicht duften und nur in der Gruppe richtig Eindruck machen. Der Glanz ihrer Erscheinung liegt eindeutig in ihren herrlichen Blüten.

Ist ihre Schönheit ihr Schicksal? Tulpen wären sicher nicht zu Statussymbolen, zu Spekulationsobjekten, zu Schnittblumenlieblingen geworden, wenn sie nicht so aufsehenerregende Blüten in immer neuen Formen und Farben hätten. Doch das blumige Spektakel kann nicht allein den Ruhm der Zwiebelgewächse begründet haben. Sicher trägt auch dazu bei, dass die Blütenwunder innerhalb kürzester Zeit aus unscheinbaren Organen hervorgehen, die die meiste Zeit des Jahres verborgen unter der Erde verharren.

„Ich liebe Tulpen mehr als jede andere Frühlingsblume; sie sind die Verkörperung wacher Fröhlichkeit und ordentlicher Anmut, und neben einer Hyazinthe sehen sie aus wie ein gesundes, frisch gebadetes junges Mädchen neben einer stämmigen Dame, deren jede Bewegung die Luft mit Patchouli beschwert." So begeistert äußerte sich die britische Schriftstellerin und Gartenfreundin Elizabeth von Arnim (1866–1941).

Geraten Sie doch auch ins Schwärmen!

Karin Greiner und Simone Braun

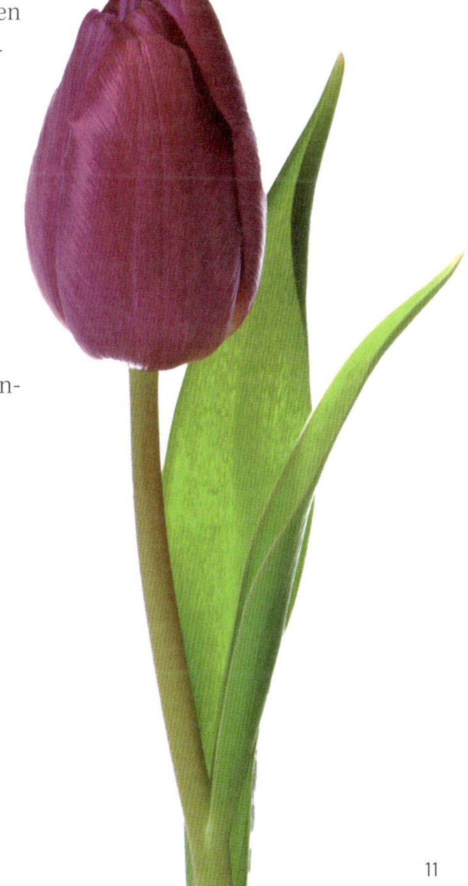

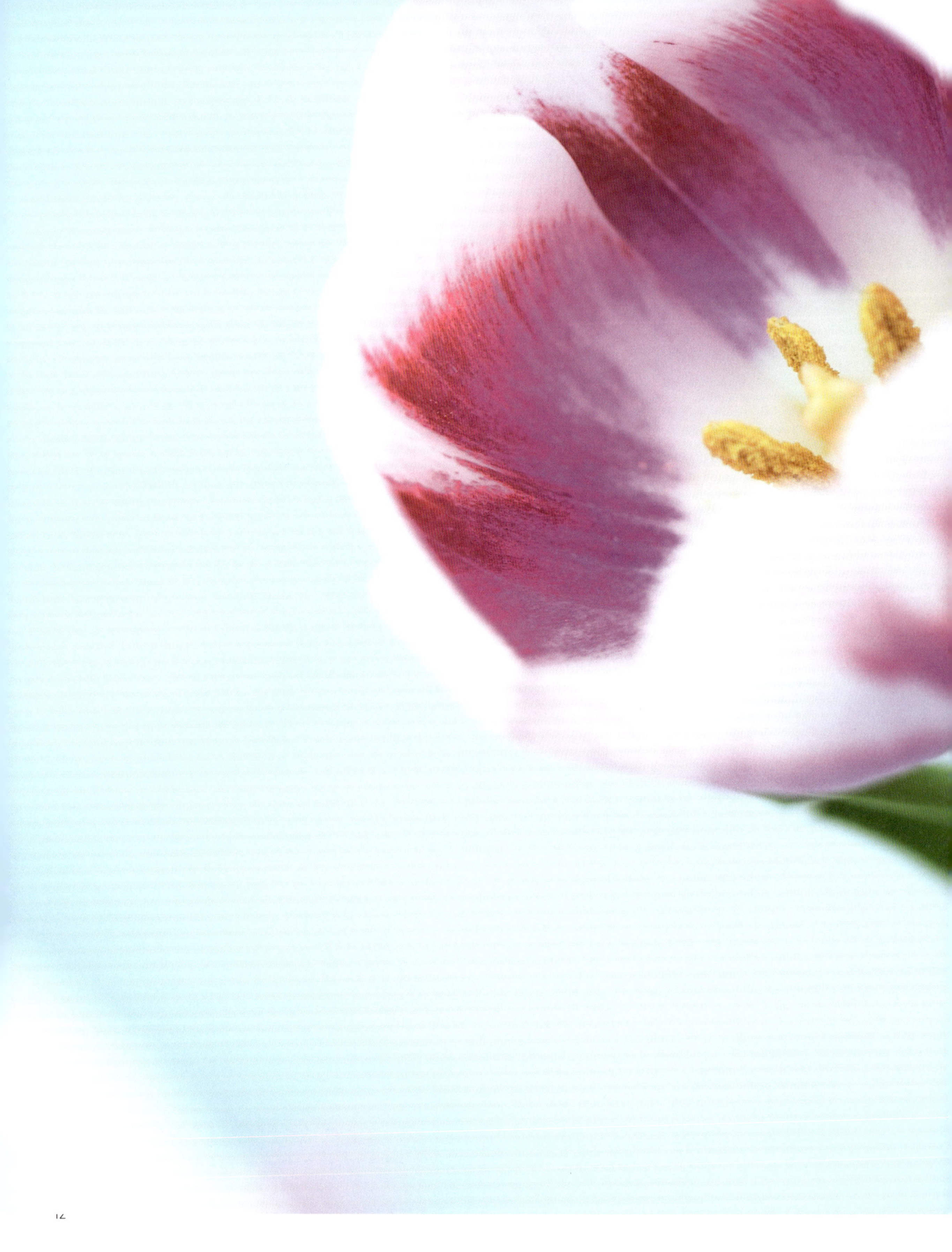

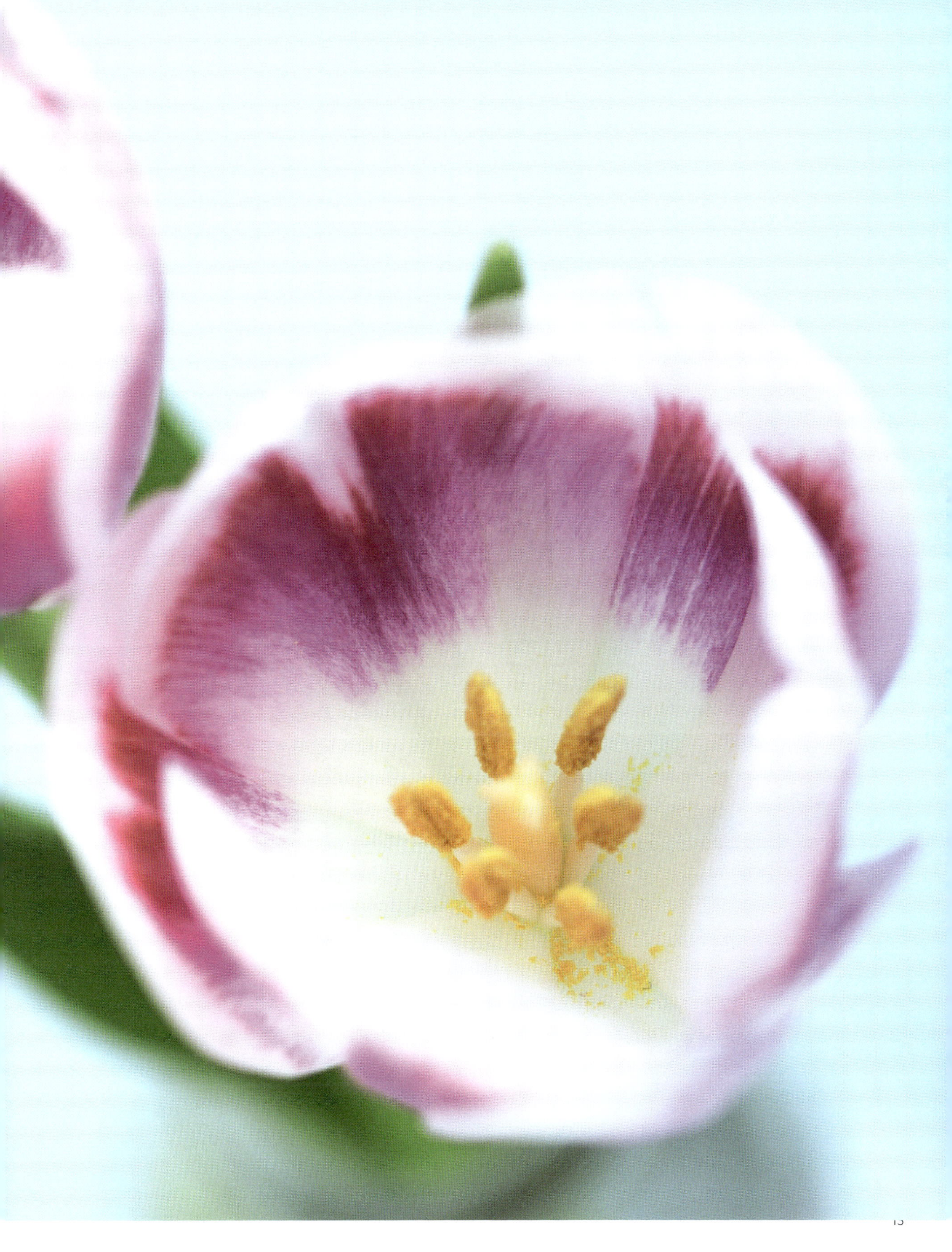

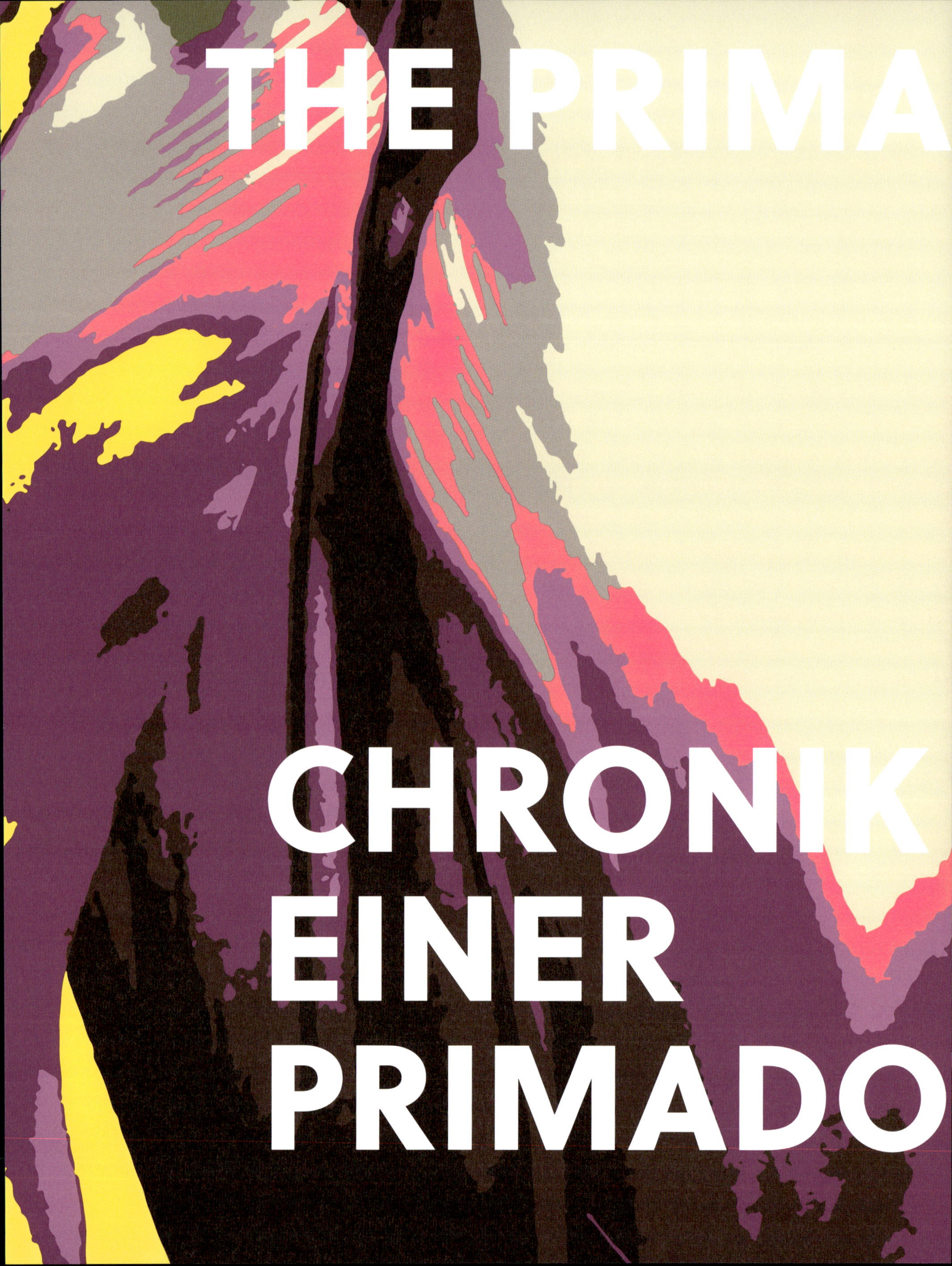

THE PRIMA
CHRONIK
EINER
PRIMADO

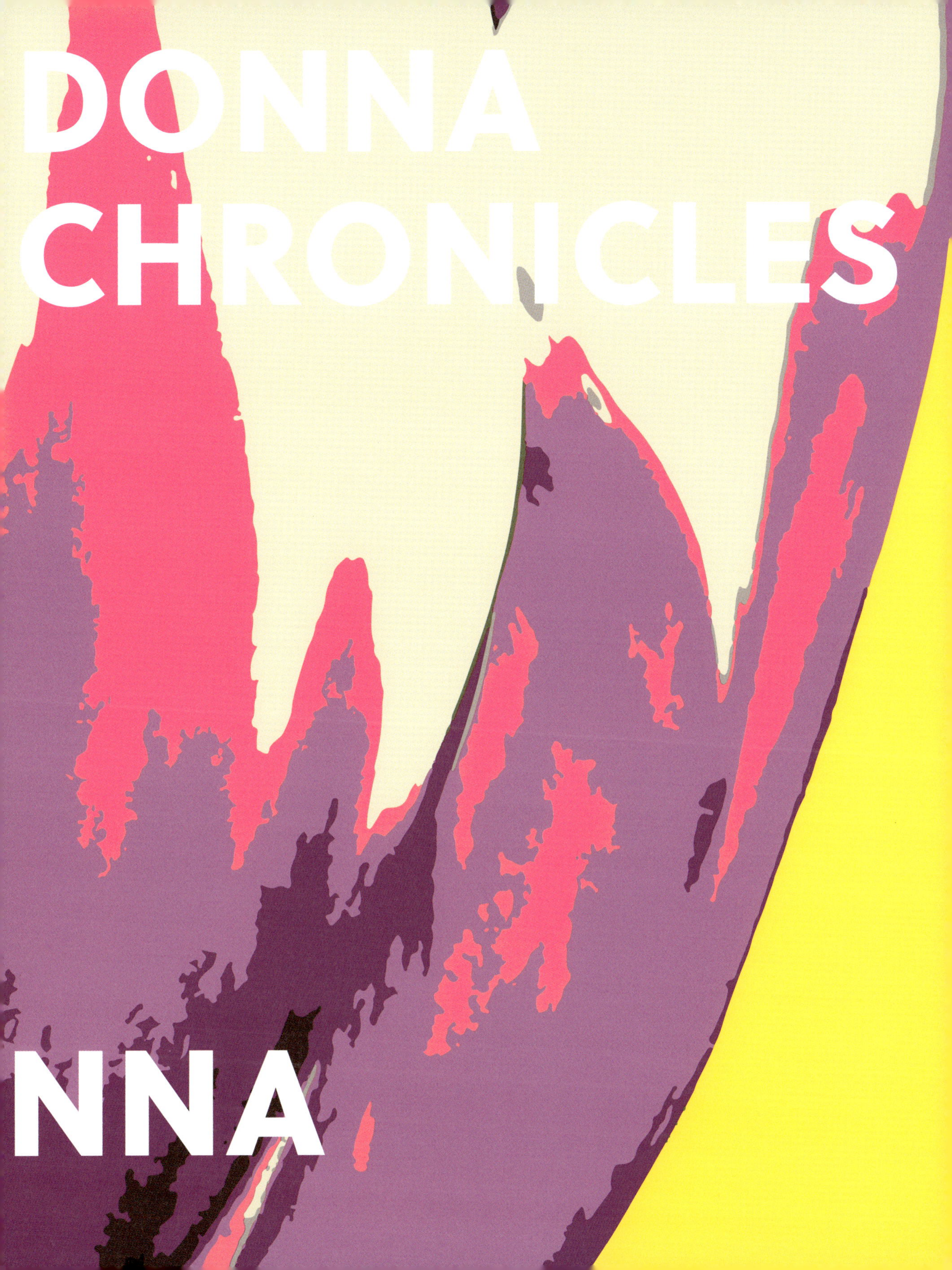
DONNA
CHRONICLES
NNA

Short-lived splendor

VANITAS: FLOWER OF TRANSIENCE

TULIPS OFFER A GRAND, BUT BRIEF SPECTACLE— FORTUNATELY, IT ALWAYS RETURNS

Tulips seem to appear out of nowhere in spring. Green buds bloom into brightly shimmering chalices or colorful bowls. They open in the morning and close in the evening. Then, after just a few days, the magnificent petals wither away and drop—a morbid yet elegant display. Soon, the green leaves also fade, and the plant withdraws back beneath the earth, where it lingers, resting inside a bulb in Morpheus' arms.

Similar to cherry blossoms in Japan, tulips symbolize not only the beauty of life but also its transience. Hope rests in their green leaves and in the underground bulbs. Just as we know that tulips will bloom every spring, we trust life itself to move in a constant circle of resurrection and renewal.

According to a Persian legend, tulips first sprung from the blood of a desperate young man. He took his own life when he was misled to believe that his beloved had been killed. Where his blood gathered on the earth, a tulip sprouted. Thus, blood-red tulips are considered symbols of eternal and unconditional love. Later, tulips were seen to represent chastity because they close their blossoms in what appears to be modesty. However, like life itself, love is fleeting, and modesty cannot last forever ...

Volle Pracht für kurze Zeit

VANITAS: BLUME DER VERGÄNGLICHKEIT

TULPEN BIETEN EIN GRANDIOSES, ABER KURZES SCHAUSPIEL – EIN GLÜCK, DASS ES IMMER WIEDERKEHRT

Scheinbar aus dem Nichts tauchen Tulpen im Frühling auf. Grüne Knospen erblühen zu bunt schillernden Kelchen oder farbenprächtigen Schalen. Öffnen sich morgens, schließen sich abends. Doch es dauert nur wenige Tage, dann welken die prunkvollen Blütenblätter dahin und fallen in morbider Eleganz ab. Bald vergehen auch die grünen Blätter, zieht sich die Pflanze unter die Erde zurück. Verharrt in der Zwiebel in Morpheus' Armen.

Ähnlich wie Kirschblüten in Japan symbolisieren Tulpen deshalb die Schönheit des Lebens, aber auch dessen Vergänglichkeit. In ihren grünen Blättern wie in den unterirdischen Zwiebeln steckt die Hoffnung. Wie die Tulpe jedes Frühjahr neue Blüten bildet, so vertraut man auf Auferstehung und Erneuerung des Lebens.

Einer persischen Legende zufolge entstanden Tulpen aus dem Blut eines verzweifelten Jünglings. Er nahm sich das Leben, als er fälschlich erfahren hatte, dass seine Geliebte getötet worden sei. Wo sein Blut sich auf der Erde sammelte, wuchs eine Tulpe empor. Insbesondere blutrote Tulpen gelten seitdem als Symbole für ewige und bedingungslose Liebe. Später sah man in Tulpen mehr das Sinnbild für Keuschheit, weil sie ihre Blüten sittsam verschließen. Doch wie das Leben selbst ist auch Liebe flüchtig, und Sittsamkeit währt ebenfalls nicht ewig …

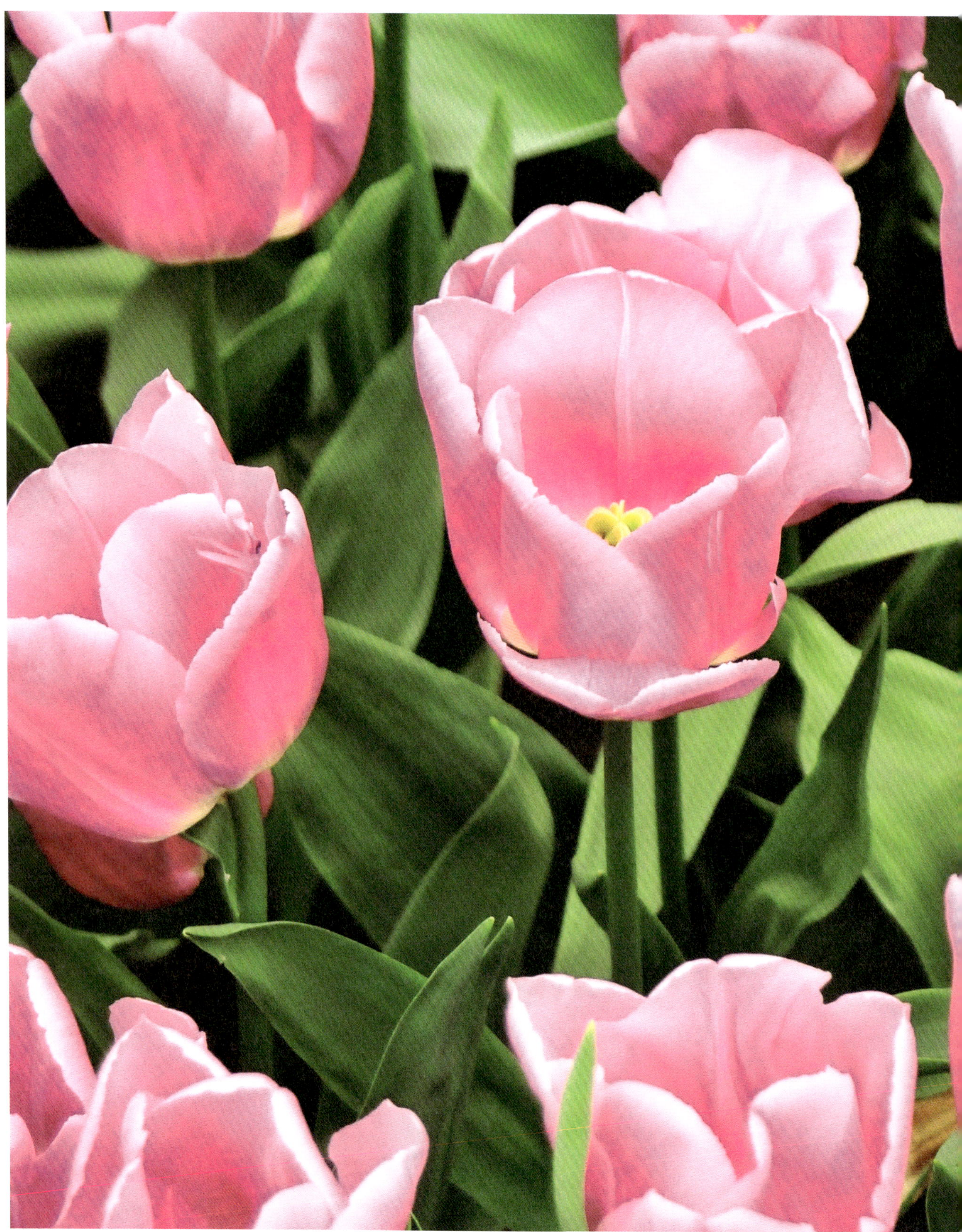

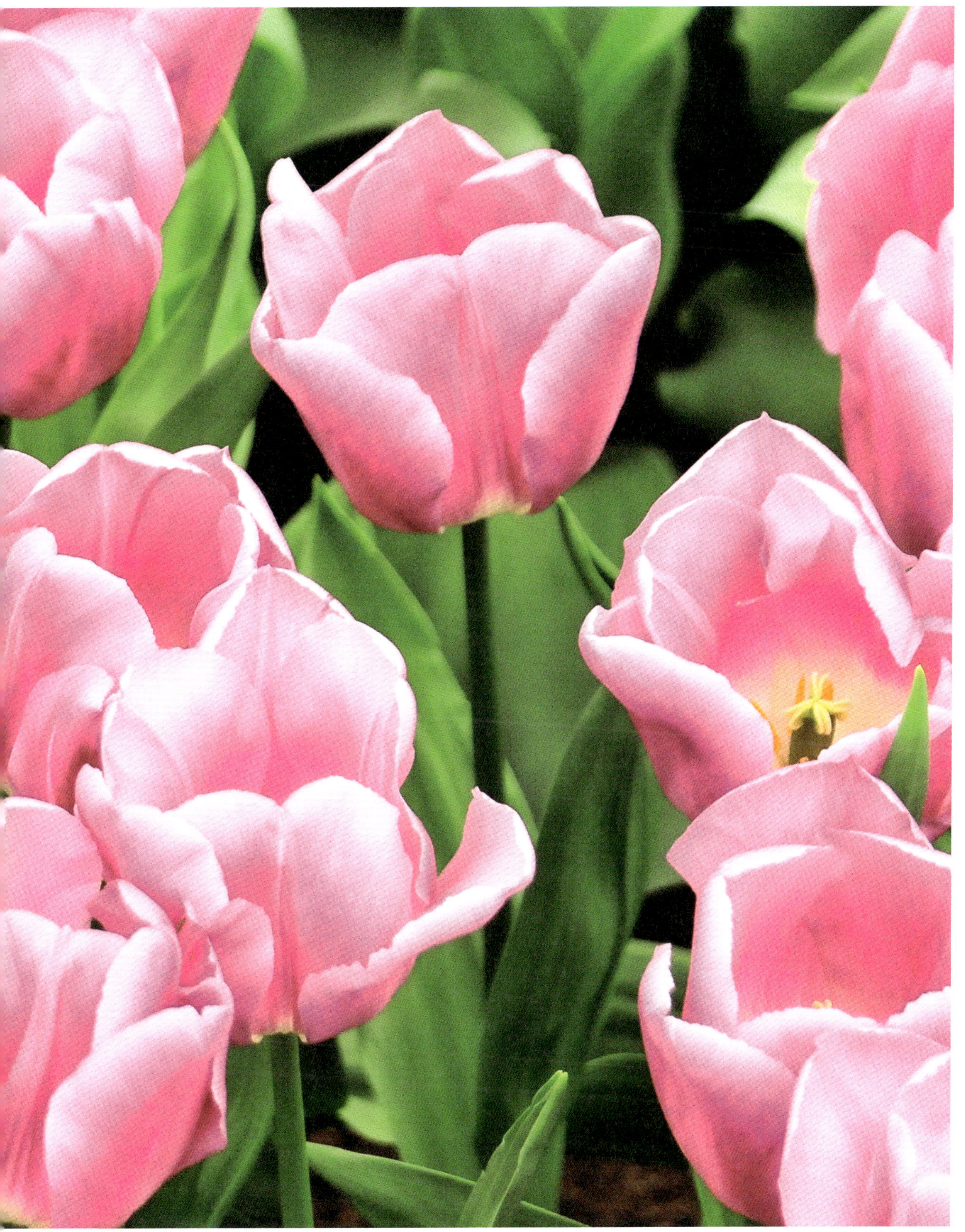

Eastern origins

ENCHANTED BLOSSOMS FROM THE ROOF OF THE WORLD

TULIPS CAME FROM HIGH-MOUNTAIN ASIA TO THE MESOPOTAMIAN PLAINS

The mountain ranges of Central Asia, one of the most inhospitable regions on Earth, are characterized by snow-covered mountains and wind-whipped plains. Icy in winter and hot in summer, they are barren and rocky. Only the daring venture to explore their sparse, treeless, and barely passable vegetation. Yet right here, before winter has fully retreated to the snow-capped summits, a miracle occurs every year in early spring: thousands of plants bloom in dazzling colors on the barren slopes. The sight of steppes and mountain slopes covered in blossoms must have enchanted everyone.

Especially vibrant red tulips would have appeared as a beacon of hope, as omens of life, and as messengers of joy in these desolate regions. It seems possible that the biblical Rose of Sharon—a flower revered and loved by all—was, in fact, a tulip, but we do not know for sure. Likewise, the exact journey of tulips from the east to the west cannot be traced.

Nomads and traders must have facilitated the spread of wild tulips beyond their native regions. Tulips were already revered in ancient times in Persia and Afghanistan, as can be seen from stylized depictions of flowers on signet rings, clothing, carpets, paintings, and reliefs from the Sasanian Empire from late antiquity until the early Middle Ages. Tulips were admired and probably cultivated in those regions. The spectacular bulbous plants then continued to spread, especially westward, to Mesopotamia, the Middle East, and as far as North Africa.

Ursprung Orient

BLÜTENZAUBER VOM DACH DER WELT

TULPEN KAMEN VON ASIATISCHEN HOCHGEBIRGEN IN DIE EBENEN DES ZWEISTROMLANDS

Das Hochland von Zentralasien, eine der unwirtlichsten Gegenden der Erde – geprägt von schneebedeckten Bergen und windgepeitschten Ebenen. Eisig im Winter, heiß im Sommer. Karg und steinig. Spärlich bewachsen, baumlos, kaum passierbar, nur von Wagemutigen erkundet. Doch eben hier, wenn sich der Winter noch gar nicht richtig auf die Höhen der Berggipfel zurückgezogen hat, vollzieht sich jedes Jahr im beginnenden Frühling ein Wunder: An den kahlen Hängen blühen abertausende Pflanzen in gleißenden Farben auf. Der Anblick von blumenübersäten Steppen und Bergflanken muss die Menschen verzaubert haben.

Vor allem leuchtend rote Tulpen wirkten in diesen trostlosen Regionen wie ein Fanal der Hoffnung, als Omen des Lebens, als Boten des Glücks. Ob es sich bei der in der Bibel erwähnten Rose von Scharon – eine Blume, die von allen geehrt und geliebt wird – um eine Tulpe gehandelt hat? Mag sein, doch genau wissen wir es nicht. Ebenso wenig lässt sich nachvollziehen, wie der genaue Weg der Tulpen aus dem Morgenland ins Abendland verlief.

Nomaden und Händler haben die Verbreitung wilder Tulpen aus den Ursprungsgebieten sicher gefördert. Schon in antiker Zeit wurden Tulpen in Persien und Afghanistan verehrt. Das beweisen stilisierte Abbildungen von Blüten auf Siegelringen, Kleidungsstücken, Teppichen, Gemälden und Reliefs des sassanidischen Reichs von der Spätantike bis ins Frühmittelalter. Tulpen wurden dort allseits bewundert und wohl auch kultiviert. Immer weiter verbreiteten sich die spektakulären Zwiebelgewächse, vor allem Richtung Westen, ins Zweistromland, nach Vorderasien und bis nach Nordafrika.

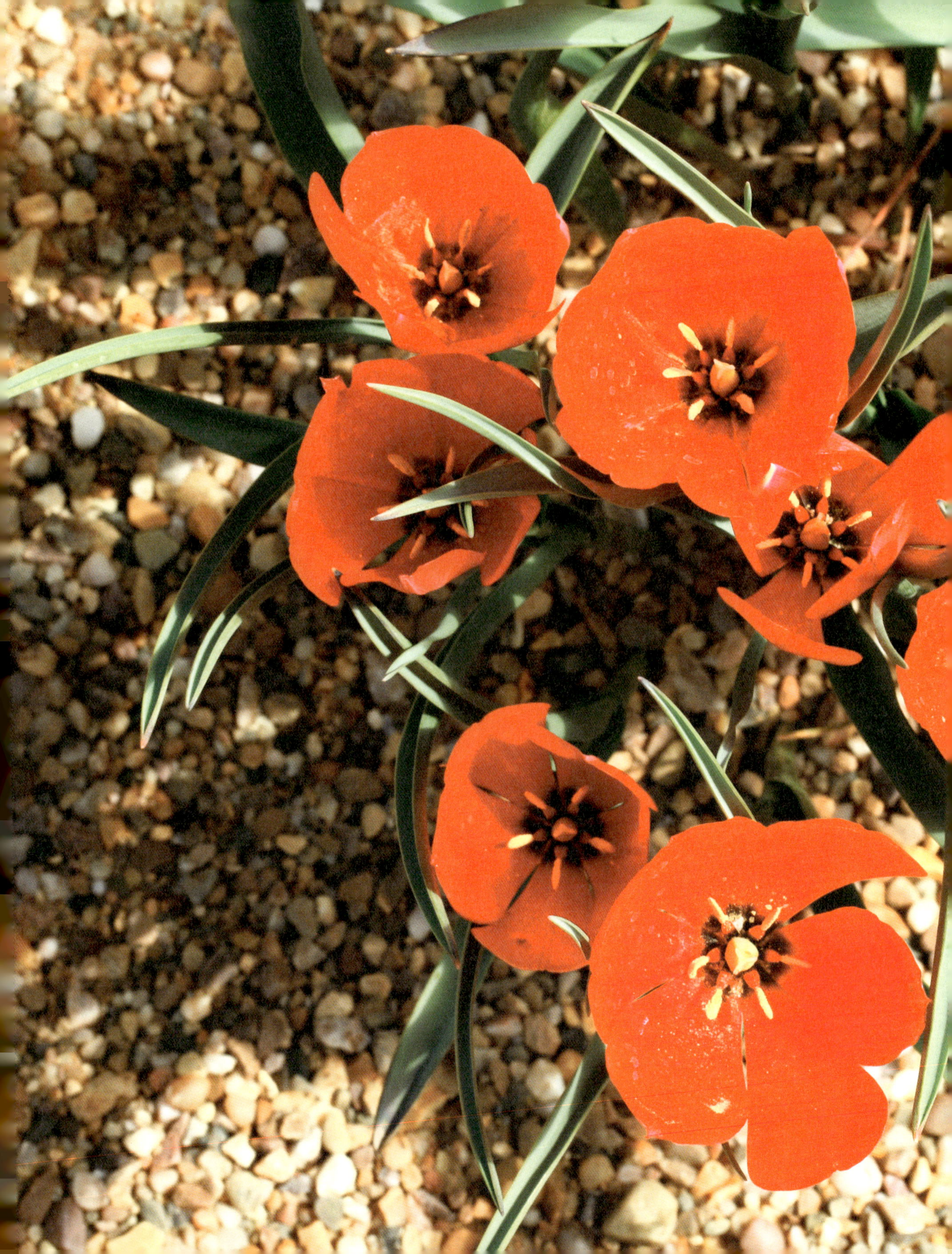

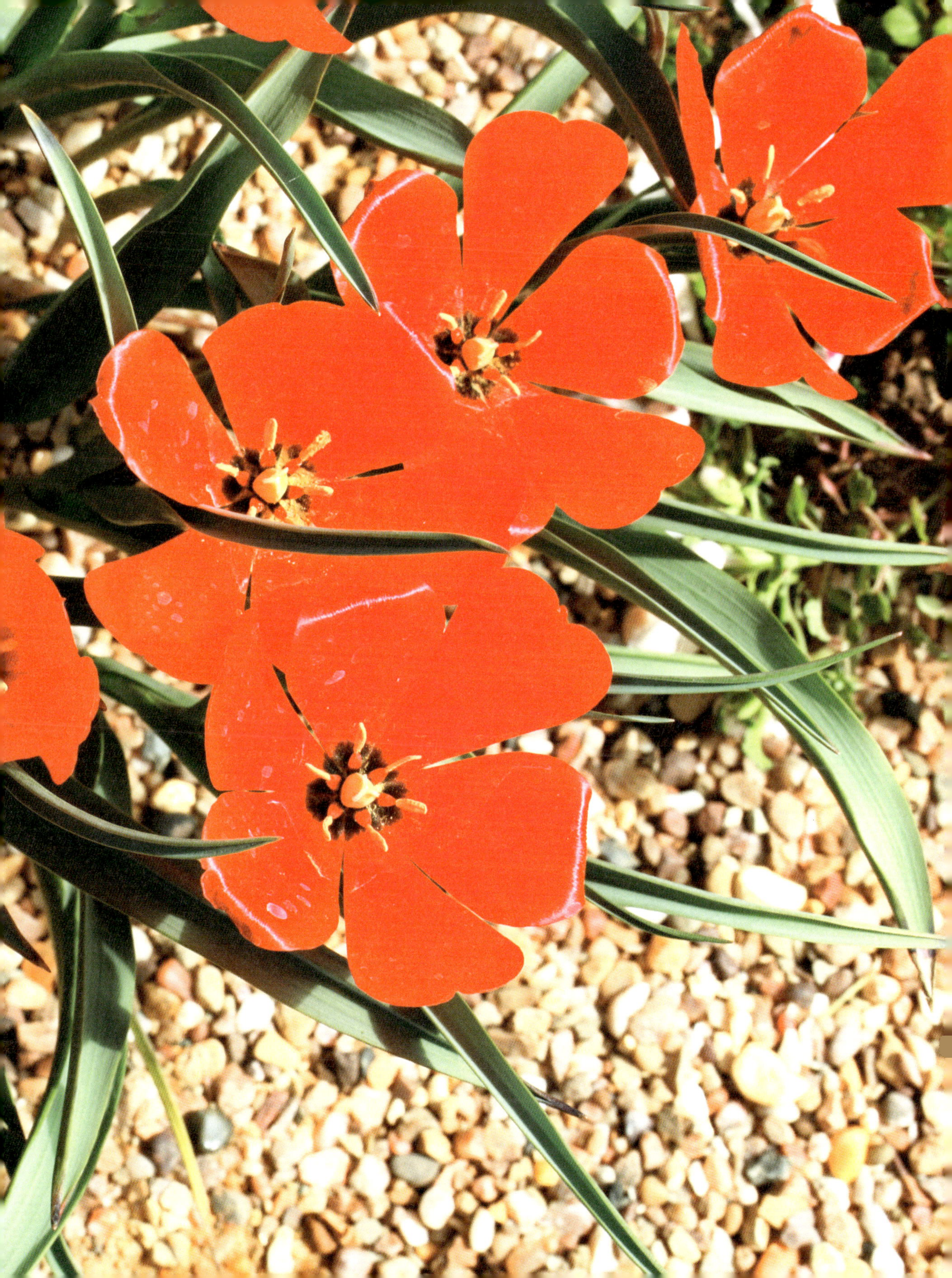

Garden ornament

CENTERPIECE IN TURKISH GARDENS

PRECIOUS FLOWERS ELEVATE YOUR PUBLIC IMAGE

In Persia, wild tulips were revered, whereas in the Ottoman Empire, cultivated tulips in gardens were seen as more desirable. During the Seljuk Empire in the Middle Ages, tulips made their way through trade routes from Isfahan to Istanbul, spreading across Anatolia and the eastern Mediterranean. In times of wealth and prestige, tulips were regarded as symbols of nobility and status; they became a firmly established insignia of Turkish grandeur.

Gartenzierde

BLICKFANG IN TÜRKISCHEN GÄRTEN

MIT DEN EDLEN BLUMEN HOB MAN DAS EIGENE IMAGE AN

Während in Persien vor allem wild wachsende Tulpen verehrt wurden, begeisterte man sich im Osmanischen Reich vielmehr für Tulpen in Gärten. Unter den Seldschuken waren Tulpen im Mittelalter über Handelsrouten von Isfahan nach Istanbul gelangt, hatten sich in Kleinasien und im östlichen Mittelmeerraum ausgebreitet. In Zeiten von Reichtum und Prestigedenken galten Tulpen als Wahrzeichen von Noblesse und Ansehen, etablierten sich als Insignien der türkischen Großmacht.

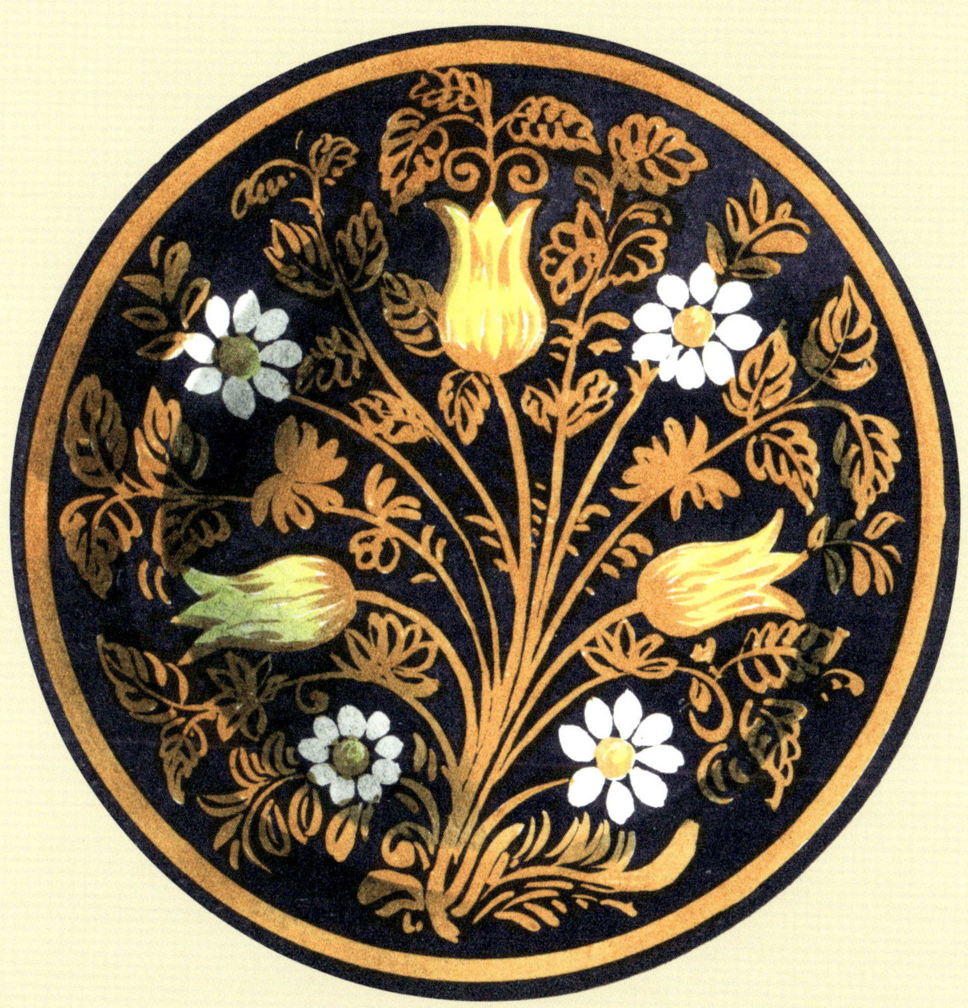

Persian ornamental plate from Nevers, France,
decorated with tulips and foliage. Hand-finished
chromolithograph by Oscar-Edmond Ris-Paquot
from his "General History of Ancient French and
Foreign Glazed Pottery", 1874

Persischer Zierteller mit Tulpen und Blättern.
Handgefertigte Chromolithographie von
Oscar-Edmond Ris-Paquot aus einem Werk
über französische und ausländische glasierte
Töpferwaren, 1874

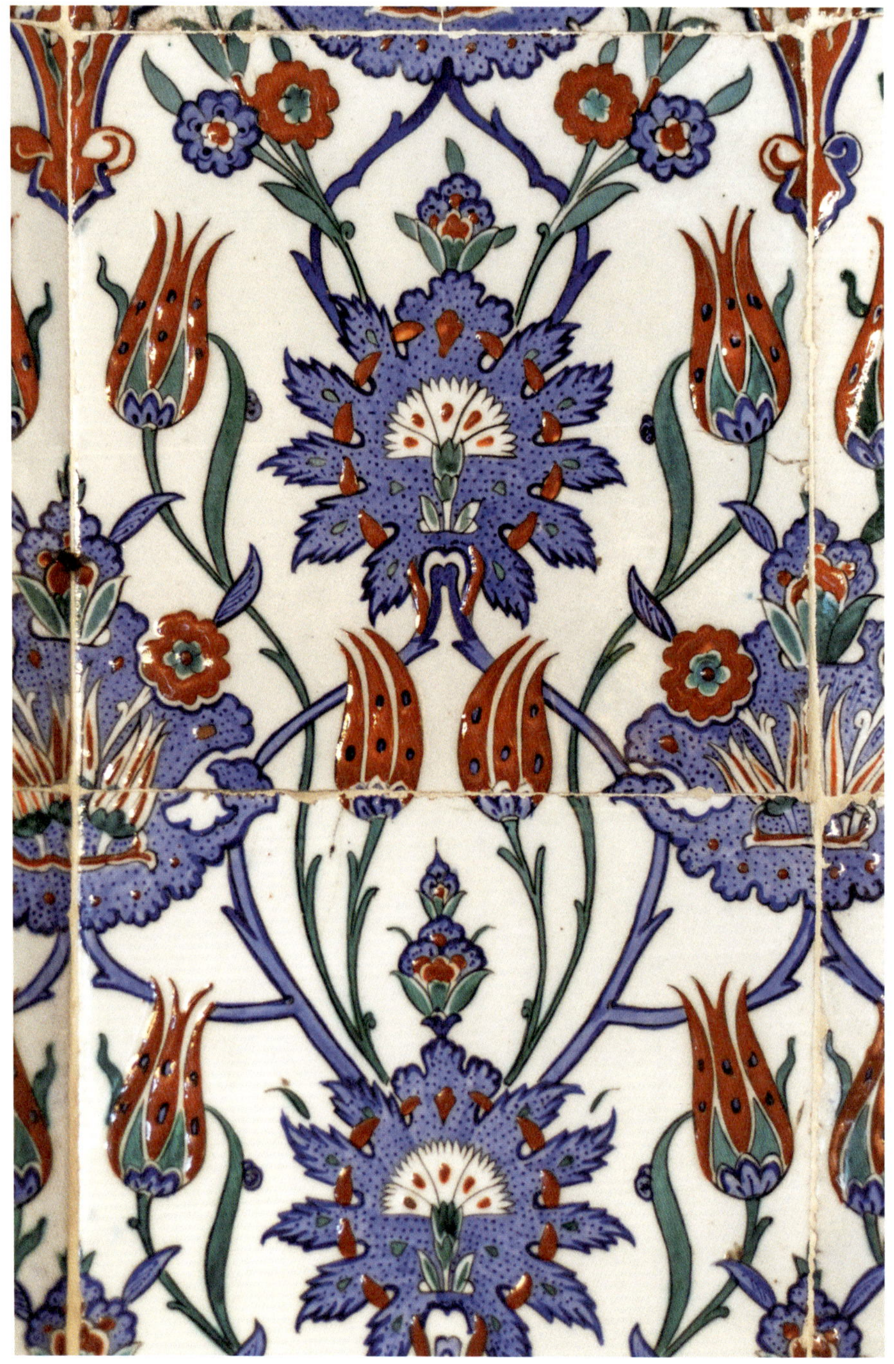

Tulip ornament inside the Takkeci İbrahim Ağa
Camii mosque in Istanbul, which was built in the
16th century

Tulpenmuster in der Takkeci İbrahim Ağa
Moschee in Istanbul. Sie wurde im
16. Jahrhundert erbaut.

Symbolism

DIVINE PERFECTION

TULIPS ARE CONSIDERED SACRED IN THE EAST DUE TO THEIR ETHEREAL BEAUTY

In the rich symbolism of the east, tulips were allegories for the divine. Due to their spiritual significance, they are deeply rooted in Turkish history and culture. The tulip is found in the Ottoman coat of arms as a symbol of life and fertile land. According to legend, a red tulip sprouted from the blood of every warrior who died for the empire. To this day, the tulip remains the national flower of Turkey.

Symbolik

GÖTTLICHE VOLLKOMMENHEIT

TULPEN GELTEN IM ORIENT MIT IHRER ÜBERIRDISCHEN SCHÖNHEIT ALS GEHEILIGT

In der reichen Symbolsprache des Orients galten Tulpen als Allegorien für das Göttliche. In ihrer spirituellen Bedeutung sind sie tief in der türkischen Geschichte und Kultur verankert. Im Wappen der Osmanen findet sich die Tulpe als Sinnbild des Lebens und der Fruchtbarkeit des Landes. Aus dem Blut jedes Kriegers, der für das Reich starb, spross eine rote Tulpe – so erzählt es eine Legende. Bis heute ist die Tulpe die Nationalblume der Türkei.

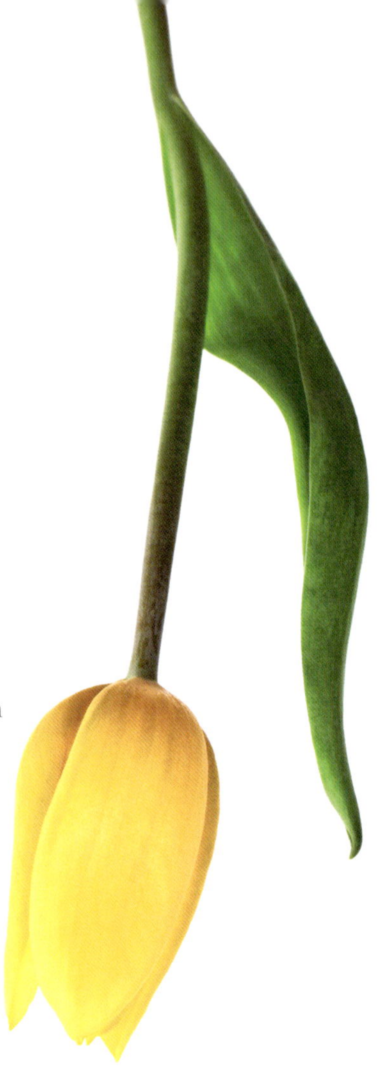

Etymology

THE NAME OF THE TULIP

ARE BLOSSOMS RESEMBLING A TURBAN THE ORIGIN OF ITS NAME?

The Persian word *delband* means "to bind the heart" and is often used to refer to one's beloved; what a charming reference for anyone presenting a bouquet of tulips!

Whether the term "tulip" can be traced back to the Turkish word *tülbent*, meaning turban cloth, is unclear. These flowers used to be very popular in the east, and people would tuck them into the folds of their turbans. At the same time, the blossoms themselves bear a resemblance to this form of headdress. Yet the desire to connect the term "turban" to the flower seems to reflect a more European perspective, perhaps even stemming from a misunderstanding.

In the 1653 hymn, *"Geh aus, mein Herz, und suche Freud"* ("Go Forth, My Heart, and Seek Joy"), the German theologian Paul Gerhardt (1607–1676) praises tulips, referring to them as "*Tulipan*, their dress so much more beautiful than Solomon's silk." In the mid-16th century, the term *Tulipan* was in use in the German language, whereas the term *Tulpe* (tulip) appeared only as late as the mid-17th century.

In its place of origin, the tulip was called *laleh* in Persian and *lale* in Turkish, both of which are popular names for women even today. In Arabic script, the name of the sultan's holy flower is composed of the same characters as the name of Allah, making *lale* a mystical symbol for the creative and life-giving power of God. The six petals represent the six articles of faith in Islam.

Etymologie

DER NAME DER TULPE

IHRE BLÜTE ÄHNELT EINEM TURBAN, DOCH IST DAS DER URSPRUNG IHRER BENENNUNG?

Das persische *delband* bedeutet so viel wie „das Herz binden" und ist bedeutungsgleich mit Geliebter/Geliebte. Was für eine passende Vorstellung, wenn man einen Tulpenstrauß überreicht!

Ob Tulpe sich auf das türkische Wort *tülbent* für Turbantuch zurückführen lässt, erscheint zweifelhaft. Man pflegte im Orient eine große Leidenschaft für die Blumen, steckte die Blüten in die Falten des Turbans. Tulpenblüten weisen aber auch selbst eine Ähnlichkeit zu dieser Kopfbedeckung auf. Die Übertragung des Begriffs Turban auf die Pflanze entspricht eher einer europäischen Sichtweise, ist vielleicht gar auf ein Missverständnis zurückzuführen.

Als „Tulipan, die ziehen sich viel schöner an als Salomonis Seide" besingt der Theologe Paul Gerhardt (1607–1676) im 1653 veröffentlichten Lied „Geh aus, mein Herz, und suche Freud" die Tulpen. „Tulipan" als Name war im deutschen Sprachgebrauch ab Mitte des 16. Jahrhunderts gebräuchlich. Die Bezeichnung Tulpe manifestierte sich im Deutschen erst Mitte des 17. Jahrhunderts.

Originär hieß die Tulpe im Persischen *Laleh*, im Türkischen *Lale*, beides heute auch als weiblicher Vorname vertraut. In der arabischen Schrift setzt sich der Name der heiligen Blume der Sultane aus denselben Zeichen zusammen wie der Name Allahs, daher gilt Lale als mystisches Symbol für die schöpferische und lebensspendende Macht Gottes. Die sechs Blütenblätter repräsentieren die sechs islamischen Glaubensbekenntnisse.

Reverence in the east

LÂLE DEVRI: THE TULIP ERA

MORE THAN A FAIRY TALE FROM ONE THOUSAND AND ONE NIGHTS

The reign of Sultan Suleiman I (1494/1495/1496–1566), known as "the Magnificent," marked the dawn of a special era. He initiated an unprecedented tulip boom, adorning his silk and brocade garments with tulip embroidery and adding the flowers to his emblem. Naturally, tulips with names such as "Light of Paradise," "Instiller of Passion," or "Diamond's Envy," featured in his gardens.

Verehrung im Orient

LÂLE DEVRI: DIE TULPENÄRA

MEHR ALS EIN MÄRCHEN AUS TAUSENDUNDEINER NACHT

Mit Sultan Süleyman I. (1494/1495/1496–1566), genannt „der Prächtige", begann eine besondere Epoche. Er sorgte für einen bislang nicht dagewesenen Tulpen-Boom. Seine Gewänder aus Seide und Brokat waren mit Tulpen bestickt, sein Signum mit stilisierten Tulpen verziert. Und selbstverständlich schmückten Tulpen seine Gärten und trugen Namen wie „Licht des Paradieses", „Erweckerin der Leidenschaft" oder „Neid des Diamanten".

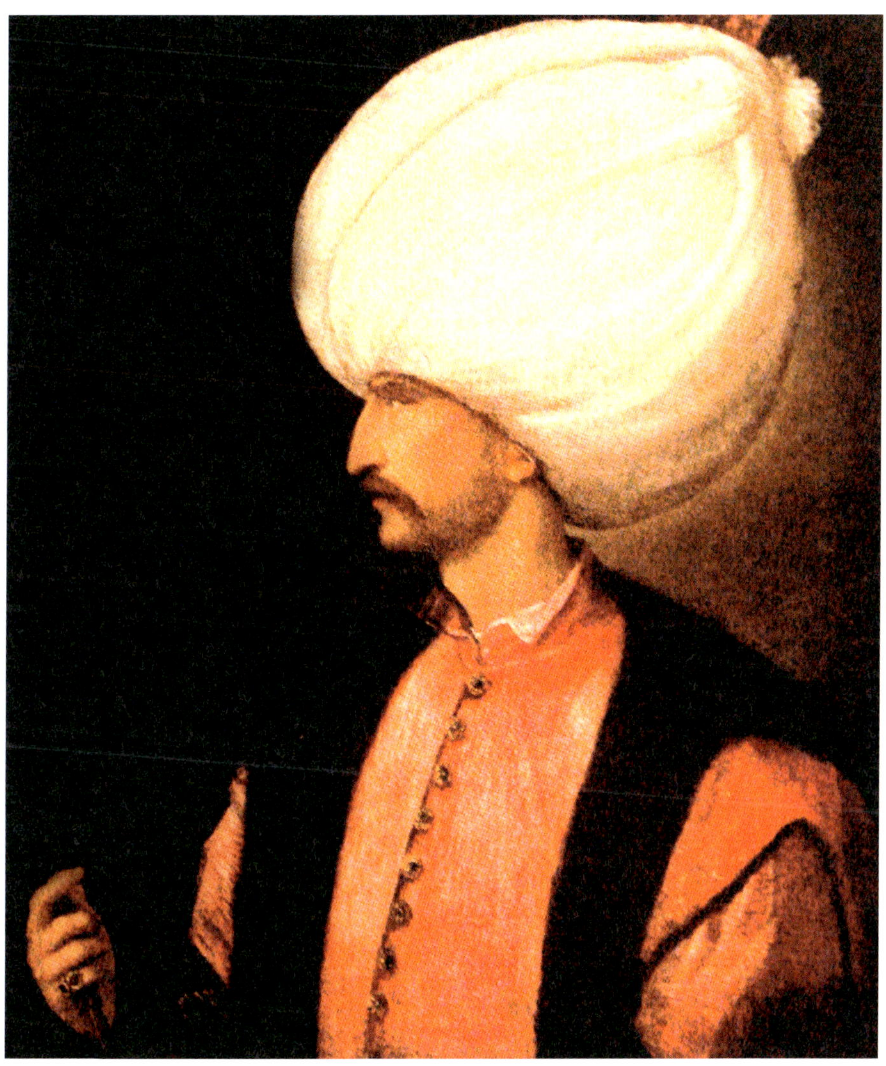

Sultan Suleiman I organized a splendid festival in honor of the tulip every year. During his reign, tulips became a symbol of power and wealth in the Ottoman Empire.

Sultan Süleyman I. veranstaltete jedes Jahr ein rauschendes Fest zu Ehren der Tulpe. Während seiner Herrschaft wurden Tulpen zum Symbol für Macht und Reichtum im osmanischen Reich.

Early breeding

TRUE PARADISE

THE RAREST, MOST BEAUTIFUL TULIPS WERE METAPHORS FOR THE WEALTHY RULER HIMSELF

In the Ottoman Empire, tulips were increasingly bred for distinctive features. Flowers with perfectly symmetrical, slender, and pointed petals were considered the epitome of beauty and perfection. Special commissions assessed the level of their excellence. The most precious tulips were as valuable as the most expensive treasures in the vaults. However, the ruler always took precautions to prevent tulips from becoming the object of speculative trade.

The rule of Sultan Ahmed III ended in 1730 with a coup by the janissaries, the Sultan's household army. This also ended the tulip era, whose decadence had long been a thorn in the side of the insurgents. Although the flower suddenly lost significance, it never faded into obscurity. To this day, it is deeply rooted in Turkish culture, grown in Anatolia, and celebrated every spring at festivals and exhibitions.

Frühe Züchtung

WAHRLICH PARADIESISCH

DIE SCHÖNSTEN UND SELTENSTEN TULPEN WAREN METAPHERN FÜR DEN REICHEN HERRSCHER SELBST

Im Osmanischen Reich wurden Tulpen mehr und mehr nach besonderen Merkmalen gezüchtet. Als Inbegriff der Schönheit und Perfektion galten Exemplare mit absolut ebenmäßigen, schlanken und spitz zulaufenden Blütenblättern. Deren Vollkommenheit wurde von eigens bestellten Kommissionen bewertet. Die kostbarsten Tulpen waren so viel wert wie die teuersten Preziosen in den Schatzkammern. Dennoch achtete man von höchster Stelle stets darauf, dass Tulpen nicht zu Spekulationsobjekten wurden.

Mit einem Putsch der Janitscharen, der Leibwache des Sultans, endete 1730 die Herrschaft von Sultan Ahmed III. und damit auch die Tulpenära, deren Dekadenz den Aufständischen schon lange ein Dorn im Auge gewesen war. Schlagartig verloren die Pflanzen an Bedeutung, gerieten aber nie in Vergessenheit. Bis heute sind sie tief in der türkischen Kultur verankert, werden in Anatolien produziert und jeden Frühling bei Festen und Schauen gefeiert.

Rising fame

EUROPEANS DISCOVER THE TULIP

THE EASTERN FLOWER INITIALLY CAPTIVATES MOSTLY SCIENTISTS

"No people understand better than the Turkish how to adorn themselves with flowers and take pleasure in them," wrote French naturalist Pierre Belon (1517–1564) in the descriptions of his journey to the Levant. He was fascinated with *lils rouges* ("red lilies") growing in Turkey in all gardens—he was clearly referring to tulips here. The Flemish Ogier Ghislain de Busbecq (1522–1592), an envoy to Istanbul during Suleiman I's reign, expressed similar enthusiasm. He marveled at daffodils, hyacinths, and especially tulips, even though they had no fragrance: "They are appreciated more for the diversity and beauty of their colors."

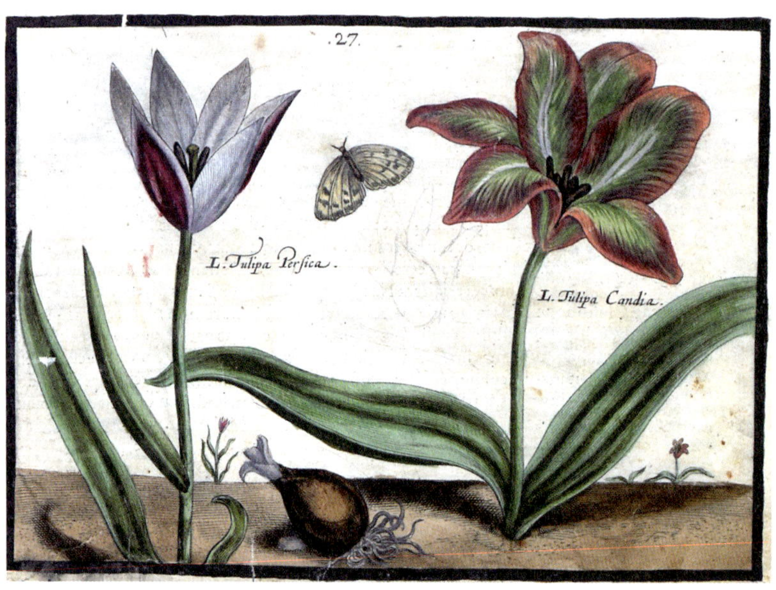

Steigende Bekanntheit

EUROPÄER ENTDECKEN DIE TULPEN

DIE ORIENTALISCHEN BLUMEN FASZINIEREN ANFANGS VOR ALLEM WISSENSCHAFTLER

„Kein Volk versteht es besser als das türkische, sich mit Blumen zu schmücken und sich an ihnen zu erfreuen", schrieb der französische Naturforscher Pierre Belon (1517–1564) in den Beschreibungen seiner Reise in die Levante. Fasziniert erzählte er von *Lils rouges* („roten Lilien"), die in der Türkei in allen Gärten wuchsen – damit meinte er zweifelsfrei Tulpen. Ähnliche Begeisterung zeigte auch der Flame Ogier Ghislain de Busbecq (1522–1592), der als Gesandter der Habsburger nach Istanbul zu Süleyman I. reiste. Er staunte über Narzissen, Hyazinthen und vor allem Tulpen, die nicht einmal dufteten: „Sie werden mehr um der Vielfalt und Schönheit ihrer Farben willen geschätzt."

LEFT PAGE | The „Hortus Floridus", a florilegium from the early 17th century by Crispin de Passe the Younger, already featured tulips.

LINKE SEITE | Im „Hortus floridus", einem Florilegium aus dem frühen 17. Jahrhundert von Crispin de Passe dem Jüngeren, tauchen bereits Tulpen auf.

Off to new lands

SULEIMAN'S GIFT

FROM EAST TO WEST: TULIPS CONQUER EUROPE

Deeply impressed by the Ottoman flowers, Belon and Busbecq (see previous page) ensured that tulips gained attention in Europe as novel and exclusive flowers. Busbecq soon sent bulbs and seeds of "tulipam" from the Sultan's court to Vienna and Prague, intending to adorn the gardens of future Emperor Ferdinand I. He also passed tulips on to various plant researchers, such as Charles de l'Écluse (see page 40).

Auf in neue Länder

SÜLEYMANS GABE

VOM MORGENLAND INS ABENDLAND: TULPEN EROBERN EUROPA

Tief beeindruckt von den Blumen der Osmanen sorgten Belon und Busbecq (siehe vorige Seite) dafür, dass Tulpen als neuartige und exklusive Gewächse in Europa Beachtung fanden. Busbecq schickte vom Hof des Sultans Süleyman I. schon bald Zwiebeln und Samen von den „tulipam" nach Wien und Prag, damit die edlen Gewächse die Gärten des späteren Kaisers Ferdinand I. schmücken sollten. Außerdem reichte er Tulpen an verschiedene Pflanzenforscher weiter, so etwa an Charles de l'Écluse (siehe Seite 42).

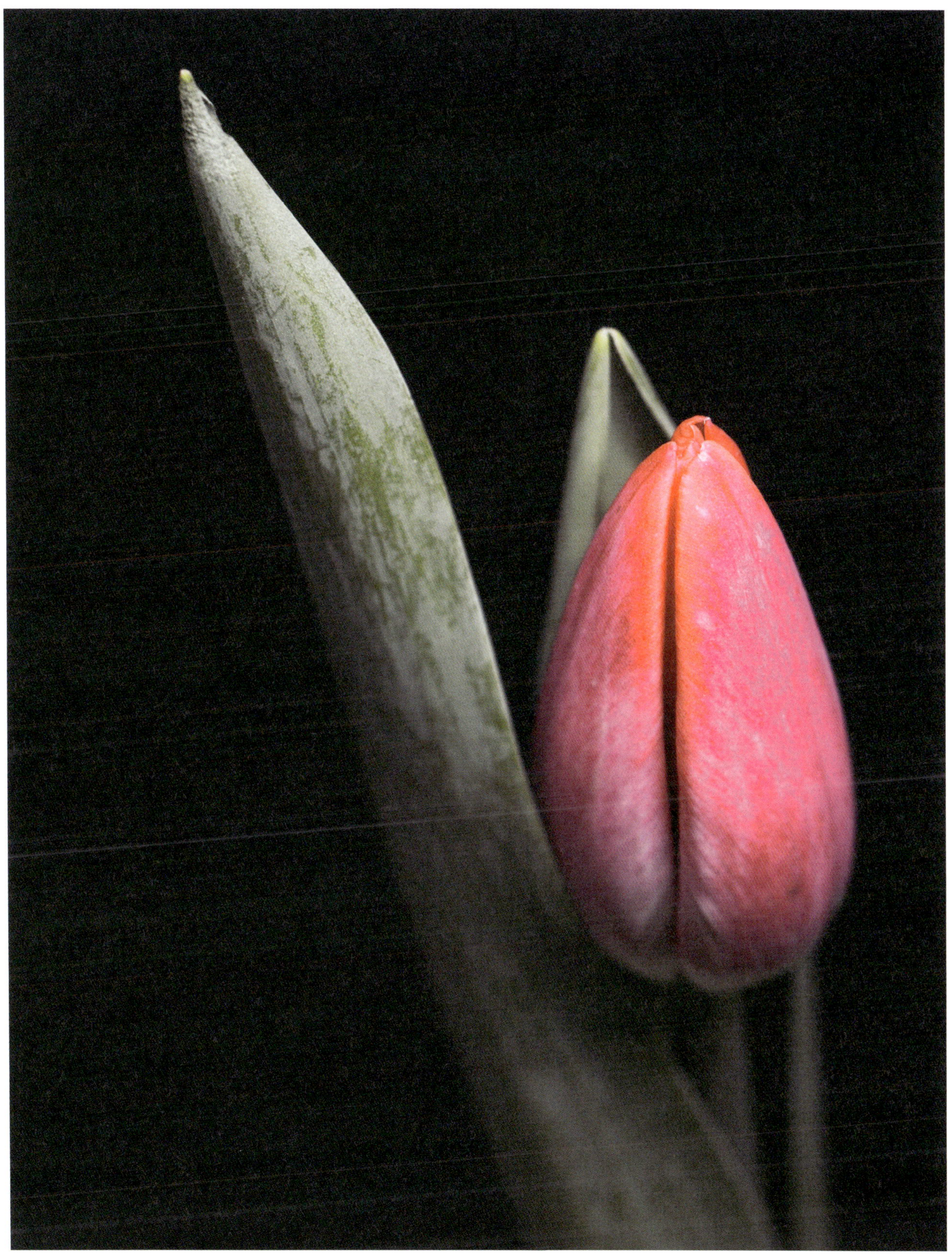

Early imports

PROVISIONS OR CURIOSITY

MANY TRAVELERS HAD ALREADY CARRIED TULIPS IN THEIR LUGGAGE—AS ONION BULBS

Neither Pierre Belon nor Ogier Ghislain de Busbecq, who encountered tulips as researchers and envoys of the Habsburgs in the 16th century (see page 34), deserve credit for introducing the flowers from the east to the west; the tulip had likely reached Venice and other European cities via the Mediterranean long before their time.

Tulip bulbs seem to have traveled through Europe on various trade routes, either as standalone goods or as a little add-on in fabrics or ceramics deliveries. Some mistakenly brought onion bulbs as vegetables to be fried or consumed with vinegar and oil, though some tulip bulbs may have made it into a vegetable garden. If they sprouted and bloomed, they were passed on as a curiosity.

Frühe Importware

WEGZEHRUNG ODER KURIOSITÄT

ALS ZWIEBELN WAREN TULPEN SCHON LÄNGER IM GEPÄCK VIELER HANDLUNGSREISENDER

Weder Pierre Belon noch Ogier Ghislain de Busbecq, die als Forscher bzw. Gesandter der Habsburger im 16. Jahrhundert auf Tulpen stießen (siehe Seite 35), gebührt die Ehre, die Blumen aus dem Orient in den Okzident eingeführt zu haben. Die Zwiebelgewächse sind wohl schon vorher übers Mittelmeer nach Venedig und in andere europäische Städte gelangt.

Tulpen scheinen auf vielen Handelswegen nach und durch Europa gereist zu sein, als eigenständige Ware oder auch als Beimischung, etwa zu Stoffen oder Keramiken. So soll mancher Tulpenzwiebel als Gemüse mittransportiert, fehlinterpretiert und sogar geröstet oder mit Essig und Öl verzehrt haben. Die eine oder andere Tulpenzwiebel wurde dann vielleicht auch in den Garten gesetzt. Kam sie zur Blüte, reichte man sie als Kuriosität weiter.

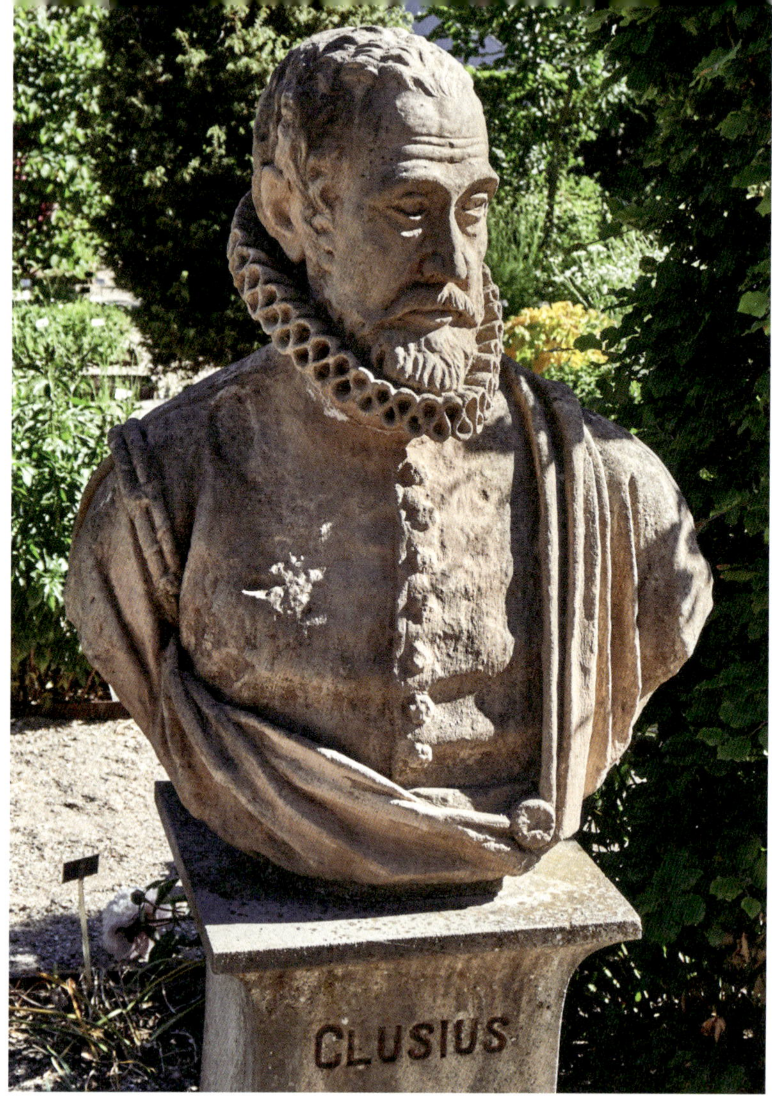

Charles de l'Écluse

THE TULIP PIONEER

THE SPREAD OF TULIPS WAS FUELED BY A PASSION FOR BOTANY AND GARDENING

Transporting tulip bulbs is extremely convenient. This fact, coupled with the exquisite plant's quick rise in popularity as a garden flower, contributed to its rapid spread across Europe. The zeitgeist also played a role: in the vibrant Renaissance era, traditional practices went hand in hand with a push towards modernity. Extensive trade relationships accelerated the exchange of goods as well as that of art and culture. Alongside the revival of classical antiquity, the sciences flourished; this included the study of living plants.

In this era of explorers and scholars, of artists and patrons, botany and gardening were all the rage. Nobles and wealthy citizens wanted to adorn their gardens with rare plants and specimens that you could not see elsewhere. Researchers were interested in both local flora and that of distant lands. In addition to the fathers of botany, Otto Brunfels (1488–1534), Hieronymus Bock (1498–1554), and Leonhard Fuchs (1501–1566), the Flemish polymath Charles de l'Écluse (1526–1609) must be mentioned—not least because he is seen as the father of tulips in Europe.

Known by his Latinized name, Carolus Clusius, he and his three aforementioned colleagues focused on accurately describing and illustrating plants. However, unlike his colleagues, he was interested in plants not for their medicinal use but solely for their own sake. A passionate and gifted gardener, Clusius acquired extensive knowledge about the cultivation of tulips, which "delight our eyes with their charming variety."

Throughout his life, Clusius traveled across Europe and worked in various centers of learning. He engaged in active exchanges with notable colleagues, sending them tulip bulbs and seeds. Thanks to him, tulips became widely known throughout Europe.

Although tulips had been planted in Holland before Carolus Clusius became a professor in the emerging university town of Leiden in 1593, he enhanced the reputation of the Netherlands as the land of tulips. Until his death, he extensively studied tulips, cultivating a mixture of wild tulips and early cultivated forms in the newly established Botanical Garden. He was continually amazed at how easily tulips could crossbreed and how effortlessly new varieties could be created.

NEXT PAGE | *Tulipa clusiana* was named in honor of
Charles de l'Écluse (see also page 141).

Charles de l'Écluse

DER TULPEN-PIONIER

BOTANISCHE NEUGIER UND GÄRTNERISCHE LEIDENSCHAFT SORGTEN FÜR DIE VERBREITUNG DER TULPEN

Wie praktisch, dass sich Tulpen so einfach als Zwiebeln befördern lassen. Das hat ebenso zu ihrer raschen Verbreitung quer durch Europa beigetragen wie das Verlangen vieler Menschen, eine solch exquisite Blume im eigenen Garten zu haben. Hinzu kam der Zeitgeist. Das schillernde Zeitalter der Renaissance verband althergebrachte Tradition mit dem Aufbruch ins Moderne. Weit reichende Handelsbeziehungen beschleunigten neben dem Austausch von Gütern auch den von Kunst und Kultur. Neben der Wiedergeburt der Ideen des klassischen Altertums lebten die Naturwissenschaften auf, darunter die Erforschung lebender Pflanzen.

In der Ära der Entdecker und Gelehrten, Künstler und Mäzene beschäftigte man sich gerne mit Botanik und Gärtnerei. Adelige wie wohlhabende Bürger bevorzugten Gewächse für ihre Gärten, die es nirgendwo sonst gab. Forscher waren sowohl an der heimischen Flora als auch an jener aus fernen Landen interessiert. Neben den Vätern der Botanik Otto Brunfels (1488–1534), Hieronymus Bock (1498–1554) und Leonhard Fuchs (1501–1566) darf der flämische Universalgelehrte Charles de l'Écluse (1526–1609) nicht unerwähnt bleiben – schon deshalb, weil er als Vater der Tulpen in Europa gilt.

Carolus Clusius, wie sein latinisierter Name lautet, befasste sich wie seine drei erwähnten Kollegen damit, die Pflanzen exakt zu beschreiben und bildlich darzustellen. Doch anders als diese betrachtete er Pflanzen nicht im Hinblick auf medizinischen Nutzen, sondern einzig um ihrer selbst willen. Überdies ein passionierter und begnadeter Gärtner, eignete sich Clusius ein breites Wissen um die Kultur der Tulpen an, die „durch ihre liebreizende Vielfalt unser Auge erfreuen".

Sein Lebtag reiste Clusius durch ganz Europa und wirkte an verschiedensten Hochburgen der Wissenschaften. Mit namhaften Kollegen unterhielt er eine rege Tauschtätigkeit und schickte ihnen auch Tulpenzwiebeln und -samen. Deshalb ist es ihm zu verdanken, dass Tulpen sehr schnell überall in Europa bekannt wurden.

Obwohl Tulpen schon früher in Holland gepflanzt worden waren, bevor Carolus Clusius 1593 als Professor in die aufstrebende Universitätsstadt Leiden kam, förderte er doch den Ruf der Niederlande als Land der Tulpen schlechthin. Bis zu seinem Tod befasste er sich umfassend mit Tulpen. Im neu geschaffenen Botanischen Garten baute er eine Mischung aus Wildtulpen und frühen Kulturformen an. Und war immer wieder verblüfft, wie leicht sich Tulpen miteinander kreuzen, wie einfach sich immer neue Spielarten ziehen ließen.

Tulipa clusiana erhielt ihren Namen zu Ehren von
Charles de l'Écluse (siehe auch S. 141).

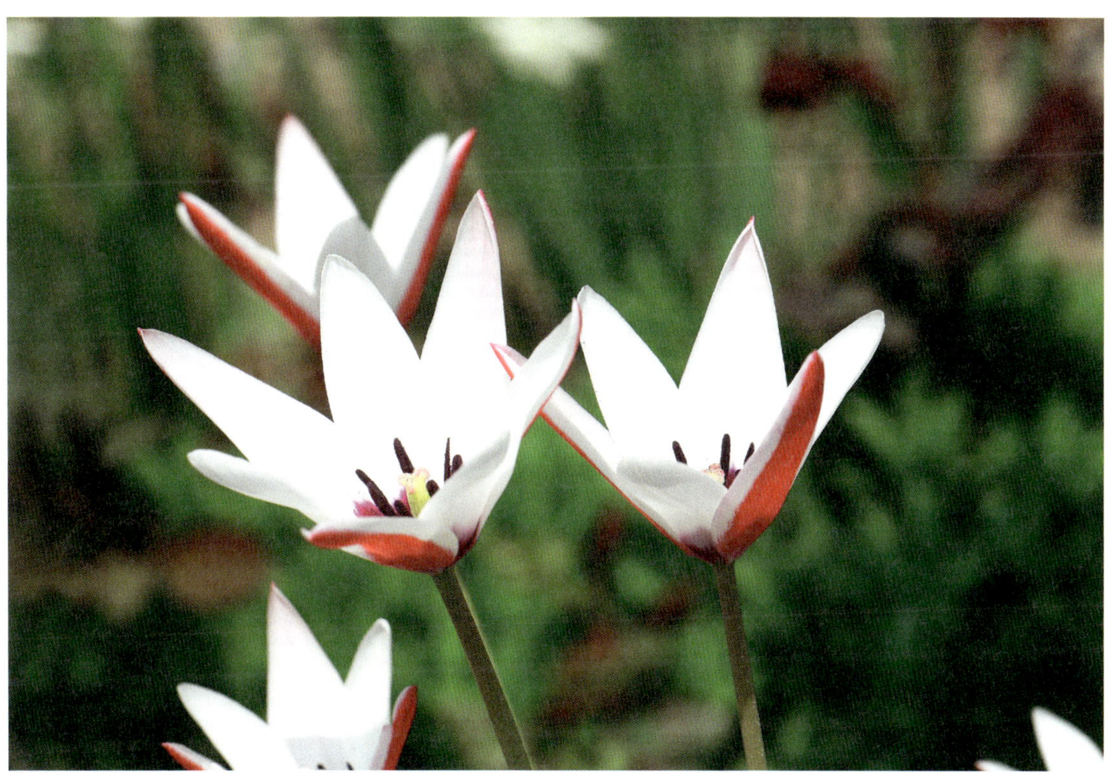

Shared passion

SUDDENLY, EVERYONE WANTS TULIPS

IN THE GOLDEN AGE OF THE NETHERLANDS, THE 17TH CENTURY, TULIPS FLOURISH

Novel, exotic, exquisite, aesthetic, and capricious—enthusiasts found many ways to describe the nature of tulips. Wanting to compete with each other and trying to surpass one another is often seen as an inherently human trait. At the beginning of the 17th century, tulips were perceived to have similar characteristics, sparking a wave of enthusiasm for the flowers; suddenly, everyone wanted tulips!

Across Europe, but primarily in the Dutch Republic, which had risen to become a global maritime and trading power, enthusiastic tulip lovers gathered, spurred on not least by role models like Carolus Clusius. The *liefhebbers* (enthusiasts) exchanged both bulbs and knowledge. Driven by rising demand, more and more commercially minded connoisseurs joined in. Unsurprisingly, it was not long before people with a more criminal disposition also got involved. Tulips became cult objects in the upper echelons of society.

Even Carolus Clusius noted with frustration that during his visits to the gardens of aristocrats, tulips which had clearly been stolen from his own gardens were presented as special treasures. Those who wanted to own such unique plants had to either procure them through expensive trade, exchange them with like-minded individuals, or acquire them through unscrupulous means.

NEXT PAGE | In the early 17th century, the Prince of Savoy-Carignan commissioned a florilegium. It depicts *Tulipa lutea centifolia* (left) whose spectacular color and shape continue to impress even today. The 1716 painting "Flowers in a Vase" by Dutch artist Margareta Haverman features, among other things, a lush "broken" tulip flower (right).

Geteilte Leidenschaft

PLÖTZLICH WILL JEDER TULPEN HABEN

IM GOLDENEN ZEITALTER DER NIEDERLANDE, DEM 17. JAHRHUNDERT, BLÜHEN TULPEN ENORM AUF

Neuartig, ausgefallen, erlesen, ästhetisch und launisch – es ließen sich noch viele Wesenszüge der Tulpen aufzählen, um das Naturell der Zwiebelgewächse aus der Sicht von Liebhabern zu umschreiben. Und es ist ein tief im Menschen verankerter Wesenszug, miteinander zu konkurrieren und andere zu überflügeln. Liebhaberei und Konkurrenzdenken trafen Anfang des 17. Jahrhunderts aufeinander und lösten eine Welle der Begeisterung für Tulpen aus. Jeder wollte welche haben!

Überall in Europa, hauptsächlich aber in den zur See- und Handelsmacht aufgestiegenen Vereinigten Niederlanden, fanden sich enthusiastische Tulpenfreunde zusammen. Die *liefhebbers* tauschten sowohl Zwiebeln als auch Kenntnisse aus. Angetrieben von steigender Nachfrage kamen mehr und mehr kommerziell denkende Connaisseurs hinzu. Und, wie könnte es anders sein, auch solche mit krimineller Energie. Tulpen wurden zu Kultobjekten der oberen Gesellschaftsschichten.

Schon Carolus Clusius ärgerte sich, dass er bei Besuchen in herrschaftlichen Gärten Tulpen als besondere Schätze vorgeführt bekam, die vorher aus seinen Beeten gestohlen worden waren. Wer solche ausgefallenen Pflanzen sein Eigen nennen wollte, musste sich entweder mit kostspieliger Ware aus exklusivem Handel versorgen, mit Gleichgesinnten tauschen oder auf unlauterem Weg zu den Objekten der Begierde kommen.

NÄCHSTE SEITE | Prinz von Savoyen-Carignan ließ im frühen 17. Jahrhundert ein Florilegium anlegen – bis heute beeindruckt die spektakuläre Farbe und Form der darin festgehaltenen *Tulipa lutea centifolia* (links). Das Gemälde „Blumen in einer Vase" der niederländischen Künstlerin Margareta Haverman von 1716 zeigt unter anderem eine üppige „gebrochene" Tulpenblüte (rechts).

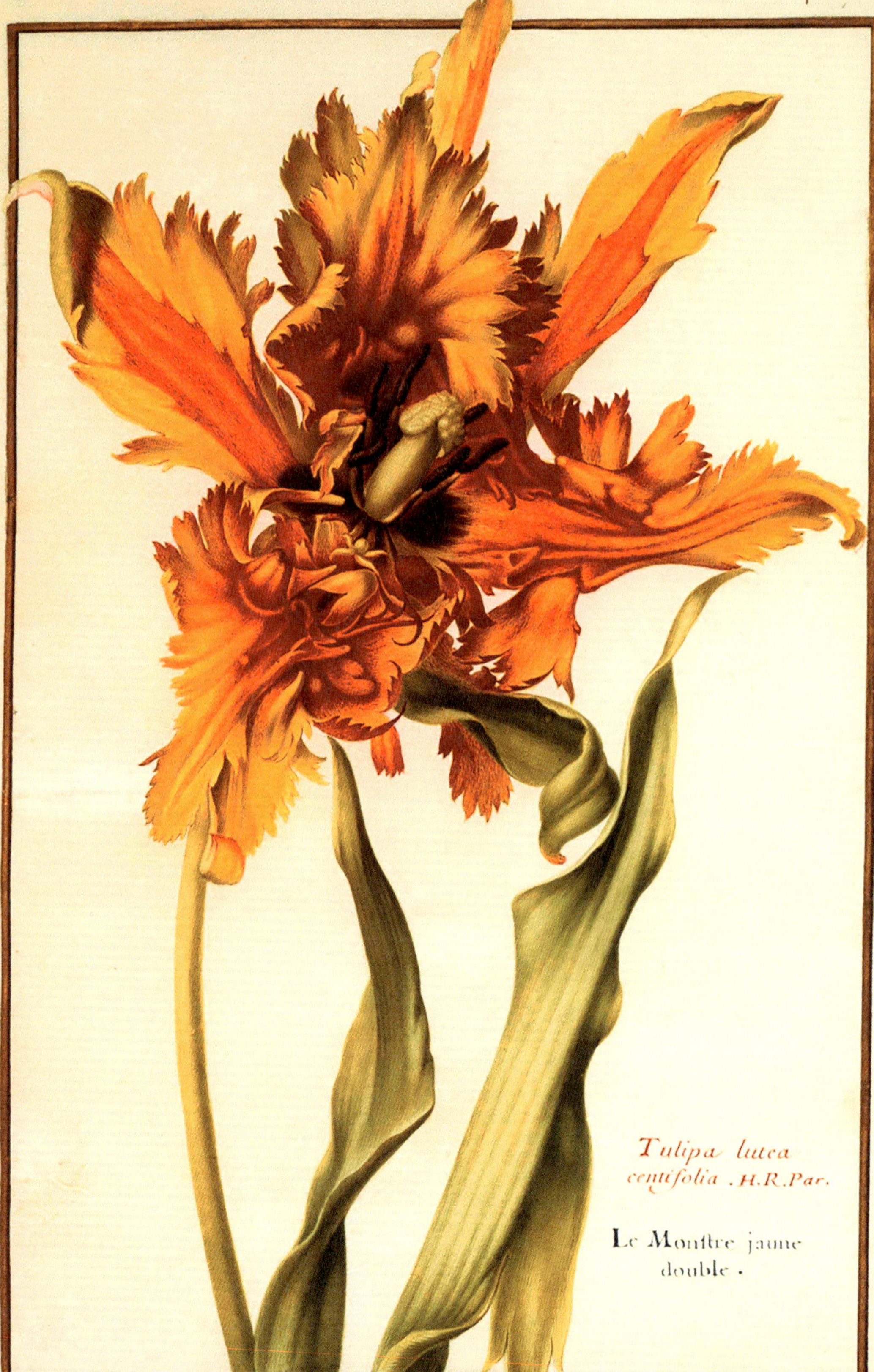

Tulipa lutea
centifolia . H.R.Par.

Le Monftre jaune
double .

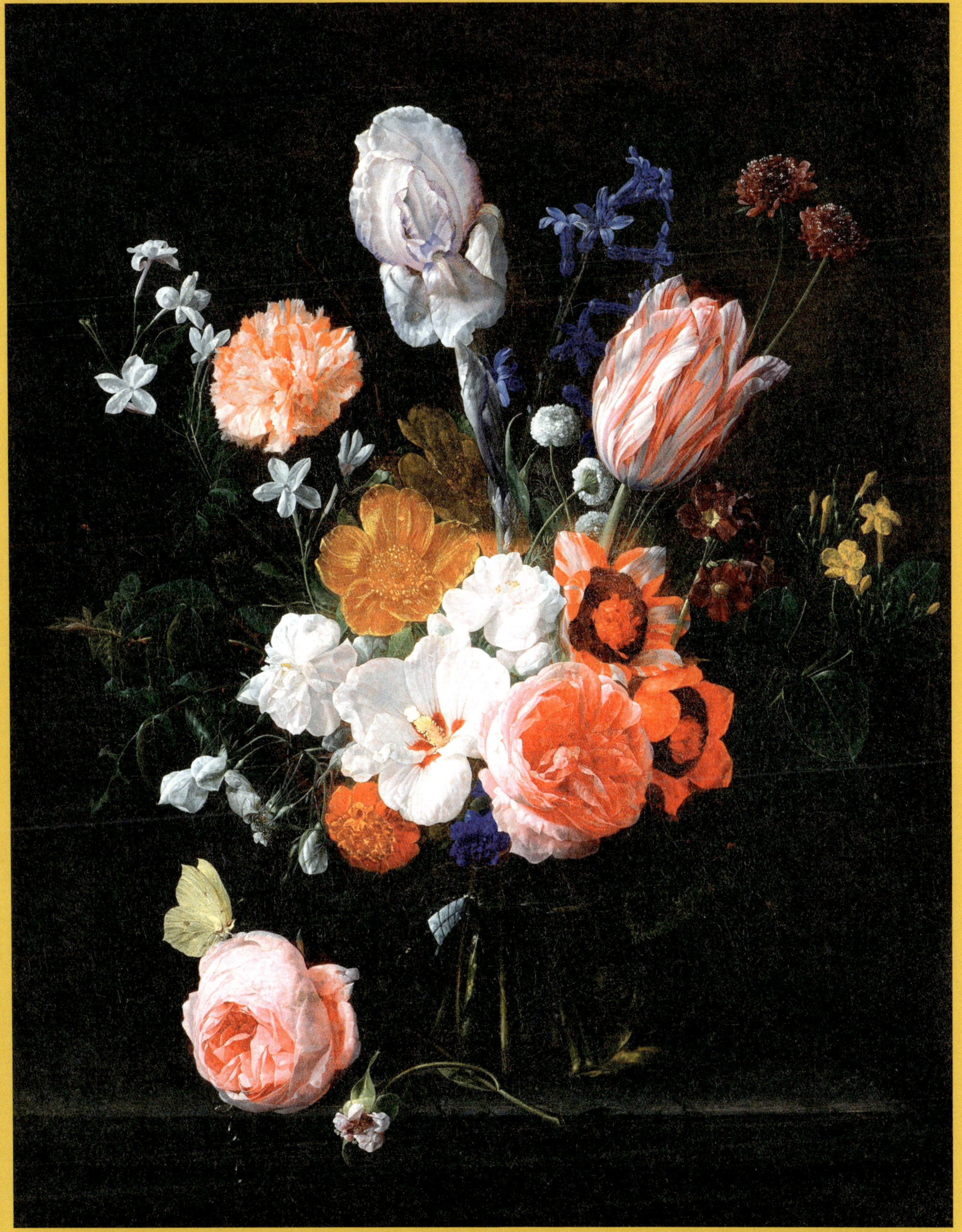

A piece of art

PRECIOUS AND ECCENTRIC DISPLAYS

EASTERN FLOWERS BREAK AWAY FROM THE NORM IN EVERY RESPECT

From the 17th century onwards, tulips were no longer seen as mere botanical rarities; they became beacons of exclusivity. Wealthy citizens in Amsterdam placed them in geometric gardens, with areas of bare earth surrounding each tulip like a picture frame, as if it were a work of art. But tulips were used to impress outside of gardens, too: some enthusiasts set up a mirror cabinet to display a single tulip, as this seemed more sophisticated than a whole bed full of tulips.

People who had tulips depicted or catalogued were seen as distinguished. Countless paintings from that time feature tulips, either alone or in the company of other exotic floral beauties. These were carried out by lesser-known and famous artists alike, the list including names such as Jan Brueghel the Elder, Jan van Huysum, or Balthasar van der Ast.

Finally, there were the cabinets of curiosities. For the wealthy, the trading of tulip bulbs and the cultivation and description of tulips were exclusive hobbies; likewise, collecting and displaying other rarities and curiosities was a respected pastime. Display cabinets filled with ostrich eggs, narwhal horns, corals, crystals, and shells increasingly also contained tulip bulbs, illustrations, ceramics, or porcelain featuring tulips.

NEXT PAGE | Amsterdam and tulips—an intimate
relationship then and now

Kunstobjekte

KOSTBARKEITEN UND SKURRILE SCHAUSTÜCKE

DIE ORIENTALISCHEN BLUMEN FALLEN IN JEDER HINSICHT AUS DEM RAHMEN

Von botanischen Raritäten verwandelten sich Tulpen ab dem 17. Jahrhundert zu exklusiven Repräsentanten. Reiche Bürger in Amsterdam setzten sie in geometrische Gärten, wobei Flächen blanker Erde wie Bilderrahmen jede Tulpe umgeben, als sei sie ein Kunstwerk. Doch nicht immer musste es ein Tulpengarten sein, um Eindruck zu schinden. Mancher errichtete ein Spiegelkabinett und stellte eine einzelne Tulpe hinein. Das wirkte mondäner als ein ganzes Beet voller Tulpen.

Profilieren konnte sich auch derjenige, welcher Tulpen abbilden und katalogisieren ließ. Unzählige Gemälde von weniger bekannten wie von berühmten Künstlern wie Jan Brueghel dem Älteren, Jan van Huysum oder Balthasar van der Ast aus der Zeit zeigen Tulpen, entweder solo oder in Gemeinschaft mit weiteren exotischen Blütenschönheiten.

Schließlich waren da noch die Wunderkammern. So wie das Tauschen von Tulpenzwiebeln, deren Gartenkultur und Beschreibung exklusive Hobbys für Leute mit Geld waren, stellte auch das Sammeln und Zurschaustellen von Raritäten und Kuriositäten einen angesehenen Zeitvertreib dar. Neben Straußeneiern, Narwalhörnern, Korallen, Kristallen und Muscheln nahm man auch Tulpenzwiebeln, -abbildungen, Keramik oder Porzellan mit Tulpen in diese Kabinette auf.

NÄCHSTE SEITE | Amsterdam und die Tulpen – damals
wie heute eine innige Beziehung

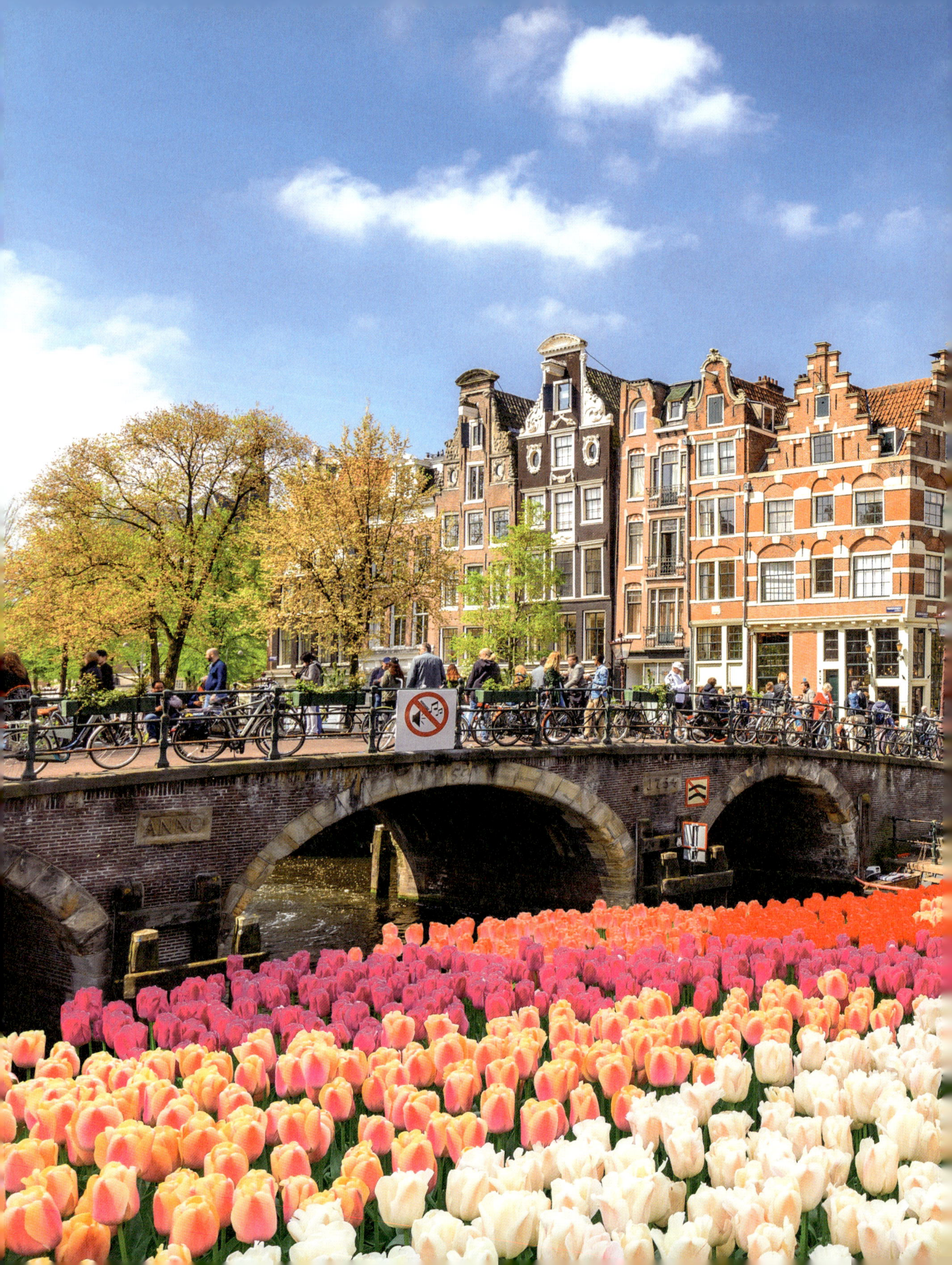

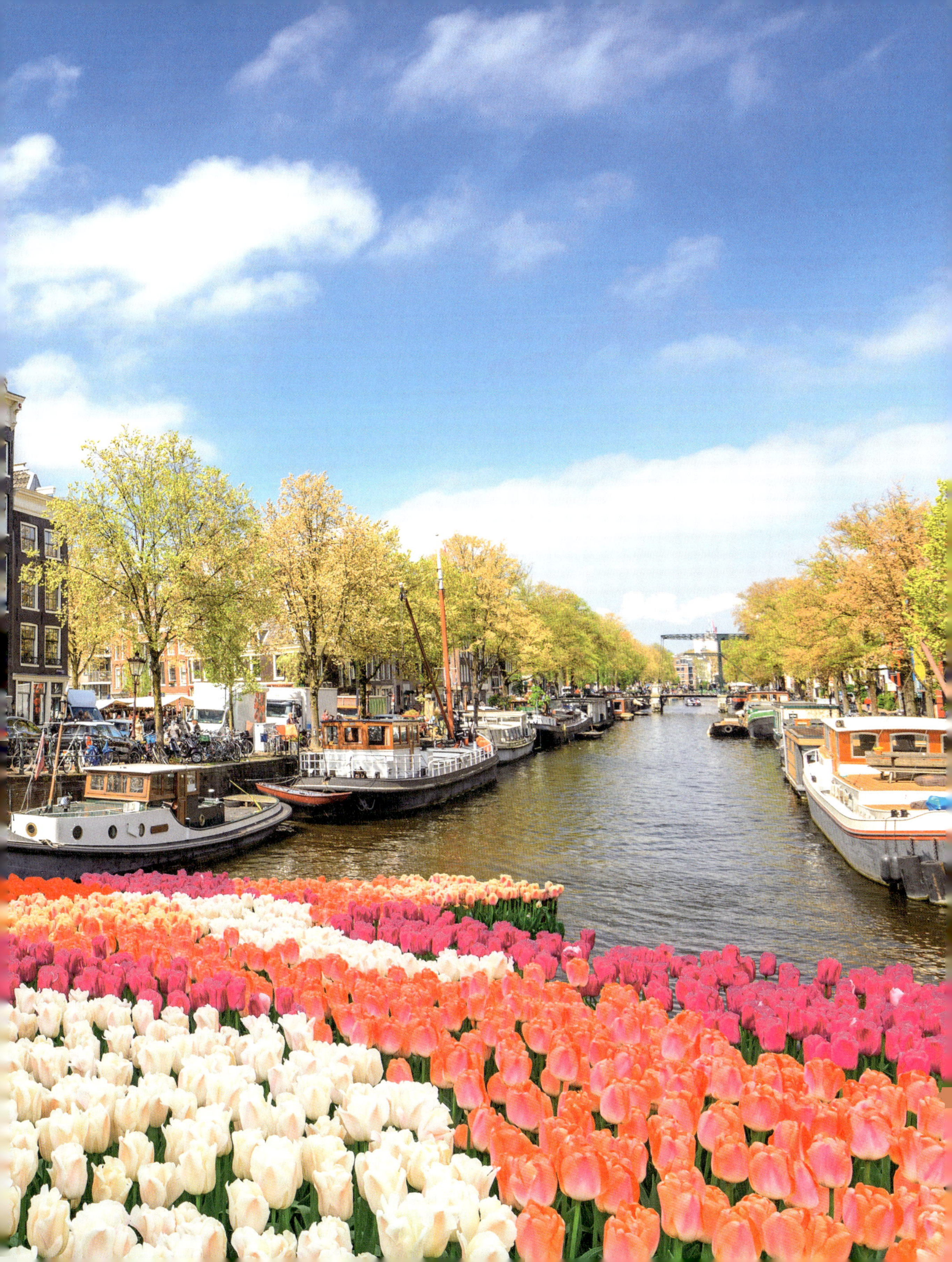

Buzz around bulbs

TULIP MANIA

FROM AMAZEMENT AND CURIOSITY TO ADMIRATION AND, ULTIMATELY, DESIRE

At the threshold from the Middle Ages to the modern era, two completely different worlds collided: Europe and the Orient. With the Ottoman advance into the heart of the European continent, people regarded this "Turkish threat" with a mixture of concern and fascination for this entirely foreign culture. Sensational objects from previously unknown lands reached Europe: delicate spices, precious fabrics, the finest silk rugs, exquisite ceramics, and, of course, peculiar plants. Paintings like the portrait of Sultan Mehmed II by the Venetian painter Gentile Bellini (1429–1507), as well as travel reports and scientific exchanges, all contributed to this general fascination for the east. It was the perfect backdrop for magnificent, previously unknown flowers like tulips to make an appearance.

Tulips characterized the so-called Oriental Period of garden culture between 1560 and 1620, during which plants from Southern Europe, the Middle East, and Western Asia increasingly adorned European estates. Booming trade brought wealth to many people, and soon, the flowers of the east, with their unique colors and forms, were considered must-haves, especially among the upper class.

A match made in heaven: exotic tulips and the highly popular Delft ceramics inspired by Chinese porcelain

Der Hype um Zwiebeln

DIE TULPEN-HAUSSE

AUS STAUNEN UND NEUGIER WERDEN BEWUNDERUNG UND SCHLIESSLICH BEGIERDE

An der Schwelle vom Mittelalter zur Neuzeit trafen zwei völlig unterschiedliche Welten aufeinander: Europa und der Orient. Mit dem Vormarsch der Osmanen ins Herz des europäischen Kontinents waren die Menschen nicht nur durch die „Türkengefahr" beunruhigt, sondern auch fasziniert von dieser gänzlich anderen Kultur. Sensationelle Dinge aus bislang unbekannten Ländern gelangten nach Europa: delikate Spezereien, kostbare Stoffe, feinste Seidenteppiche, erlesene Keramiken und natürlich auch skurrile Gewächse. Gemälde wie das Porträt des Sultans Mehmed II. vom venezianischen Maler Gentile Bellini (1429–1507) trugen ebenso zur allgemeinen Faszination bei wie Reiseberichte und Wissenschaftsaustausch. Da kamen prächtige, bis dato unbekannte Pflanzen wie Tulpen gerade recht.

Tulpen prägten die sogenannte Orientalische Periode der Gartenkultur zwischen 1560 und 1620, in der Pflanzen aus Südeuropa, dem Nahen Osten und Vorderasien vermehrt europäische Anwesen zierten. Boomender Handel machte viele Menschen reich, und bald galten die Blumen des Orients, die mit so einzigartigen Farben und Formen aufwarteten, schon bald als *must haves* vor allem der gehobenen Gesellschaft.

Zwei, die die Menschen begeisterten: exotische Tulpen und die ausgesprochen erfolgreiche, von chinesischem Porzellan inspirierte Keramik aus Delft

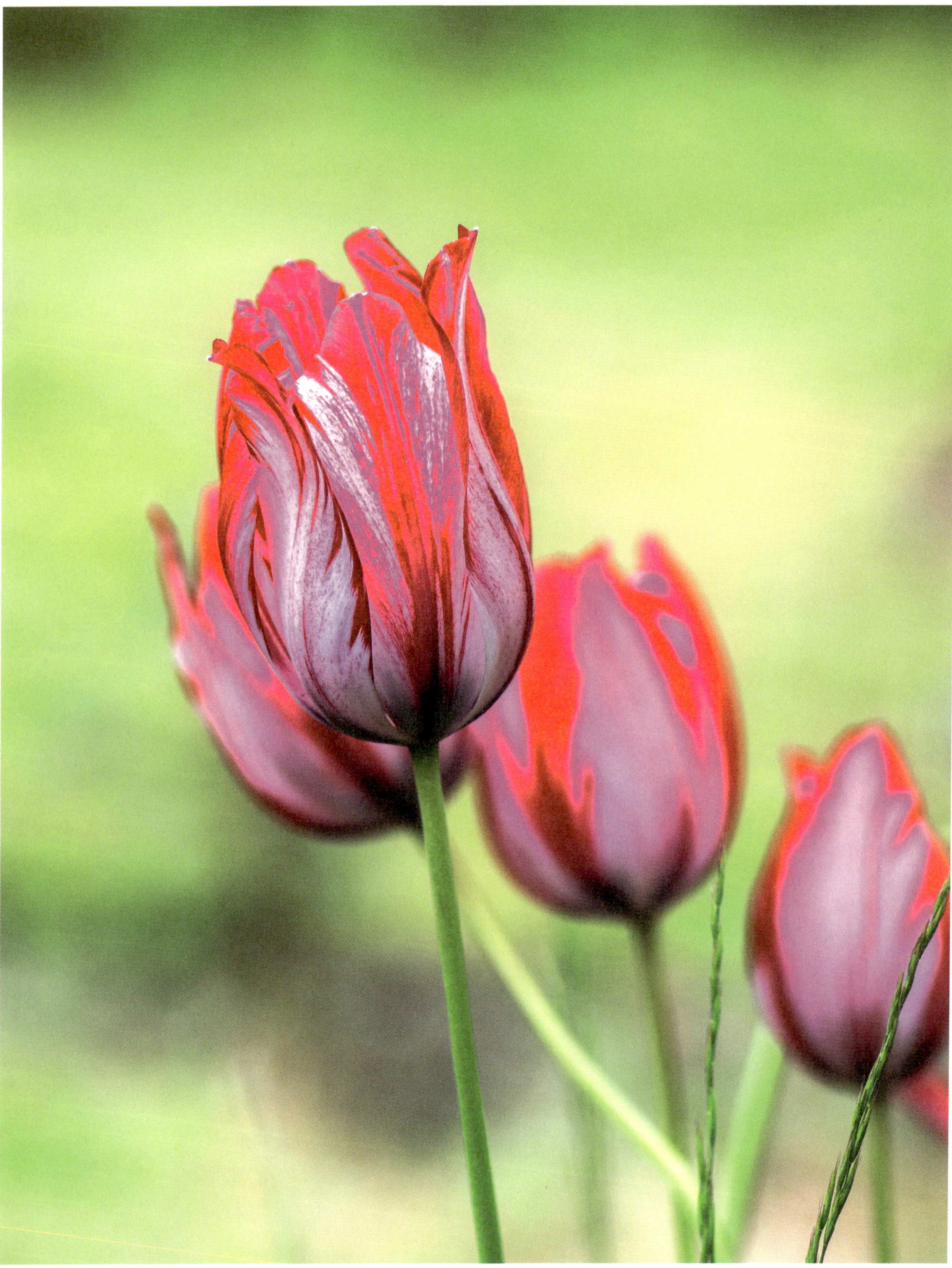

A "magical" phenomenon

A VIRUS FUELS THE FEVER

"BROKEN" TULIPS BREAK ALL RECORDS

Spontaneously occurring variations made tulips even more exclusive: some specimens suddenly produced flowers with speckles, streaks, stripes, dots, flames, or feathered patterns in contrasting colors. The cause of the "breaking" of the tulip blossom, now known as the Tulip Breaking Virus (TBV) or Tulip Mosaic Virus, was a mystery at that time, and it was considered magic. Of course, this only increased the general passion for tulips as well as their value.

Ein „magisches" Phänomen

EIN VIRUS SCHÜRT DAS FIEBER

„GEBROCHENE" TULPEN BRECHEN ALLE REKORDE

Spontan auftretende Varianten machten Tulpen noch exklusiver: Manche Exemplare trugen plötzlich Blüten mit Sprenkeln, Schlieren, Streifen, Tupfen, Flammen- oder Federmustern in kontrastierenden Farben. Dass ein Virus, genauer der Tulip Breaking Virus (TBV) oder Tulpen-Mosaik-Virus, die Ursache für das „Brechen" der Tulpenblüte war, wusste man damals natürlich nicht und hielt es für Magie. Was die Leidenschaft für Tulpen und deren Wert selbstverständlich abermals steigerte.

Mania, part 1

TULIP MANIA AND BULB FRENZY

A FLOWER SHAKES THE ECONOMY OF AN ENTIRE NATION

Solid colors? No, thanks; plain tulips are just too cheap and pedestrian. Bizarden with colorful markings on a yellow background? That's more like it. Bijbloemen or Rozen? These white-and-purple-colored or white-and-red-patterned tulips were all the rage! They really were exceedingly popular. Among all the tulips flooding the market, everyone sought to acquire the most beautiful, unique, and, most importantly, rarest specimens. This passion developed into a pathological obsession in the Netherlands in the early 17th century.

In the rush to obtain the highest-quality tulip, trading was no longer reduced to tulip planting season in the fall but took place year-round. You could consider yourself lucky if you received a presentable bulb by the agreed delivery date. If a tulip then bloomed in the desired color composition, your trade had paid off. Yet who could predict this kind of desirable outcome just by looking at a bulb? It was pure speculation. Options on bulbs were often resold multiple times without anyone even having seen the bulb itself or the flower it was to produce.

Rozen- and Bijbloemen tulips became
bestsellers when tulip fever struck.

Wahn, Teil 1

TULPENRAUSCH UND ZWIEBELWAHN

EINE BLUME BRINGT DIE WIRTSCHAFT EINER GANZEN NATION INS WANKEN

Couleurs? Nein danke, einfarbige Tulpen sind bloß billige Allerweltsware. Bizarden, bunte Zeichnung auf gelbem Grund? Schon eher. Bijbloemen oder Rozen? Her mit solchen Tulpen, die weiß-violett bzw. weiß-rot gemustert sind! Das waren die wahren Schlager. Unter all den Tulpen, die auf dem Markt angeboten wurden, suchte ein jeder die schönste, ausgefallenste und vor allem seltenste zu ergattern. Die Leidenschaft entwickelte sich in den Niederlanden des frühen 17. Jahrhunderts ins Krankhafte.

Im Wahn, die hochwertigste Tulpe zu erstehen, handelte man bald nicht mehr zur Pflanzzeit der Tulpen im Herbst, sondern ganzjährig. Bekam man zum vereinbarten Liefertermin eine ansehnliche Zwiebel, konnte man zufrieden sein. Blühte eine Tulpe dann noch in der gewünschten Farbkomposition auf, hatte sich der Handel gelohnt. Doch wer wollte das vorhersagen oder gar an den Zwiebeln erkennen? Reine Spekulation. Nicht selten wurden Optionen auf Zwiebeln mehrfach weiterveräußert, ohne dass jemand Zwiebel oder Blüte zu Gesicht bekommen hätte.

Rozen- und Bijbloemen-Tulpen
gehörten zu den Verkaufsschlagern,
als das Tulpenfieber um sich griff.

Mania, part 2

THE BAROQUE ERA'S BITCOIN

PLAIN BULBS BECOME MORE VALUABLE THAN GOLD

Were tulips the Bitcoin of the Baroque era? Think bulbs on option contracts, flowers as futures. Yes, in the 17th century, the Netherlands were fertile ground for an obsessive market around flowers; trading became increasingly heated and took on bizarre dimensions. According to some reports, an investor had bought a special tulip for a considerable amount of money. When he learned that a simple craftsman also owned such a tulip, he bought it from him at a high price—and stepped on it. He told the craftsman he would have paid ten times the agreed price for it; upon hearing this, the craftsman hanged himself.

How much money were people willing to invest in a tulip? Unbelievable sums that multiplied within a short period. One of the most famous and expensive tulip varieties called 'Semper Augustus' cost 1,200 guilders per bulb in 1624, 5,500 guilders in 1633, and in 1637, it went for a staggering 13,000 guilders.

The annual earnings of a carpenter at that time were around 250 guilders, and a property along the Amsterdam canals cost 10,000 guilders. Rembrandt van Rijn (1606–1669), who never painted tulips but participated in the tulip gamble and lost everything, received a salary of 1,600 guilders for his famous painting "The Night Watch". By today's standards, a 'Semper Augustus' would now be worth more than one million US dollars ...

Wahn, Teil 2

DIE BITCOINS DES BAROCKS

SCHLICHTE BLUMENZWIEBELN WERDEN WERTVOLLER ALS GOLD

Tulpen, die Bitcoins des Barocks? Zwiebeln auf Optionsscheinen? Blüten als Futures? Ja, in den Niederlanden etablierte sich im 17. Jahrhundert ein besessener Markt rund um die floralen Objekte, der sich immer weiter aufheizte und skurrile Blüten trieb. Es wird berichtet, dass ein Investor für eine stattliche Menge Geld eine besondere Tulpe gekauft hatte. Als er erfuhr, dass ein einfacher Handwerker ebenfalls eine solche Tulpe besaß, kaufte er ihm diese zu einem hohen Preis ab – und zertrampelte sie. Er hätte glatt das Zehnfache dafür bezahlt, ließ er den Handwerker wissen, der sich daraufhin erhängte.

Und was investierte man für eine Tulpe? Unglaubliche Summen, die sich innerhalb kurzer Zeit vervielfachten. Eine der berühmtesten und teuersten Tulpensorten mit dem Namen 'Semper Augustus' kostete im Jahr 1624 pro Zwiebel 1200 Gulden, 1633 schon 5500 Gulden und 1637 wurden gar 13 000 Gulden dafür geboten.

Der Jahresverdienst eines Zimmermanns lag damals bei rund 250 Gulden, ein Anwesen an den Amsterdamer Grachten bei 10 000 Gulden. Rembrandt van Rijn (1606–1669), der niemals ein richtiges Tulpenbild malte, sich jedoch an den Hasardspielen um Tulpen beteiligt und alles verloren hatte, erhielt für sein berühmtes Gemälde „Die Nachtwache" ein Salär von 1600 Gulden. Nach aktuellen Maßstäben müsste man für eine 'Semper Augustus' heute rund eine Million Euro hinblättern …

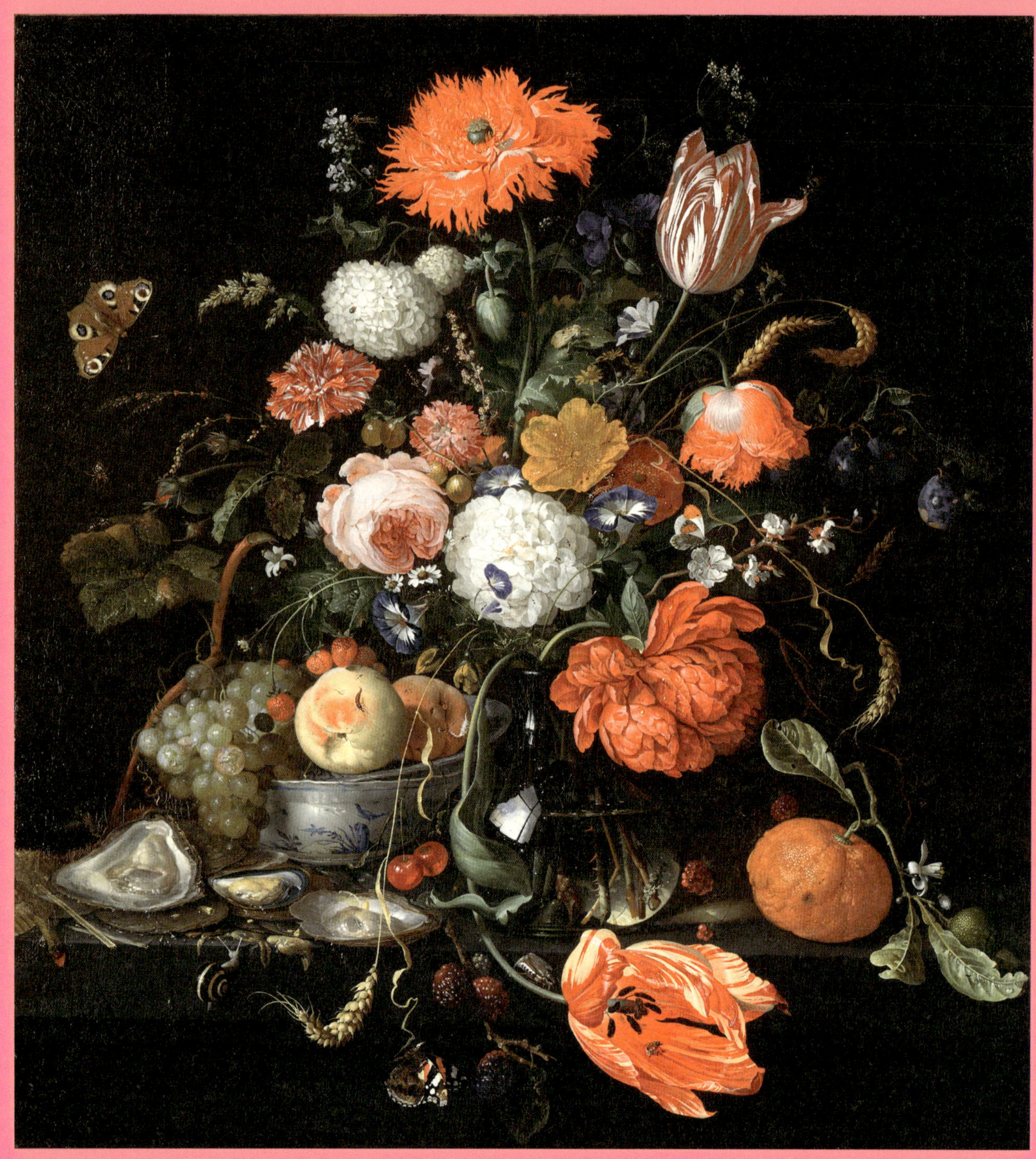

Still life by Jan Davidszoon de Heem, Rembrandt's contemporary—featuring tulips, of course (left). Object of unrestrained desire: tulip variety 'Semper Augustus' (right)

Stillleben von Jan Davidszoon de Heem, einem Zeitgenossen Rembrandts – natürlich unter anderem mit Tulpen (links). Objekt zügelloser Begierde: Tulpensorte 'Semper Augustus' (rechts)

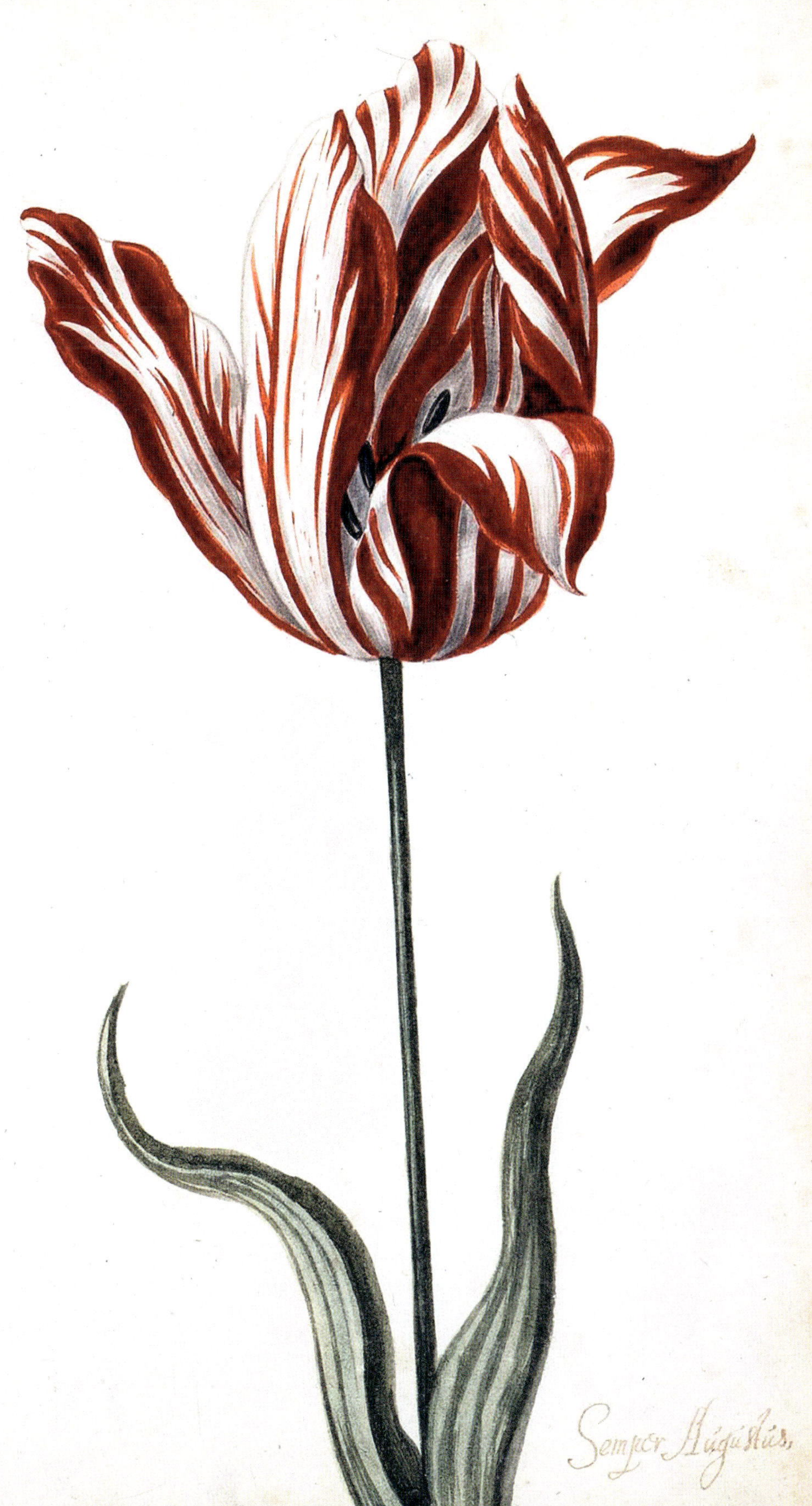
Semper Augustus.

The tulip bust

THE SHOW IS OVER

TULIP FEVER COMES TO AN ABRUPT END

Tens of thousands of Dutch people were suffering from tulip fever, which had only been rampant for a few years but had spread across all social classes. Sensible people warned against the madness of this speculative trade, yet *tulpenmanie* was spreading like a pandemic.

Gamblers firmly believed that the value of a tulip bulb would double by evening or by the next day at the very latest; one day, someone got cold feet. In early February 1637, an auction of tulip bulbs collapsed. No one wanted to bid on the specimens on offer. Panicked traders tried to sell; prices plummeted. The speculative bubble burst faster than the Great Wall Street Crash of 1929, the most famous financial disaster in history.

Yet this did not mark the end of the passion for tulips. Breeding, cultivation, and trade regained momentum. Gradually, a stable business sector emerged, and the Netherlands became the ultimate tulip exporter.

In an amusing reversal of history, Dutch tulip bulbs were imported on a large scale back into Turkey. There, under Sultan Ahmed III (1673–1736), a new kind of tulip mania erupted, with the ruler himself owning entire fields of tulips. Due to his extravagance at the expense of the suffering population, he had to abdicate in 1730.

NEXT PAGE | In his painting, "Allegory of Tulipomania", Jan Brueghel the Younger humorously mocks his contemporaries' obsession with tulips. There are monkeys weighing tulip bulbs with gold, and urinating on the most expensive specimens amidst much haggling, stealing, and fighting.

Die Tulpen-Baisse

SCHLUSS MIT DEM SPEKTAKEL

DAS DRAMA DES TULPENFIEBERS NIMMT EIN JÄHES ENDE

Zehntausende Niederländer waren vom Tulpenfieber befallen, das erst seit wenigen Jahren grassierte, aber in allen Bevölkerungsschichten verbreitet war. Vernünftige Menschen warnten vor dem Irrsinn des wilden Handels. Doch die Tulipomanie breitete sich epidemisch aus.

Die Glücksspieler glaubten fest daran, dass sich der Wert einer Tulpenzwiebel bis abends, spätestens bis zum nächsten Tag verdoppeln würde. Bis der Erste kalte Füße bekam. Anfang Februar 1637 platzte eine Auktion mit Tulpenzwiebeln. Niemand wollte den Preis für die angebotenen Exemplare bieten. Panisch versuchten die Händler zu verkaufen. Die Preise fielen ins Bodenlose. Die Spekulationsblase platzte schneller als beim großen Wallstreet-Crash von 1929, dem berühmtesten Finanzdebakel der Geschichte.

Doch wer glaubt, dass dies das Ende der Leidenschaft für Tulpen war, liegt falsch. Züchtung, Anbau und Handel kamen wieder in Schwung. Allmählich bildete sich ein stabiler Geschäftszweig aus, und die Niederlande wurden zum Tulpenland schlechthin.

Ironie der Geschichte: Holländische Tulpenzwiebeln wurden im großen Stil in die Türkei reimportiert. Dort kam es unter Sultan Ahmed III. (1673–1736) zu einer Art Tulpenrausch, der Herrscher selbst besaß ganze Tulpenfelder. Wegen seiner Verschwendungssucht zu Lasten der leidenden Bevölkerung musste er 1730 abdanken.

NÄCHSTE SEITE | In seinem Gemälde „Allegorie der Tulipomanie" macht sich Jan Brueghel der Jüngere auf derbe Art und Weise über seine den Tulpen verfallenen Zeitgenossen lustig. Da gibt es Affen, die Tulpenzwiebeln mit Gold aufwiegen, wieder andere urinieren auf die teuersten Exemplare, es wird geschachert, gestohlen und sich geprügelt.

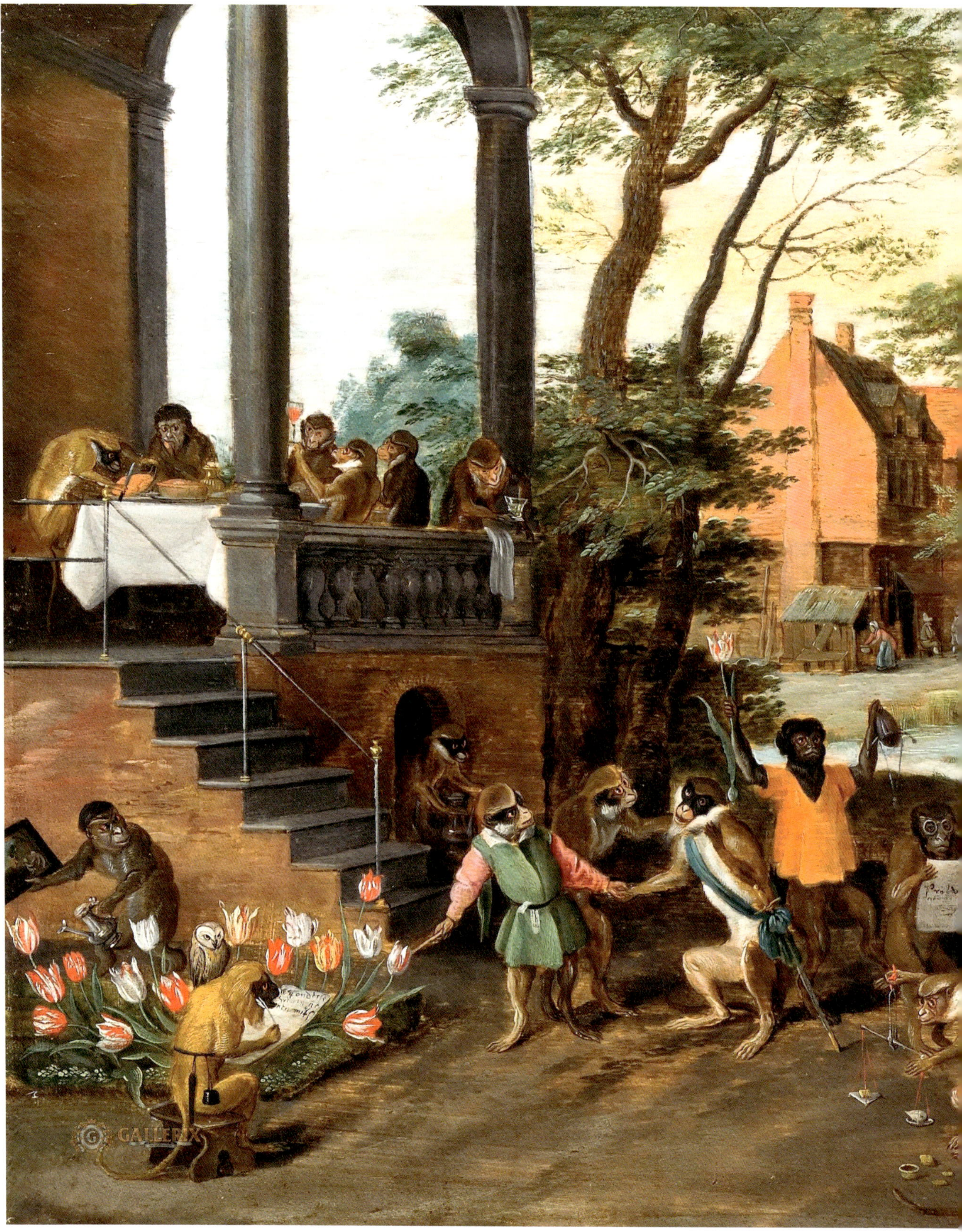

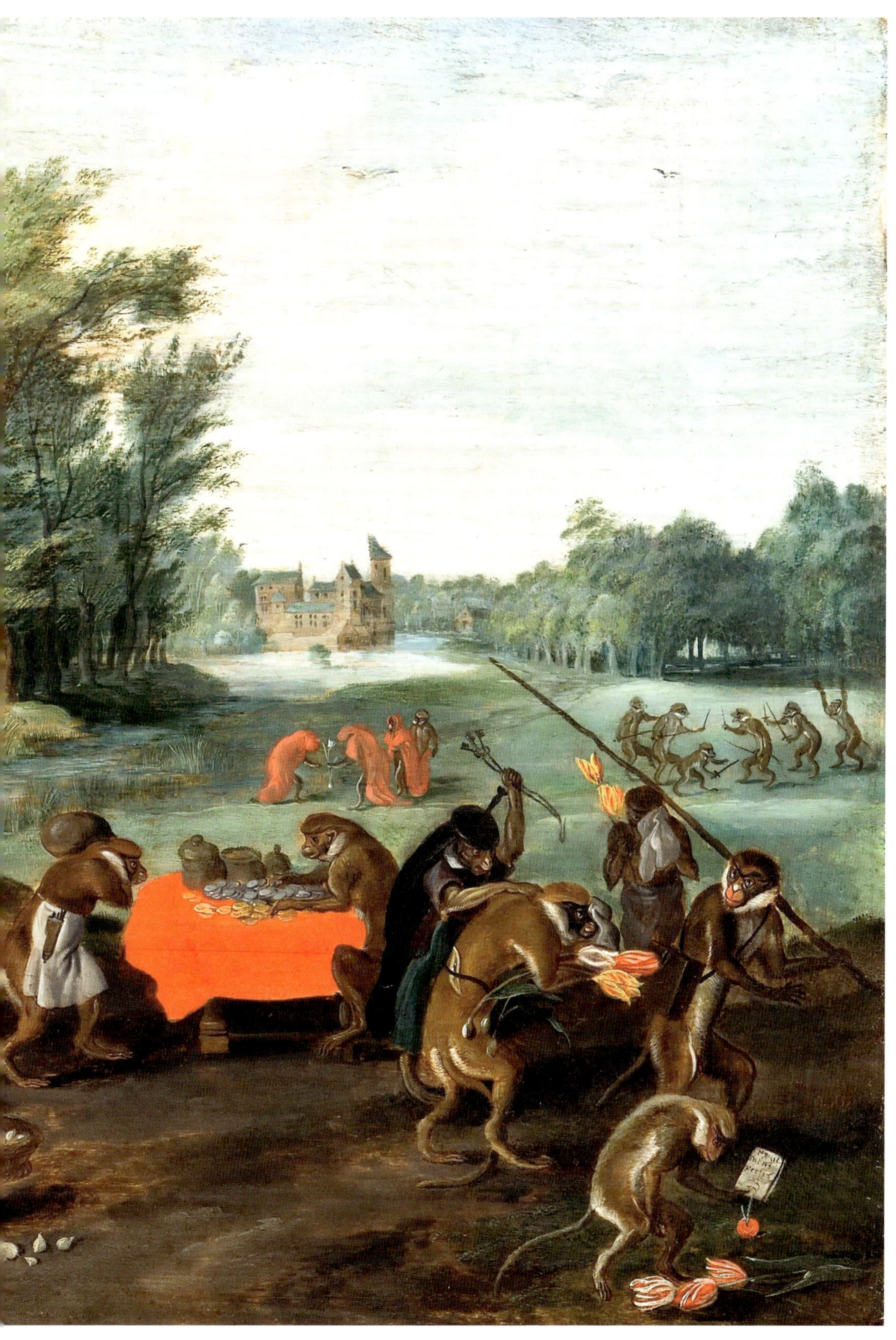

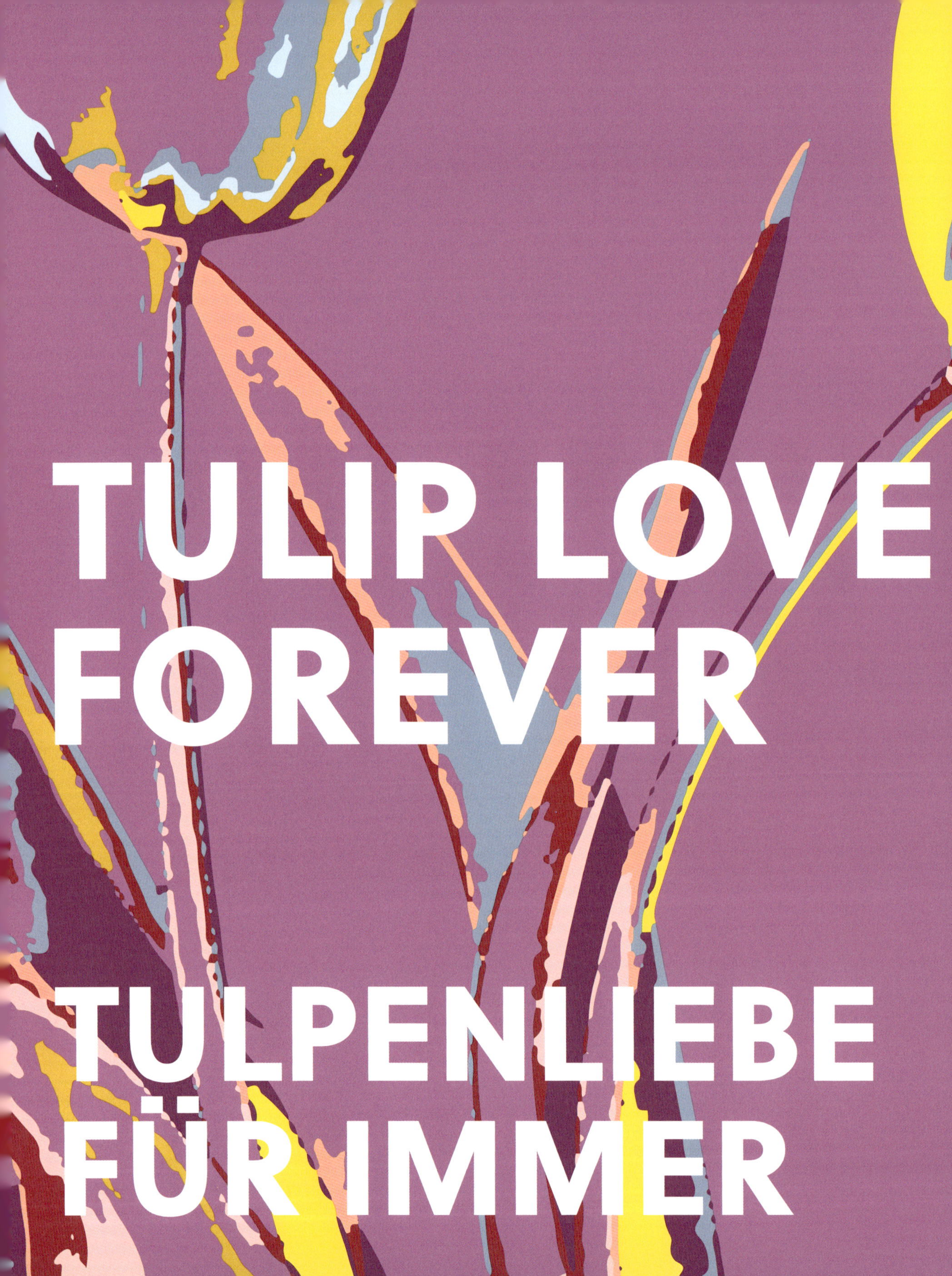
TULIP LOVE
FOREVER

TULPENLIEBE
FÜR IMMER

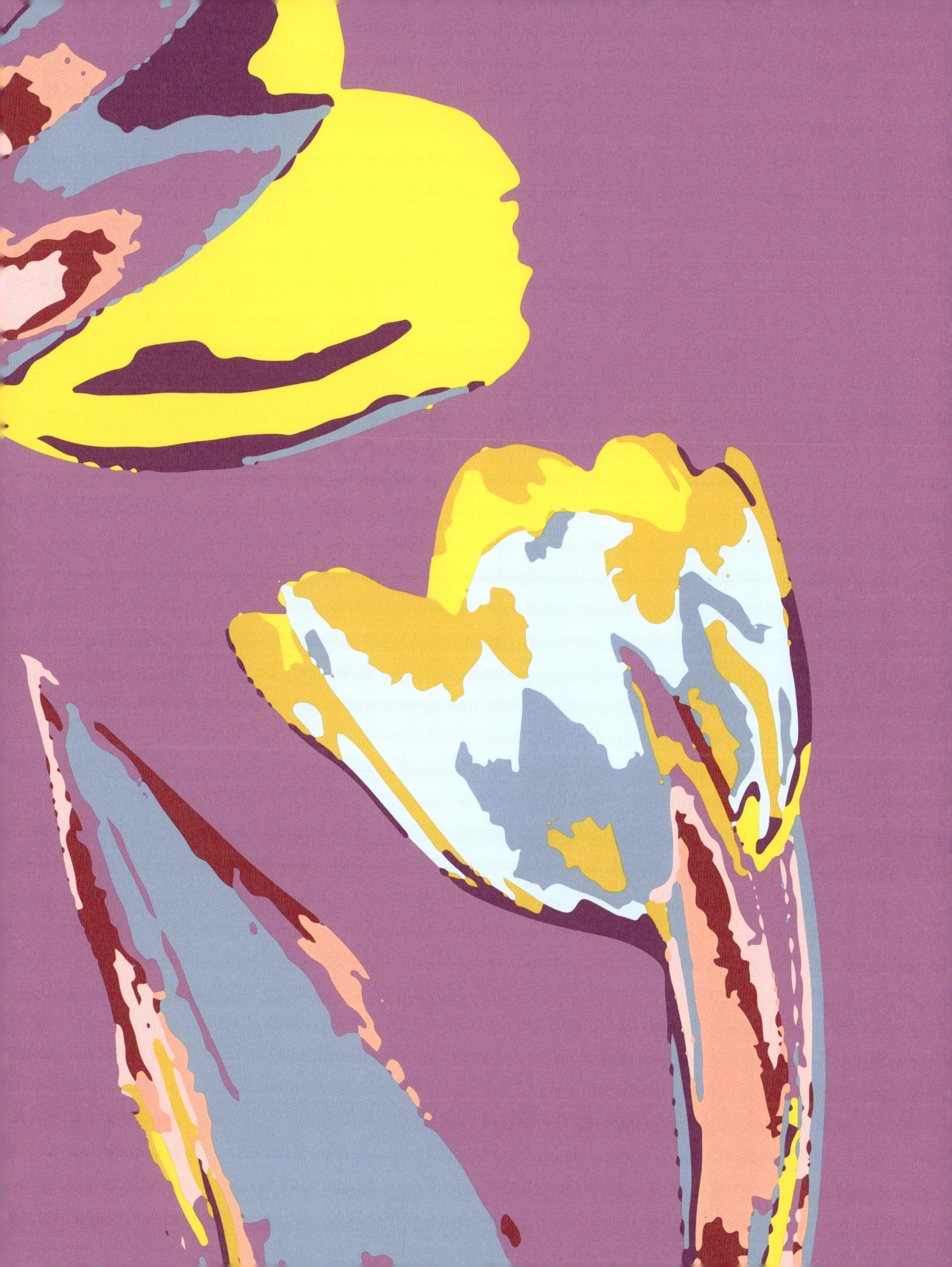

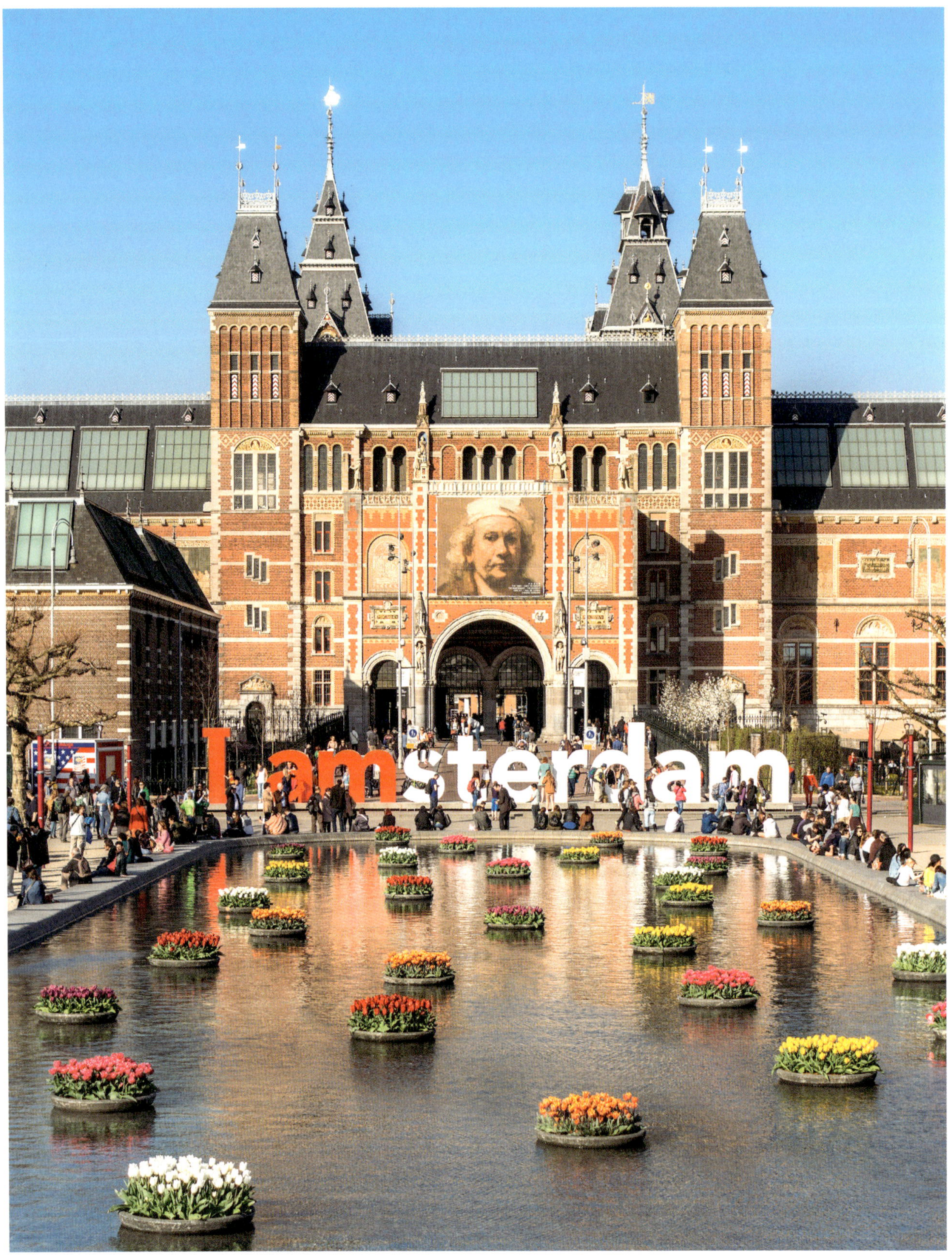I amsterdam

Festivals, parks, and gardens

SPRING, THY NAME IS TULIP

APRIL'S HERALDS: TULIPS IN AMSTERDAM

Every year, millions of people attend enchanting exhibitions and festivals celebrating tulips. In the Netherlands, the beginning of spring is traditionally marked in April with the Amsterdam Tulip Festival. Tulips are displayed in full bloom at 85 locations in the city. Many of these events attract crowds of visitors from all over the world. What joy getting back into a lively hustle and bustle and enjoying leisurely strolls through spring gardens after the long winter months!

Festivals, Parks und Gärten

FRÜHLING, DEIN NAME IST TULPE

SPRICHWÖRTLICH: DIE TULPEN IN AMSTERDAM

Jedes Jahr wieder berauschen sich Millionen von Menschen bei Ausstellungen und Festen an den Tulpen. In den Niederlanden wird der Beginn des Frühlings traditionell im April mit dem Amsterdamer Tulpenfestival begrüßt. An 85 Orten der Stadt blühen Tulpen. Viele Veranstaltungen locken Besucherscharen aus aller Herren Länder an. Nach den Wintermonaten kommt man im lebhaften Treiben und beim genüsslichen Schlendern durch frühlingshafte Parks und Gärten wieder in Schwung!

Keukenhof

SPLENDOR IN THE "KITCHEN GARDEN"

ANCIENT GARDEN FOR CULTIVATED HERBS

Many hours, if not days, can be spent in the famous Keukenhof garden. The world's largest spring garden is only open 53 days a year, and it opens its doors for the 75th time in 2024. One hundred breeders select their most magnificent spring flowers and plant them in the fall on an area equivalent to 45 soccer fields: over seven million flower bulbs, all hand-planted. Until mid-May, flower carpets drape over the city, dazzling visitors from near and far.

Keukenhof

BLÜTENPRACHT IM „KÜCHENHOF"

EINST WURDEN HIER KRÄUTER ANGEBAUT

Viele Stunden, nein, Tage, kann man in der berühmten Gartenanlage Keukenhof verbringen. Der weltgrößte Frühlingsgarten öffnet an nur 53 Tagen im Jahr seine Pforten, 2024 zum 75. Mal. Hundert Züchter wählen ihre prächtigsten Frühjahrsblumen aus und pflanzen sie im Herbst auf einer Fläche von umgerechnet 45 Fußballfeldern. Über sieben Millionen Blumenzwiebeln, in Handarbeit versteht sich. Bis Mitte Mai versetzen Blumenteppiche Menschen aus Nah und Fern in helles Staunen.

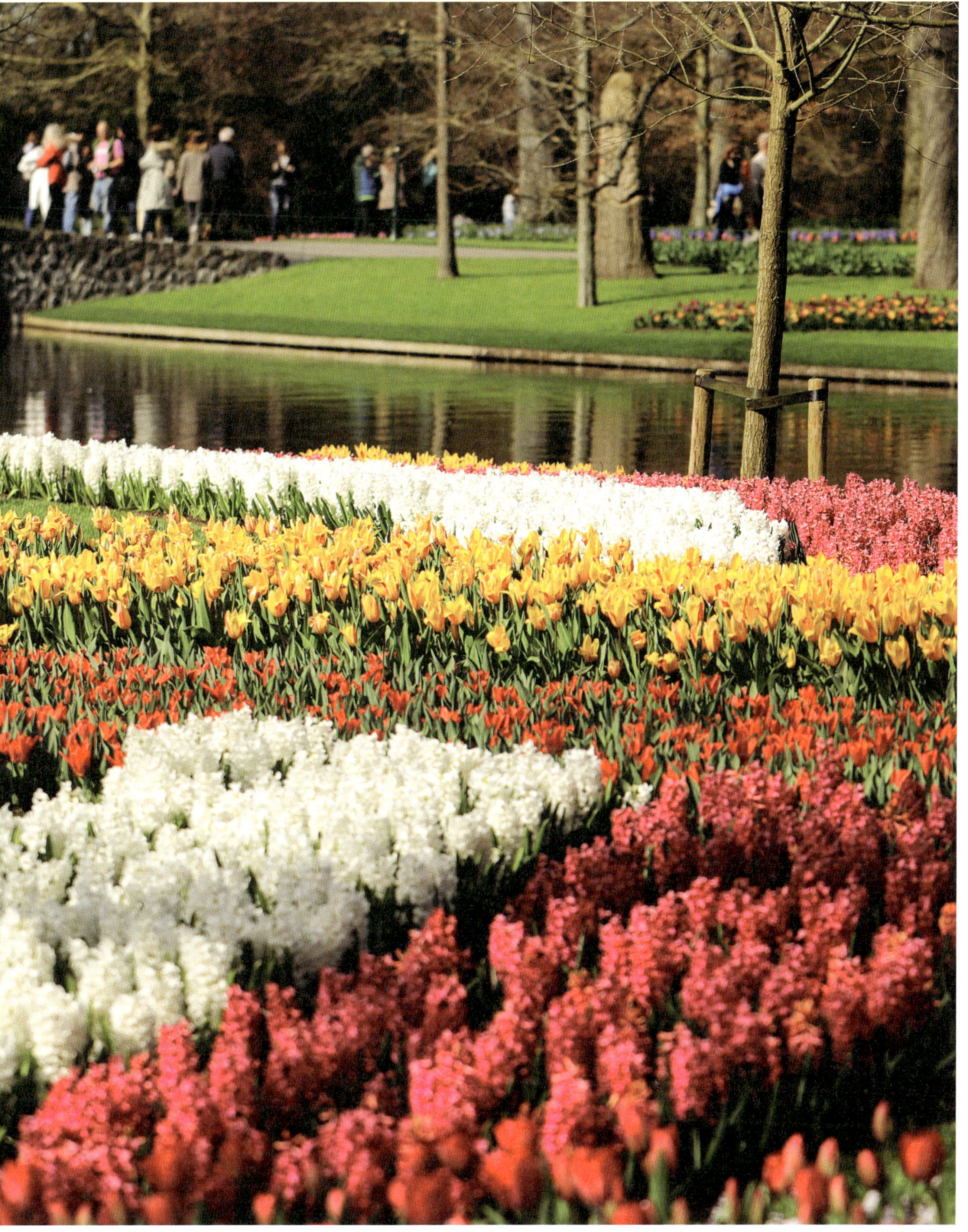

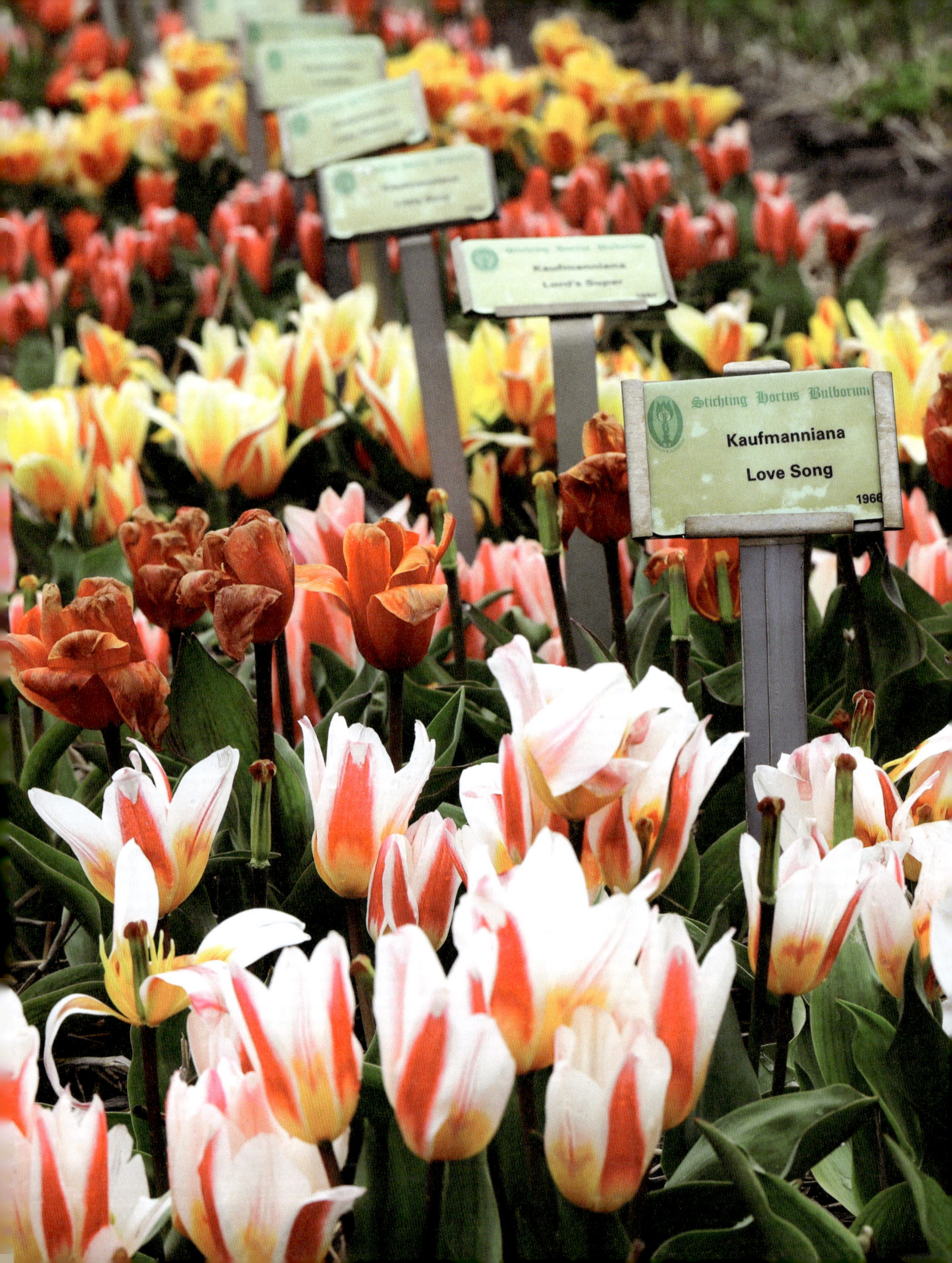

Stichting Hortus Bulborum
Kaufmanniana
Love Song
1966
Kaufmanniana
Lord's Super

Hortus Bulborum

HEIRLOOM
BLOEMBOLLEN

GARDEN MUSEUM WITH AN IMPRESSIVE COLLECTION

Hortus Bulborum in Limmen is impressive. Visitors wander through seas of tulips, daffodils, hyacinths, and crown imperials. The garden is a collection housing tulip treasures like 'Duc van Tol Red and Yellow' (1595), 'Zoomerschoon' (1620), and a long list of other old varieties from before 1900. It is a unique gene bank, a cultural-historical gem that the Hortus Bulborum Foundation cares for with great dedication and that is open to the public.

Hortus Bulborum

HISTORISCHE
BLOEMBOLLEN

MUSEUMSGARTEN MIT SEHENSWERTER SAMMLUNG

Beeindruckend ist ein Besuch im Hortus Bulborum in Limmen. Besucher wandeln durch einen Teppich aus Tulpen, Narzissen, Hyazinthen und Kaiserkronen. Das Besondere: Dieser Kollektionsgarten beherbergt Tulpen-Schätze wie 'Duc van Tol Red and Yellow' (1595), 'Zoomerschoon' (1620) sowie eine Vielzahl alter Sorten von vor 1900. Eine einzigartige Genbank, ein kulturhistorisches Juwel, das die Stiftung Hortus Bulborum mit viel Herzblut hegt und pflegt und einem breiten Publikum zugänglich macht.

Bloemencorso Bollenstreek

FLORAL PARADE

MILLIONS OF SPECTATORS FOLLOW THE ANNUAL FLOWER PARADE FROM NOORDWIJK TO HAARLEM

When the tulip fields are in full bloom in the second half of April, the highlight of the Dutch spring is celebrated with the Bloemencorso Bollenstreek, a parade of oversized figurines or sculptures covered in densely packed flowers. An incredible sweet fragrance announces the lavishly decorated floats as the world-famous flower parade makes its 40-kilometer journey from Noordwijk, passing Keukenhof, to the historic city of Haarlem.

Bloemencorso Bollenstreek

BLUMIGE PARADE

EIN MILLIONENPUBLIKUM VERFOLGT JEDES JAHR DEN PRÄCHTIGEN UMZUG VON NOORDWIJK NACH HAARLEM

Wenn die Tulpenfelder in der zweiten Aprilhälfte in voller Blüte stehen, wird der Höhepunkt des niederländischen Frühlings mit dem Bloemencorso Bollenstreek gefeiert. Dicht an dicht gesteckte Blüten bilden überlebensgroße Figuren. Unvorstellbar, was für ein lieblicher Duft den üppig verzierten Prahlwagen vorauseilt, wenn sich die weltberühmte Blumenparade von Noordwijk über Lisse, vorbei am Keukenhof auf den 40 Kilometer langen Weg in die historische Stadt Haarlem macht.

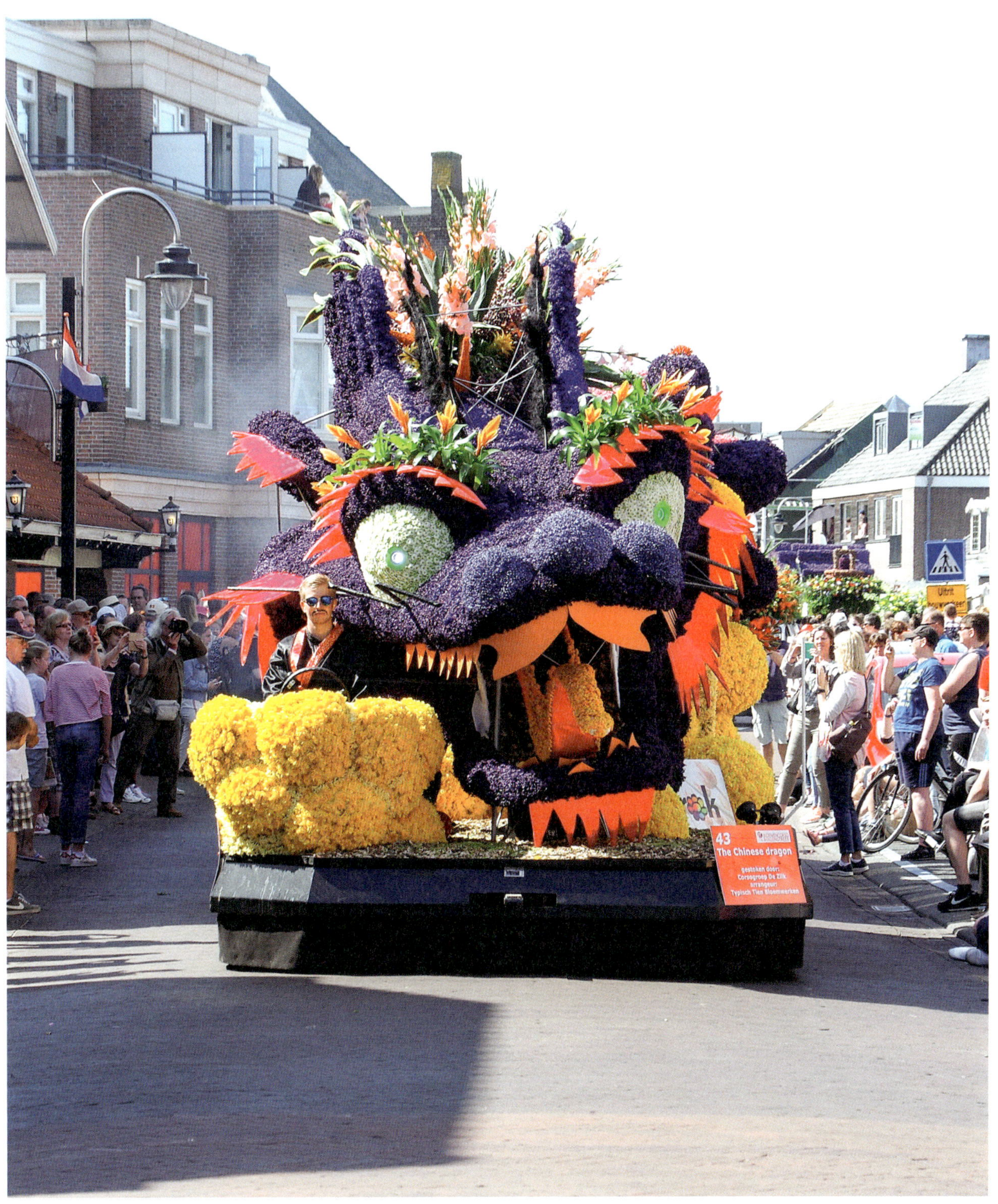
43
The Chinese dragon
gestoken door:
Corsogroep De Zilk
arrangeur:
Typisch Tien Bloemwerken

Tulip breeding in history

TULIP FEVER IN ENGLAND

RACE FOR THE GLORY OF HAVING BRED THE PERFECT TULIP

To display these precious floral jewels, a flower garden should be designed like a cabinet of curiosities, according to the English breeder John Rea (1605[?]–1677). Which of these jewels stood out the most? The queen of bulbous plants, of course: the tulip.

In mid-18th-century England, hundreds of florists' and tulip societies sprang up, with the main purpose of evaluating the aesthetics of tulip breeds according to defined rules. Eventually, a competition for the perfect tulip emerged, and in the 1840s, a kind of tulip war erupted. At the heart of the battle was a biting essay entitled "On the Perfect Form of the Tulip" by the physician and tulip enthusiast Dr. George Hardy (1801–1875). Hardy mocked divergent views from Henry Groom, John Slater, and George Glenny with sharp comments.

'Dr. Hardy', a tulip featuring red flames on yellow ground from the "bizarre" color class, was named in honor of Dr. George Hardy and bred by the railroad worker and flower enthusiast Tom Storer.

Tulpenzucht einst

TULPENFIEBER IN ENGLAND

DAS WETTEIFERN UM DEN RUHM, DIE PERFEKTE TULPE GEZÜCHTET ZU HABEN

Um die unschätzbaren „Edelsteine" der Natur zu beherbergen, möge ein Blumengarten wie ein Raritätenkabinett gestaltet sein, äußerte der englische Züchter John Rea (1605[?]–1677). Welches Juwel am meisten herausragte? Die Königin der Zwiebelgewächse natürlich: die Tulpe.

In England schossen Mitte des 18. Jahrhunderts hunderte Floristen- und Tulpenvereine aus dem Boden, mit dem Zweck, die Perfektion von Tulpenzüchtungen nach definierten Regeln zu bewerten. Schließlich entstand ein Wetteifern um die perfekte Tulpe, bis in den vierziger Jahren des 19. Jahrhunderts ein wahrer Tulpenkrieg entbrannte. Im Zentrum der Schlacht: der scharf formulierte Essay „Über die vollendete Form der Tulpe" des Arztes und Liebhabers Dr. George Hardy (1801–1875). Abweichende Vorstellungen von Henry Groom, John Slater und George Glenny wurden von Hardy mit bissigen Kommentaren verspottet.

'Dr. Hardy', eine auf gelbem Grund rot geflammte Tulpe aus der Farbklasse der Bizarren, wurde zu Ehren von Dr. George Hardy benannt, gezüchtet vom Eisenbahner und Blumenfreund Tom Storer.

Tulip breeding today

A SCIENCE OF ITS OWN

FASTER, BETTER, BLACKER: CHANGING VARIOUS TRAITS OF TULIPS

Today, tulip breeding aims not only to make aesthetic changes but also to increase resistance to disease and the durability of cut tulips. The traditional craft of tulip breeding has always been a lengthy endeavor: it takes six years from germination to the first bloom, and another fifteen years until a new variety reaches the market. Laboratory propagation (*in vitro* culture) rarely, if ever, works in tulips.

Thus, unsurprisingly, science is attempting to use new technologies for accelerated and more sustainable tulip breeding and production. Tulips possess one of the largest genomes in the plant kingdom; their genetic material, estimated to consist of about 34 billion base pairs, is almost eleven times larger than the human genome (with a comparatively meager 3.2 billion base pairs).

Despite this broad range of options for genetic transformation, breeding black tulips remains elusive. This holy grail for Dutch breeders has only once become a reality: in Alexandre Dumas' novel "La Tulipe Noire" (The Black Tulip). The tulip variety 'Queen of Night' (1944) shimmers in a deep, dark purple thanks to a disordered nanostructure on its petals, which creates an almost black spectacle.

RIGHT PAGE | The 'Queen of Night', with its purple to black shimmering flowers, is still considered the most beautiful "black" tulip.

NEXT PAGE | Duc van Tol tulips are among the oldest cultivated tulips. Various color varieties, such as the 'Violet' depicted here, are grouped in their own class.

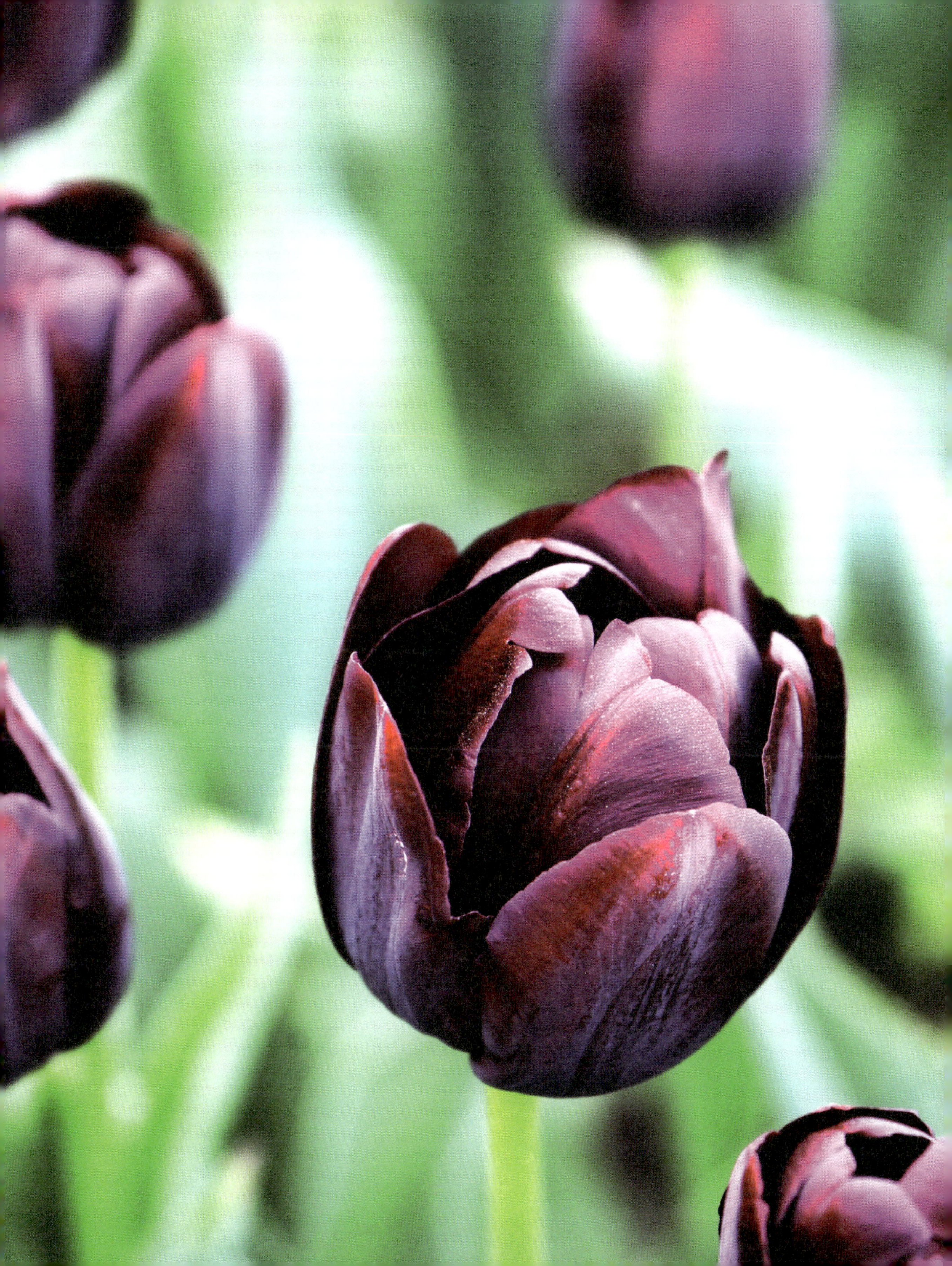

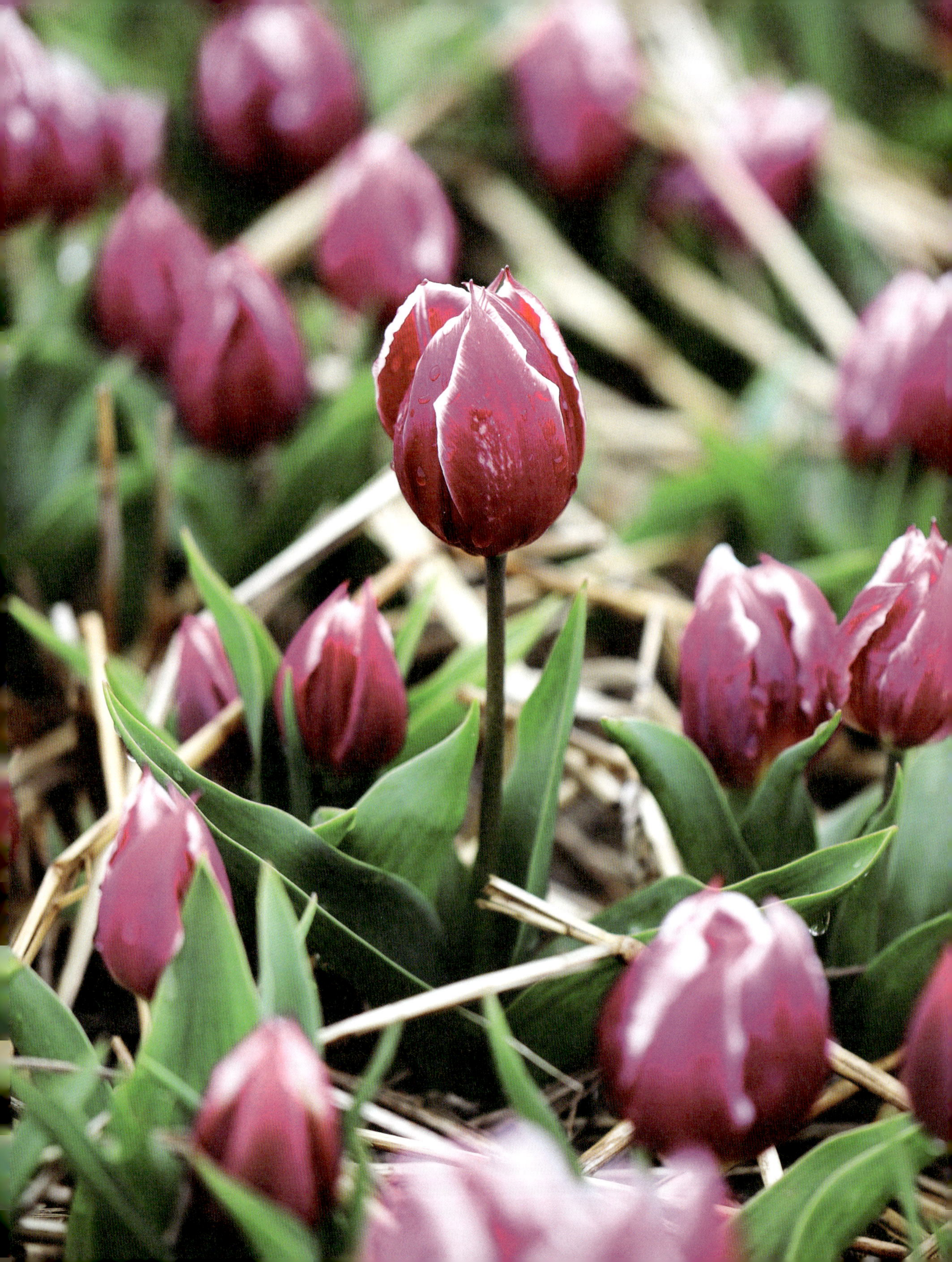

Tulpenzucht heute

EINE WISSENSCHAFT FÜR SICH

SCHNELLER, BESSER, SCHWÄRZER: VIELE EIGENSCHAFTEN DER TULPEN MÖCHTE MAN ÄNDERN

Veredelung dient heute nicht nur der Ästhetik, sondern auch der Steigerung von Resistenzen gegen Krankheiten sowie der besseren Haltbarkeit von Schnitttulpen. Das traditionelle Handwerk der Tulpenzucht ist seit jeher ein langwieriges Unterfangen: Von der Keimung bis zur ersten Blüte vergehen sechs Jahre. Und weitere fünfzehn Jahre, bis eine neue Sorte in den Handel gelangt. Eine Vermehrung im Labor (*in vitro*-Kultur) funktioniert bei Tulpen nur eingeschränkt. Wenn überhaupt.

Kein Wunder, dass sich die Wissenschaft mit neuen Technologien an einer beschleunigten und nachhaltigeren Züchtung und Produktion von Tulpen versucht. Sie besitzen eines der größten Genome im Pflanzenreich. Ihr Erbgut, das geschätzt aus etwa 34 Milliarden Basenpaaren besteht, ist fast elf Mal größer als das menschliche Genom (mit vergleichsweise mickrigen 3,2 Milliarden Basenpaaren).

Das Züchten schwarzer Tulpen will trotz genetisch breit angelegter Verwandlungsoptionen nicht gelingen. Der heilige Gral der niederländischen Züchter wurde nur im Roman „La Tulipe Noire" von Alexandre Dumas Wirklichkeit. Die 'Queen of Night' (1944) schimmert dennoch in tiefdunklem Purpur, weil eine ungeordnete Nanostruktur auf ihren Blütenblättern eine nahezu schwarze Schauwirkung erzeugt.

VORIGE SEITE | Bis heute gilt 'Queen of Night' mit ihren purpurn bis schwarz schimmernden Blüten als die wohl schönste „schwarze" Tulpe.

LINKE SEITE | Duc van Tol-Tulpen gehören zu den ältesten Kulturtulpen. Wegen ihrer historischen Bedeutung in einer eigenen Klasse geführt werden diverse Farbsorten, so wie die hier abgebildete 'Violet'.

Tulip Day

NATIONAL TULIP DAYS

THE NETHERLANDS AND THE USA: CELEBRATING TULIPS BY CELEBRATING WITH TULIPS

"It's tulip time again!" This exclamation echoes across the Netherlands on the third Saturday of January every year. It's National Tulip Day, the colorful start to the tulip season. This festival, organized by Tulpen Promotie Nederland, draws thousands of visitors to the capital's city center. People sing along to Dutch songs while gathering tulips from Amsterdam: guests can pick a bouquet from the 200,000 specially grown tulips and take some joy and cheerful color home with them.

On May 13, the United States celebrates fruit cocktails, apple pie, cough drops, frog jumps, and tulips—an eclectic mix of truly curious holidays. It is unclear who first introduced National Tulip Day in the United States and for how long it has been celebrated. In the mid-19th century, the existing trade with Europe gained rapid importance. Traveling tulip traders, called *bollenreiziger*, opened up an important market for Dutch flower growers in the USA, and exports flourished.

NEXT PAGE | The Dutch love their tulips, as we can see from this lady's headgear on National Tulip Day in Amsterdam (left). In the USA, Tulip Day celebrations are somewhat more modest (right).

Tag der Tulpen

NATIONAL TULIP DAYS

NIEDERLANDE UND USA: FEIERN FÜR DIE TULPEN, FEIERN MIT DEN TULPEN

„Es ist wieder Tulpenzeit!", erklingt es in den Niederlanden immer am dritten Samstag im Januar. Dann ist Nationaler Tulpentag, der erste farbenfrohe Auftakt in die Saison. Das von der Tulpen Promotie Nederland organisierte Fest zieht tausende Besucher ins Zentrum der Hauptstadt. Während niederländische Lieder zum Mitsingen einladen, gibt es „Tulpen aus Amsterdam": Jeder Gast darf sich von den 200 000 eigens vorgezogenen Tulpen einen Strauß pflücken und sich so etwas Freude und wohltuende Farbe mit nach Hause nehmen.

Fruchtcocktails, Apfelkuchen, Hustenbonbons, Froschsprünge und auch Tulpen werden in den USA am 13. Mai geehrt. Wahrlich kuriose Feiertage, die an diesem Tag im Kalender zu finden sind. Wie weit sich der National Tulip Day in den Vereinigten Staaten zurückverfolgen lässt und wer ihn festgesetzt hat, ist nicht bekannt. Ab Mitte des 19. Jahrhunderts gewann der bereits bestehende Handel mit Europa rasant an Bedeutung. Reisende Tulpenhändler, sogenannte *bollenreiziger*, erschlossen für die holländischen Blumenzüchter mit den USA einen wichtigen Absatzmarkt, sodass der Export immer mehr florierte.

NÄCHSTE SEITE | Niederländer lieben ihre Tulpen, das zeigt sich auch am Kopfputz dieser Dame beim Nationalen Tulpentag in Amsterdam (links). In den USA wird der Tulpentag etwas dezenter begangen (rechts).

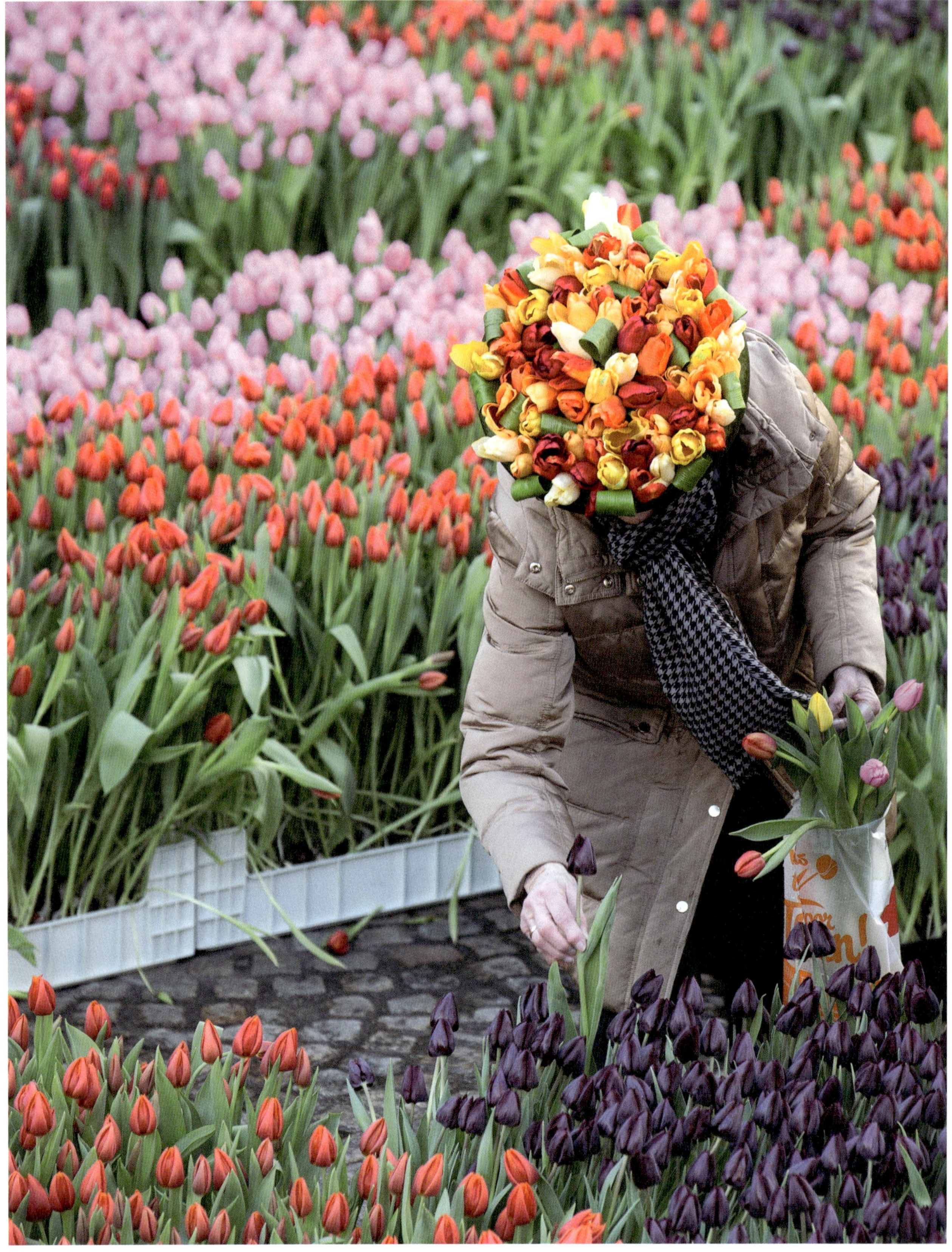

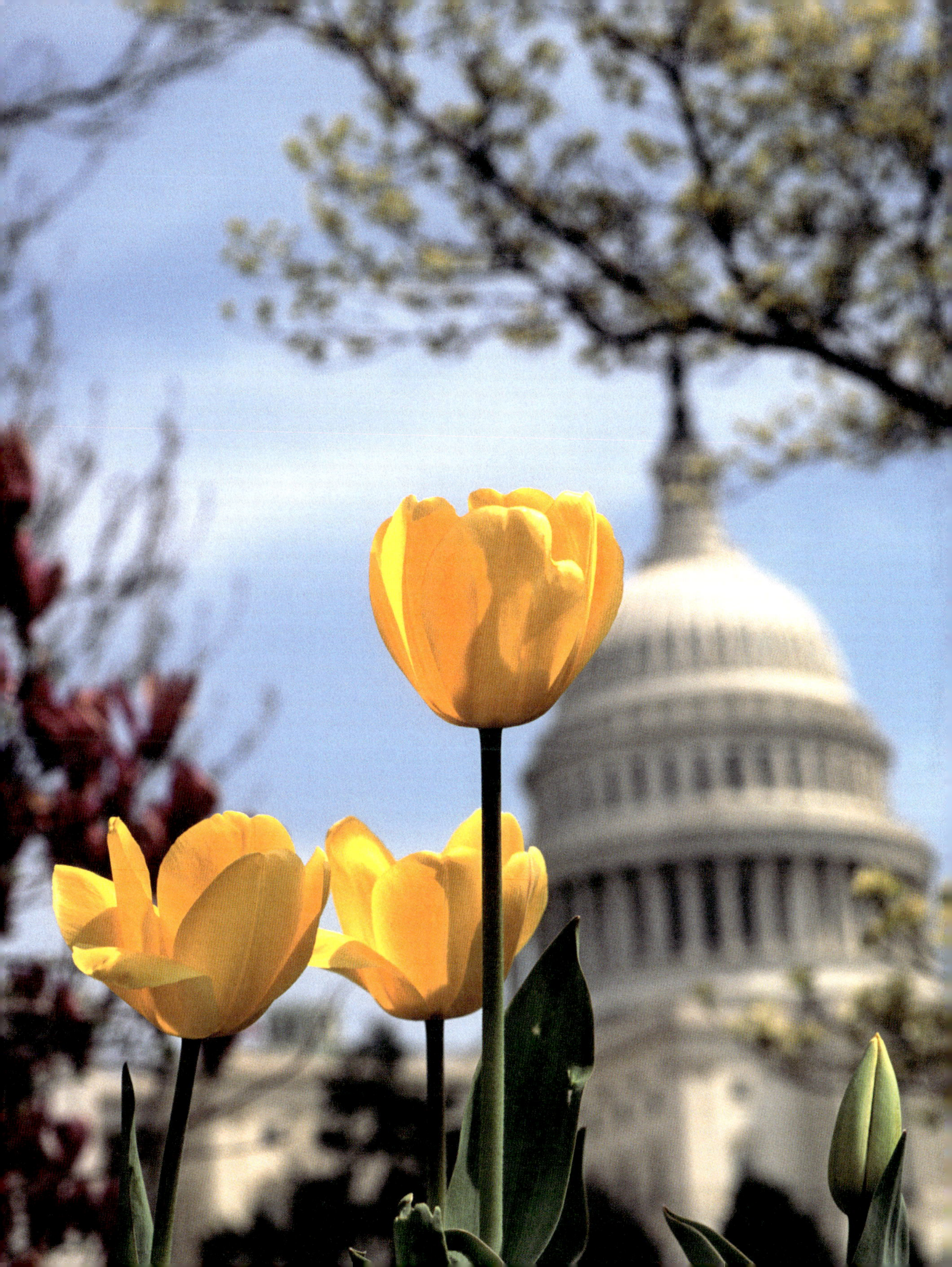

The Netherlands—an international tulip power

FROM SPECULATIVE STOCK TO SUCCESSFUL EXPORT

NO OTHER COUNTRY IN THE WORLD IS AS CLOSELY ASSOCIATED WITH TULIPS

Windmills, dikes, canals, cheese, Rembrandt, Delft Blue, *omafiets* ("granny bikes") ... all of these are typically Dutch. Should this list also include Frau Antje? Absolutely. In Germany, the blonde lady with the white lace cap has been a well-known advertising figure for cheese since 1961. What about wooden shoes *(klompen)* as souvenirs? Yes, please! The distinctive shoes made from a single piece of poplar wood keep your feet dry when you are gardening and can be repurposed as attractive plant containers. Finally, we must add tulips, the top export! As the world's largest producer, the Netherlands enjoys a dominant position in both the tulip bulb and cut flower markets.

From late April on, millions of identical flower heads stretch towards the sky along the Dutch coast in an overwhelming carpet of color. But soon, mowing machines bring an abrupt end to the dazzling splendor: the tulips are beheaded! This may seem counter-intuitive, but it is necessary to promote the development of large, robust bulbs for growing seasons to come, for cut tulips for vases are not grown in fields but in large growing halls. There, the desired blooming time is not a random occurrence; breeders can deliberately adjust the time of bloom through precise temperature control in the cooling rooms and greenhouses.

NEXT PAGE | Countless tulips cover Dutch fields in spring like a carpet (left). However, cut flowers are grown in halls (right).

Tulpenweltmacht Niederlande

VOM SPEKULATIONSOBJEKT ZUM EXPORTSCHLAGER

KEIN ANDERES LAND DER WELT WIRD SO SIGNIFIKANT MIT TULPEN VERBUNDEN

Windmühlen, Deiche, Grachten, Käse, Rembrandt, Delfter Blau, *omafiets* ... typisch niederländisch! Frau Antje fehlt in der Auflistung? Stimmt. In Deutschland ist die blonde Dame mit der weißen Spitzenhaube seit 1961 eine weithin bekannte Werbefigur für Käse. Klompen als Reisemitbringsel? Oh ja! Die markanten Schuhe aus einem einzigen Stück Pappelholz halten die Füße bei der Gartenarbeit trocken oder lassen sich als hübsches Pflanzengefäß zweckentfremden. Und natürlich Tulpen, der Exportschlager! Als weltgrößter Produzent genießen die Niederlande die Vormachtstellung auf beiden Tulpenmärkten für Zwiebeln und Schnittblumen.

Die Farbteppiche sind schier überwältigend, wenn sich ab der zweiten Aprilhälfte entlang der niederländischen Küste Millionen gleicher Blütenköpfe gen Himmel recken. Doch schon bald setzen Mähmaschinen der bunten Pracht ein jähes Ende: Die Tulpen werden geköpft! Das mag zunächst irritieren, ist aber notwendig, damit große, kräftige Zwiebeln ausgebildet werden. Schnitttulpen für die Vase werden nämlich nicht auf den Feldern, sondern in riesigen Hallen gezogen. Dort ist das Erreichen einer bestimmten Blütezeit kein Zufallsprodukt, sondern durch ideale Temperaturbehandlungen in den Kühlräumen und Gewächshäusern gezielt steuerbar.

NÄCHSTE SEITE | Riesige Tulpenteppiche überziehen im Frühling niederländische Felder (links). Schnittblumen werden allerdings in Hallen gezogen (rechts).

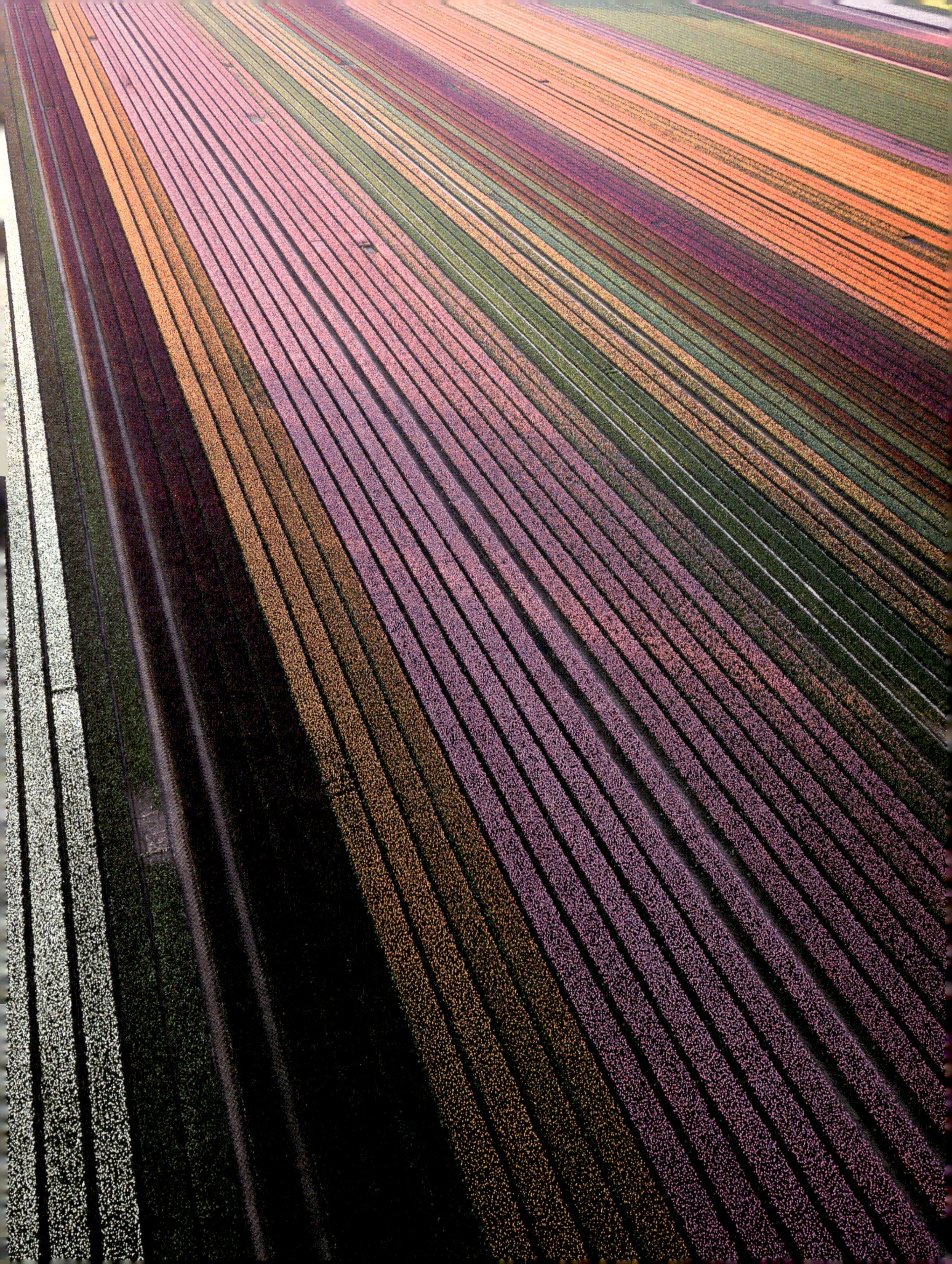

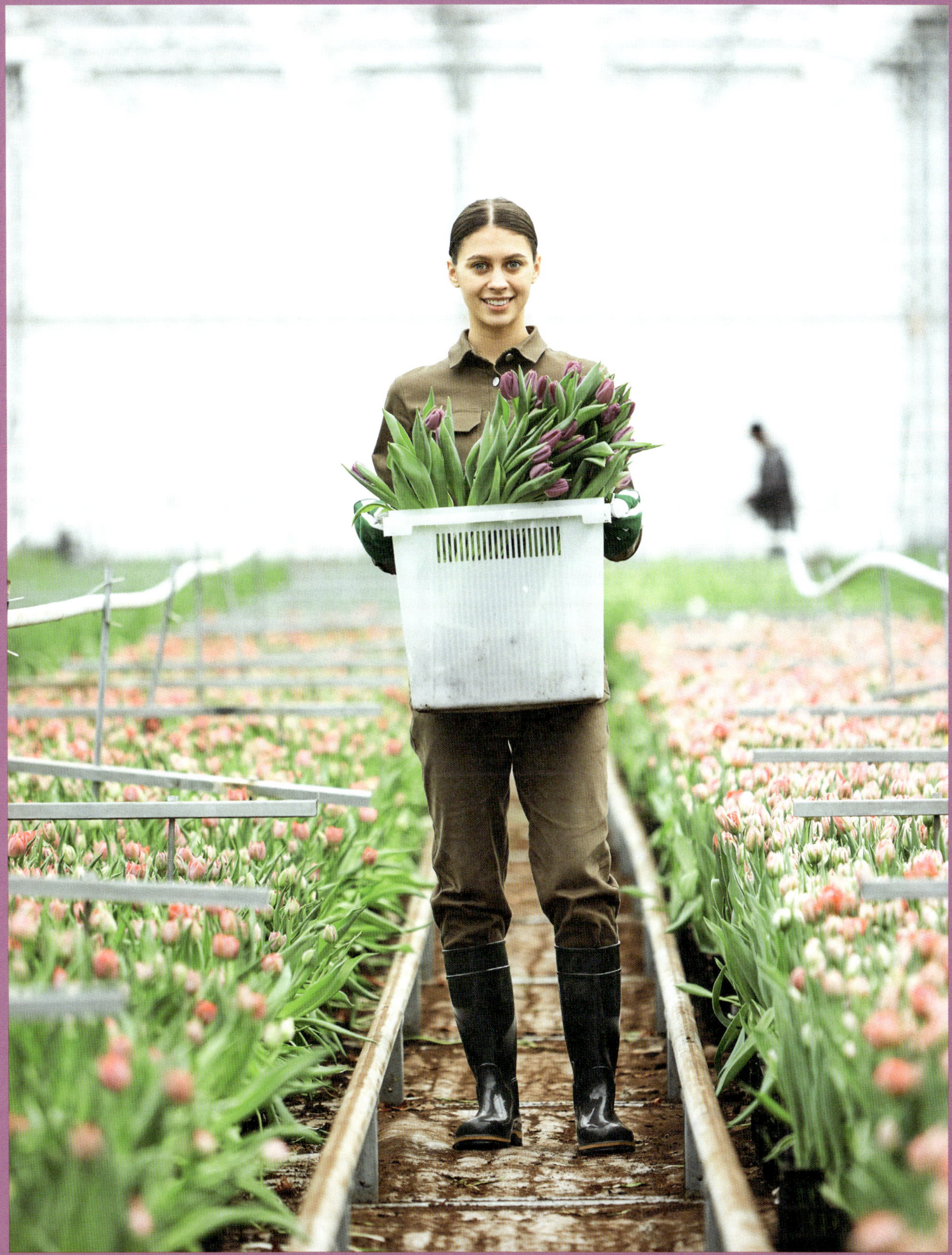

Commodity

TULIPS UNDER THE HAMMER

TULIP AUCTIONS: ADRENALINE IN FOUR-SECOND INTERVALS

Early in the morning, the vast hall is filled with bustling activity, making it appear like an anthill. Flowers of all kinds, including, of course, countless tulips, are carted around the hall on stack trolleys. We are guests at Royal FloraHolland, standing on the visitor bridge above the largest international trading platform for flowers and plants. What we see below us is only a fraction of this extraordinary place in Aalsmeer, a small town just outside Amsterdam. We can only imagine what happens here, at the world's largest flower market, 24 hours a day.

Daily from 6 a.m. onwards, millions of flowers arrive and are then auctioned off in thousands of transactions; delicate, perishable goods are under the hammer. At the center of this unique market model is a flower clock. A red dot races around the circular dial within four seconds; during this time, the price decreases, and it only stops when the first buyer bids. Sold! It is pure adrenaline; after all, the buyer wants to avoid bidding too early at too high a price. However, if they wait for too long, the lot might go to a competitor. Tough luck.

The race against time does not end there: cut flowers and plants are delivered to the dealers' loading docks as quickly as possible through a sophisticated logistics system so that they can adorn our homes the next day.

NEXT PAGE | At Royal FloraHolland, flowers are auctioned daily and immediately sent to stores.

Handelsware

TULPEN UNTER DEM HAMMER

AUKTIONEN FÜR TULPEN: STRESS IM VIER-SEKUNDEN-TAKT

Am frühen Morgen herrscht emsiges Treiben in der riesengroßen Halle, fast wie in einem Ameisenhaufen. Kreuz und quer werden allerlei Blumen, darunter natürlich auch Unmengen von Tulpen, auf Stapelwagen durch die Halle gekarrt. Als Gast stehen wir auf der Besucherbrücke von Royal FloraHolland, der größten internationalen Handelsplattform für Blumen und Pflanzen. Unter uns ist nur ein Bruchteil eines außergewöhnlichen Ortes in Aalsmeer, einer kleinen Stadt vor den Toren Amsterdams, zu sehen. Und doch lässt sich erahnen, was sich hier 24 Stunden am Tag an der weltgrößten Blumenbörse abspielt.

Ab sechs Uhr kommen täglich Millionen von Blumen in tausenden von Transaktionen unter den Hammer, die Versteigerung der leicht verderblichen Ware beginnt. Im Zentrum der besonderen Verkaufsmethode: eine Blumenuhr. Ein roter Punkt flitzt binnen vier Sekunden bei abnehmendem Preis einmal um das kreisrunde Ziffernblatt und bleibt stehen, sobald ein Käufer bietet. Gekauft. Das ist Stress pur, schließlich will ein Händler nicht zu früh bei hohem Preis kaufen. Wartet er jedoch zu lange, geht die Partie an einen Konkurrenten. Pech gehabt.

Es bleibt ein Wettlauf gegen die Zeit: Schnellstmöglich werden die Schnittblumen und Pflanzen mithilfe einer ausgeklügelten Logistik an die Verladedocks der Händler geliefert, damit sie am nächsten Tag schon unsere Wohnungen zieren können.

NÄCHSTE SEITE | Bei Royal FloraHolland werden täglich Blumen verauktioniert und unmittelbar auf die Reise in die Geschäfte geschickt.

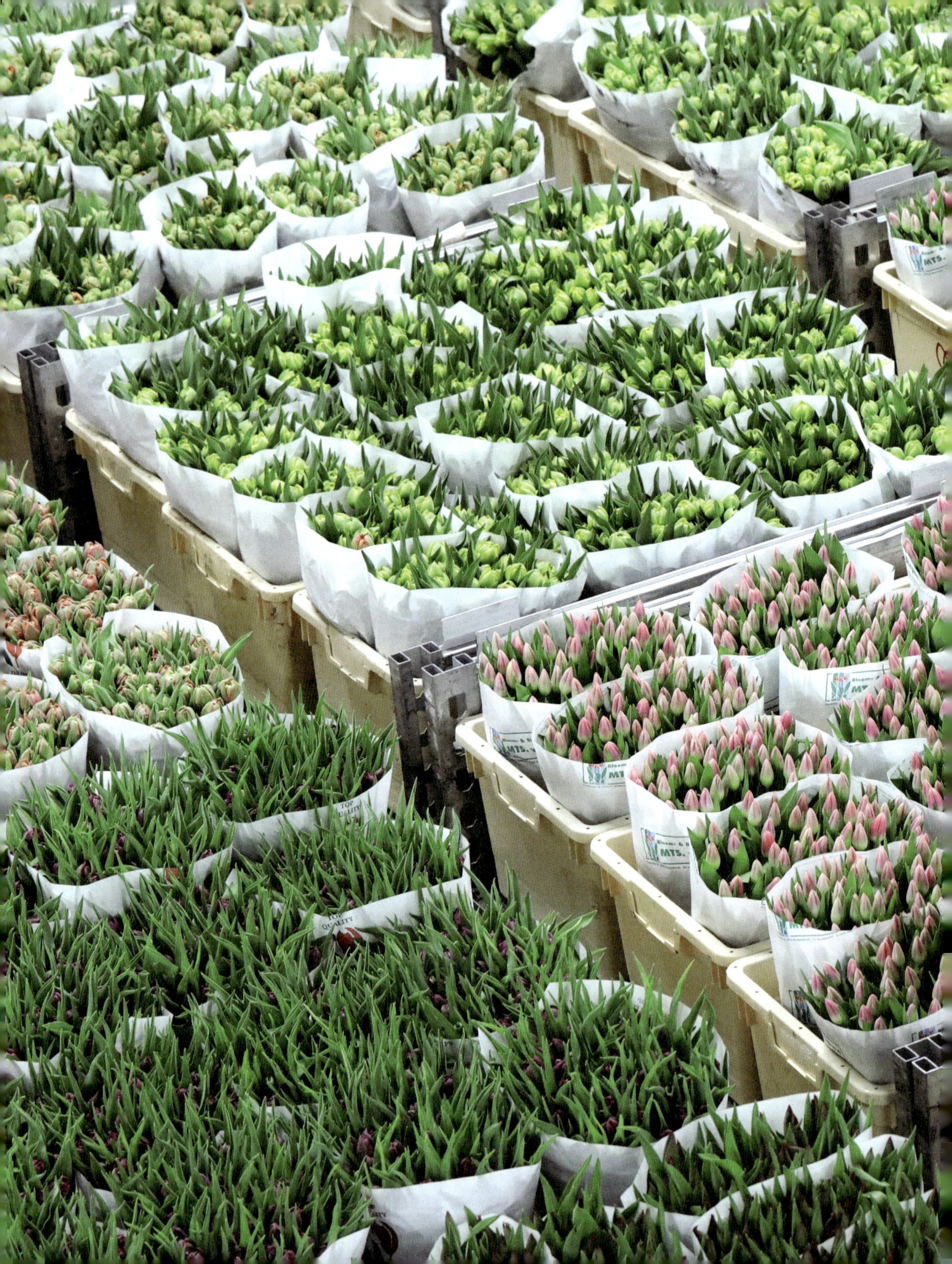

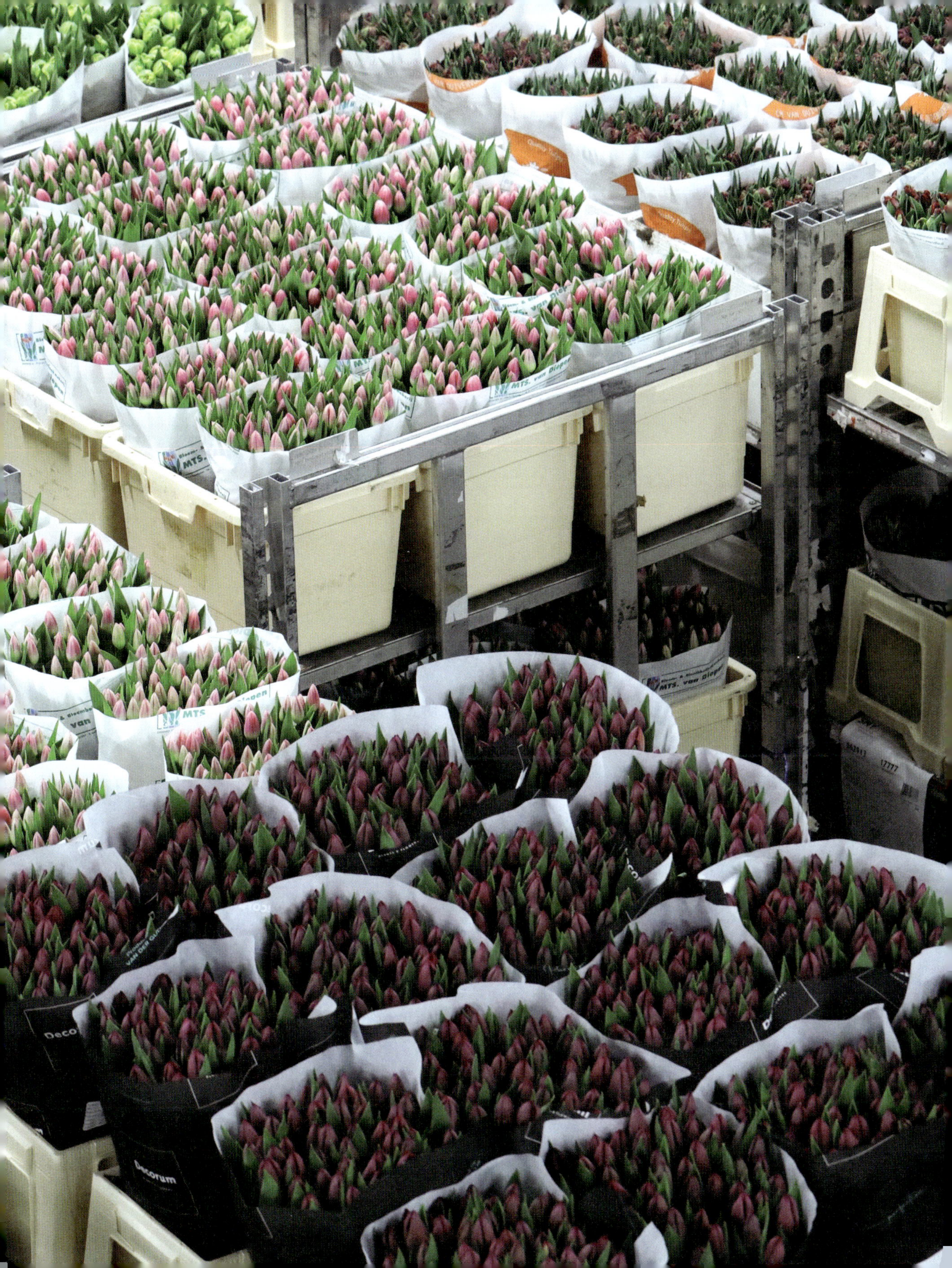

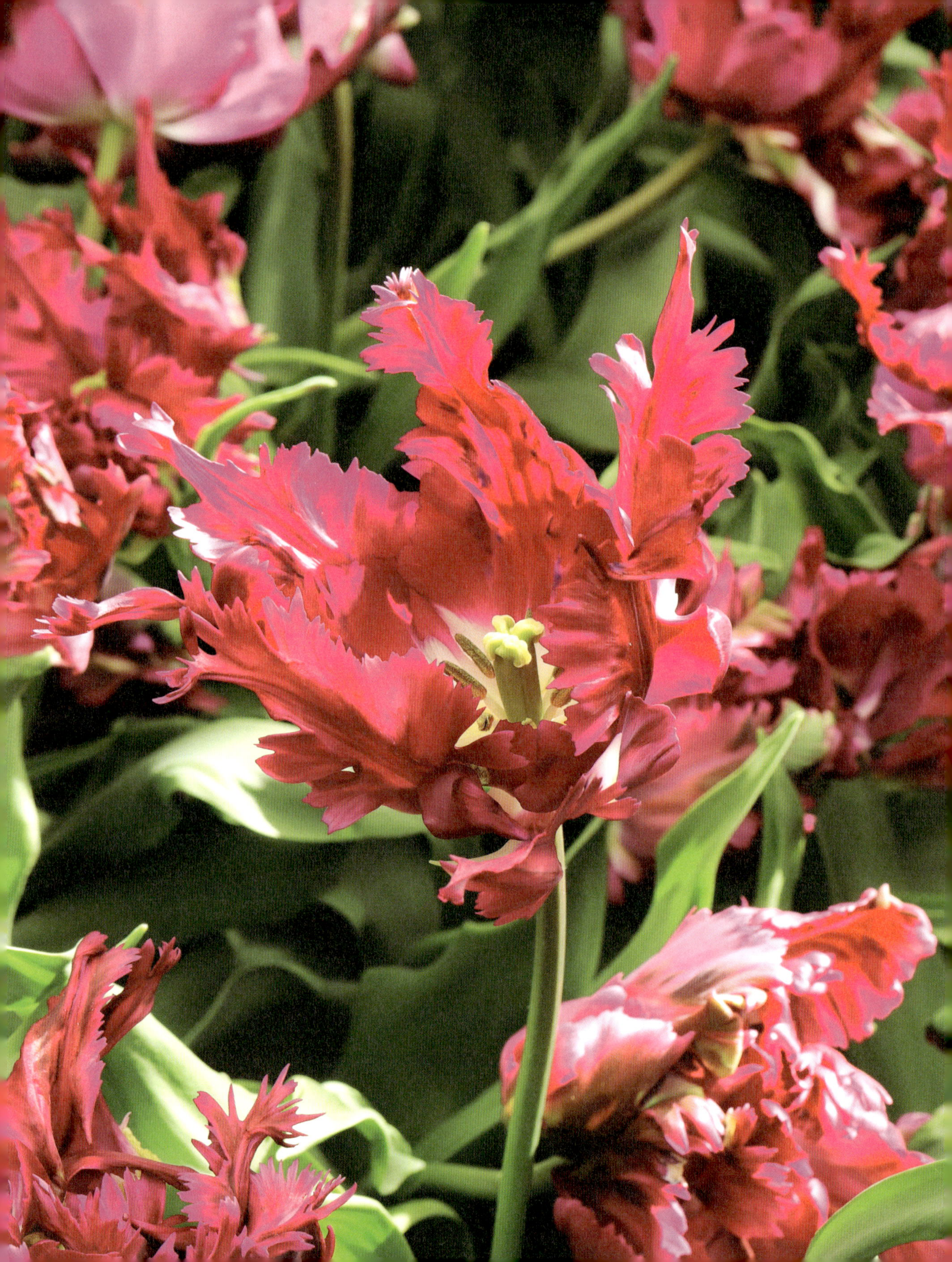

The language of flowers

COLORFUL MESSAGES

TULIPS MORE THAN SPEAK FOR THEMSELVES

In the language of flowers, tulips are full of contradictions. They can express deep disappointment as well as passionate love. A bouquet of red tulips whisks a couple away to seventh heaven. Yellow tulips express affection, and orange ones provide energy. Pink tulips whisper of newly budding fondness. Black tulips are given by those who want to express their fiery passion. White tulips are an expression of sympathy or an apology. Extravagant parrot tulips with their feathery petals are the ideal choice if you just want to bring joy to someone (as pictured on the left page).

Die Sprache der Blumen

FARBBOTSCHAFTEN

TULPEN SPRECHEN MEHR ALS NUR FÜR SICH

In der Blumensprache sind Tulpen widersprüchlich. Sie können tiefe Enttäuschung ebenso zum Ausdruck bringen wie leidenschaftliche Liebe. Ein Strauß roter Tulpen lässt ein Paar im siebten Himmel schweben. Gelbe Tulpen bekunden liebevolle Zuneigung, orangefarbene spenden Energie. Rosa spricht von gerade erwachender Liebe. Schwarze Tulpen schenken diejenigen, die heißblütige Leidenschaft empfinden. Mit weißen Tulpen entschuldigt man sich oder drückt sein Mitgefühl aus. Um jemandem eine Freude zu bereiten, sind extravagante Papageientulpen mit ihren fedrigen Blütenblättern die ideale Wahl (siehe linke Seite).

A HAPPY END FOR TULIPS

BUY SEASONAL, BUY LOCAL

Why not convey your heartfelt message through flowers? Ahead of chrysanthemums and carnations, tulips snatch the second spot each year among the most popular cut flowers, surpassed only by roses. Yet in terms of sustainability, tulips are miles ahead. Roses mostly thrive in Kenya, require an extraordinary amount of water, and travel long distances across half the globe. While most tulips are indeed grown in the Netherlands in huge heated greenhouses, solar-powered energy systems and the fact that tulips can grow in a water solution rather than soil make cut tulips more environmentally friendly than other flowers. According to manufacturers, they can even be grown without chemicals protecting against certain virus types.

Sustainability is all the rage! Ideally, buy seasonally and locally grown flowers. What could be better than visiting a pick-your-own-flowers field to create a bouquet by hand? Choose flowers whose heads are still hard and closed. You can cut the tulip stems directly above the ground; they squeak like asparagus when rubbed against each other. This is truly the freshest and, quite literally, the greenest option.

In Central Europe, roses are more common than tulips in flower bouquets, while in the US, tulips are the best-selling cut flowers.

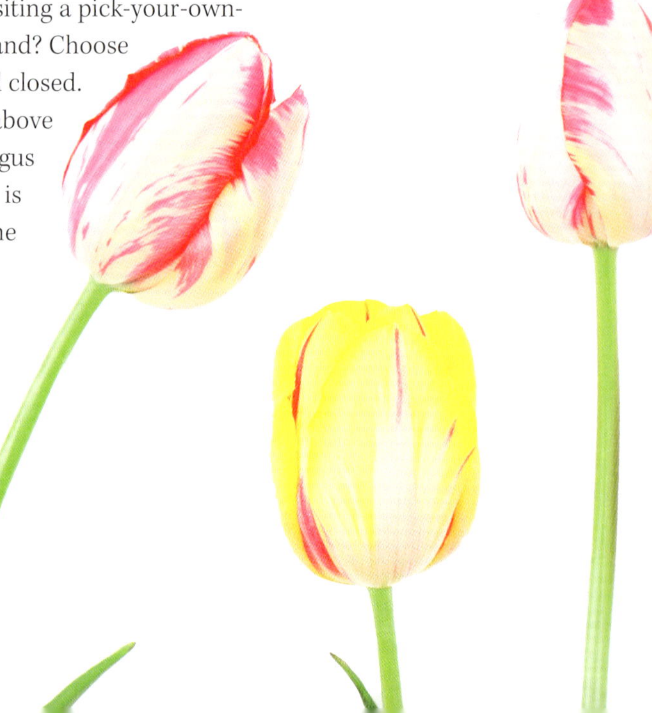

Nachhaltigkeit

TULPEN GUT, ALLES GUT

MAN KAUFT SIE ZUR PASSENDEN JAHRESZEIT, UND BESSER IN DER REGION ALS IN ÜBERSEE PRODUZIERT

Übermitteln Sie jemandem Ihre Herzensbotschaft doch durch die Blume! Vor den Chrysanthemen und Nelken ergattern Tulpen jedes Jahr den zweiten Platz bei den beliebtesten Schnittblumen, übertroffen nur von Rosen. In puncto Nachhaltigkeit liegen Tulpen sogar meilenweit vorn, da Rosen meist in Kenia gedeihen, außerordentlich viel Wasser benötigen und weite Transportwege über den halben Erdball zurücklegen. Die meisten Tulpen werden zwar in den Niederlanden in riesigen beheizten Gewächshäusern herangezogen, doch sorgen Photovoltaikanlagen und die Bepflanzung in einer Wasserlösung dafür, dass Schnitttulpen umweltverträglicher und, so die Produzenten, ohne Chemikalien gegen bestimmte Virusarten produziert werden können.

Nachhaltigkeit ist angesagt! Idealerweise wird saisonal und regional gekauft. Was gibt es folglich Besseres, als sich auf dem Selbstpflückfeld eigenhändig einen Strauß zusammenzustellen? Die Tulpenstängel mit festen und noch geschlossenen Blüten werden direkt über dem Boden abgeschnitten und knirschen wie Spargel, wenn sie aneinander gerieben werden. Frischer und „grüner" geht's nun wirklich nicht!

In Mitteleuropa finden sich häufiger Rosen als Tulpen in Blumensträußen, in den USA hingegen ist die Tulpe die meistverkaufte Schnittblume.

Beauties in vases

BEAUTIFULLY STAGED

LARGE VASES FOR A STEADY BALANCE

Vases come in all sizes, shapes, and forms: which ones are best suited to showcase a tulip bouquet? Tall and slender cylinder vases are ideal for a medium-sized bouquet. They should cover about two-thirds of the tulip's entire length, as cut tulips continue to grow in the vase. This may seem unusual, since cut flowers are technically dead, but there is a simple reason for this phenomenon. There is no actual growth through cell division; the existing cells simply swell and stretch due to water absorption.

Vasenschönheiten

SCHÖN IN SZENE

FÜR SICHEREN STAND DÜRFEN VASEN NICHT ZU KLEIN GEWÄHLT WERDEN

Vasen in allen Größen und Variationen: Welche lässt einen Tulpenstrauß am besten zur Geltung kommen? Wahre Allrounder für einen mittelgroßen Strauß sind hohe und schlanke Zylindervasen: Am besten etwa zwei Drittel der Tulpenlänge hoch, denn Schnitttulpen wachsen in der Vase weiter. Erstaunlich, denn abgeschnittene Blumen sind eigentlich tot … Der Grund ist simpel: Es ist kein Wachstum durch Zellteilung, sondern die Zellen strecken sich einfach durch Wasseraufnahme.

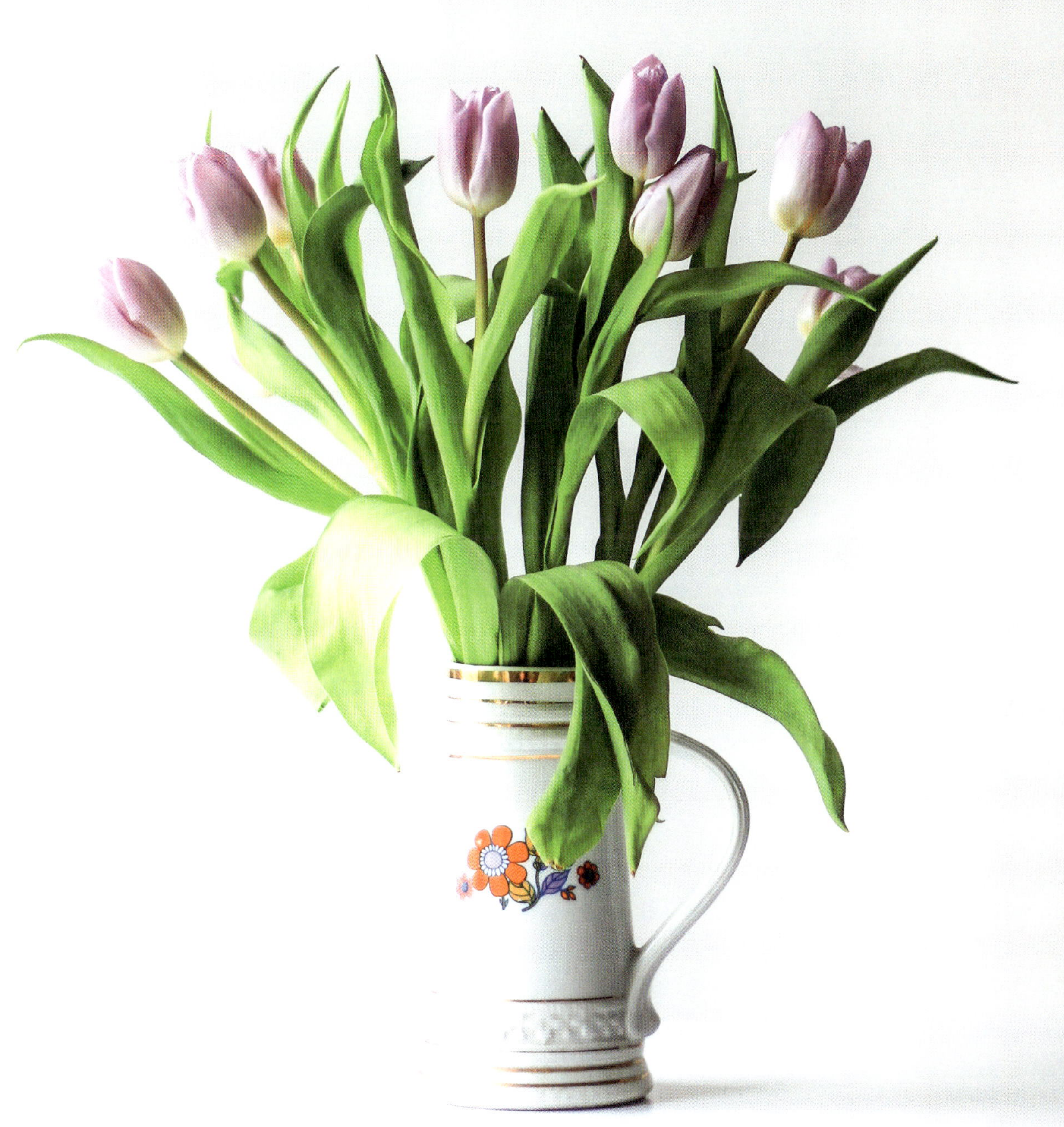

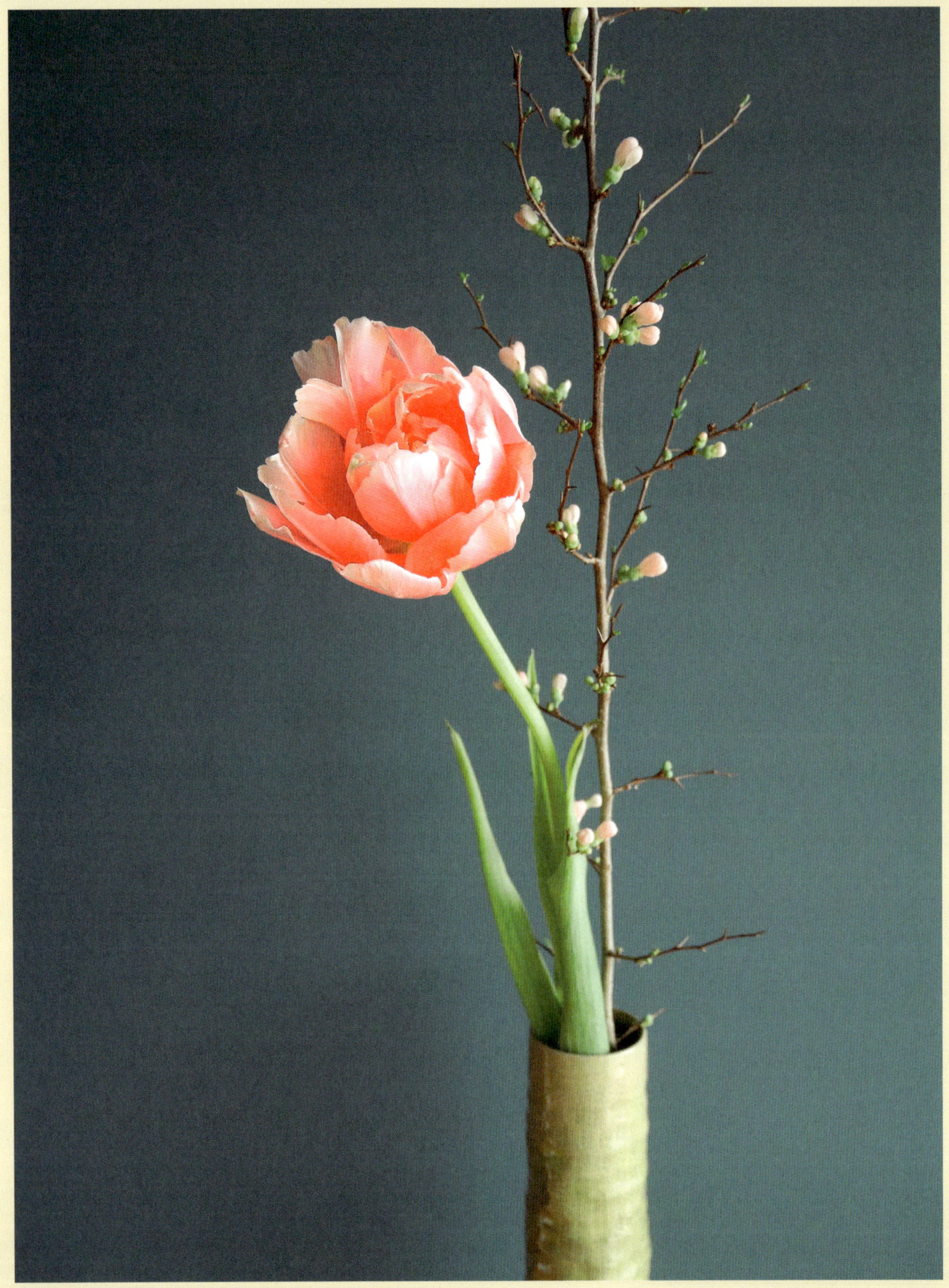

French tulips

OH, LÀ, LÀ—
THE TULIP!

NOT A DISTINCT CLASS AMONG TULIP VARIETIES,
BUT IN A LEAGUE OF THEIR OWN

French tulips are particularly tall. What sets these noble XL tulips apart are their long stems that twist and wind in their vases as they grow. Just a few of these exclusive tulips from southern France and the Netherlands are enough to create an elegant decoration, and they make a pretty display in a vase or as part of a flower arrangement.

Französische Tulpen

OH, LÀ, LÀ –
LA TULIPE!

SIE BILDEN KEINE EIGENE KLASSE UNTER DEN TULPEN-
SORTEN, SIND ABER SCHLICHTWEG KLASSE

Französische Tulpen sind *extra large*. Das Markenzeichen der edlen XL-Tulpen: lange Stiele, die sich während des Wuchses in der Vase spektakulär winden. Für eine elegante Dekoration genügen schon wenige dieser exklusiven Tulpen aus Südfrankreich und den Niederlanden, um sie in einer Vase oder in einem Blumenarrangement eindrucksvoll in Szene zu setzen.

Tulips against stress

A RELAXING SIGHT

ENGAGING CREATIVELY WITH TULIPS IS LIKE PRACTICING "FLOWER YOGA"

Receiving flowers as a gift can trigger a kind of euphoria; our brains are flooded with a surge of endorphins. Engaging creatively with flowers is like a miracle cure for stress.

All you need is time and some materials, and you can let your imagination run wild. Insert a few spring branches, such as willow catkins, cherry wood, or curly willow, into a tulip bouquet, and you can immediately see a lively interplay. Blueberry branches, grasses, or fragrant gorse sprigs also make excellent tulip companions.

Gently bending the stems in a very tall glass can create a delightful display. Drape a few tulips of varying lengths in a tall glass vase or place single tulips in individual bottles of differing heights. Short-cut tulips can be inserted into halved eggshells—the possibilities are endless …

Now, the only remaining question is how to make these beauties in vases last as long as possible. You should use a small amount of cold water, cut the stems with a sharp knife in a straight cut, remove the majority of the leaves, and choose a cool spot for them. Beyond that, the most important tip is to thoroughly enjoy their beauty while it lasts and always accept their transience.

Tulpen gegen Stress

ALLEIN DER ANBLICK ENTSPANNT

WER SICH KREATIV MIT TULPEN BESCHÄFTIGT, BETREIBT EINE ART „BLUMEN-YOGA"

Ein Blumengeschenk kann so etwas wie einen Rausch auslösen, weil unser Gehirn mit einem Schwall Glückshormonen geflutet wird. Sich kreativ mit Blumen zu beschäftigen, gilt als Wundermittel gegen Stress.

Benötigt werden nur Zeit für sich und ein paar wenige Materialien, um der Fantasie freien Lauf zu lassen: Stecken Sie in einen Tulpenstrauß ein paar Frühlingszweige, beispielsweise von Weidenkätzchen, Kirschbaum oder Korkenzieherweide, und schon erleben Sie ein lebendiges Zusammenspiel. Toll lassen sich Tulpen mit Heidelbeerzweigen, Gräsern oder duftenden Ginsterruten kombinieren.

Originell wirken Tulpen in einem sehr großen Glas, wenn die Stiele vorsichtig gebogen werden. Drapieren Sie einige wenige Tulpen in unterschiedlichen Längen in einer hohen Glasvase oder geben Sie je eine Tulpe in verschieden große Flaschen. Kurz geschnittene Tulpen können in gekappte Eierschalen gesteckt werden. Möglichkeiten gibt es mehr als genug …

Stellt sich nur noch die Frage, wie die Vasenschönheiten möglichst lange halten. Wenig kaltes Wasser, Stiele mit einem scharfen Messer gerade anschneiden, den Großteil der Blätter entfernen und einen nicht zu warmen Standort wählen. Ansonsten gilt der wohl wichtigste Tipp: Sich in jedem Moment an den Tulpen erfreuen und ihre Vergänglichkeit annehmen.

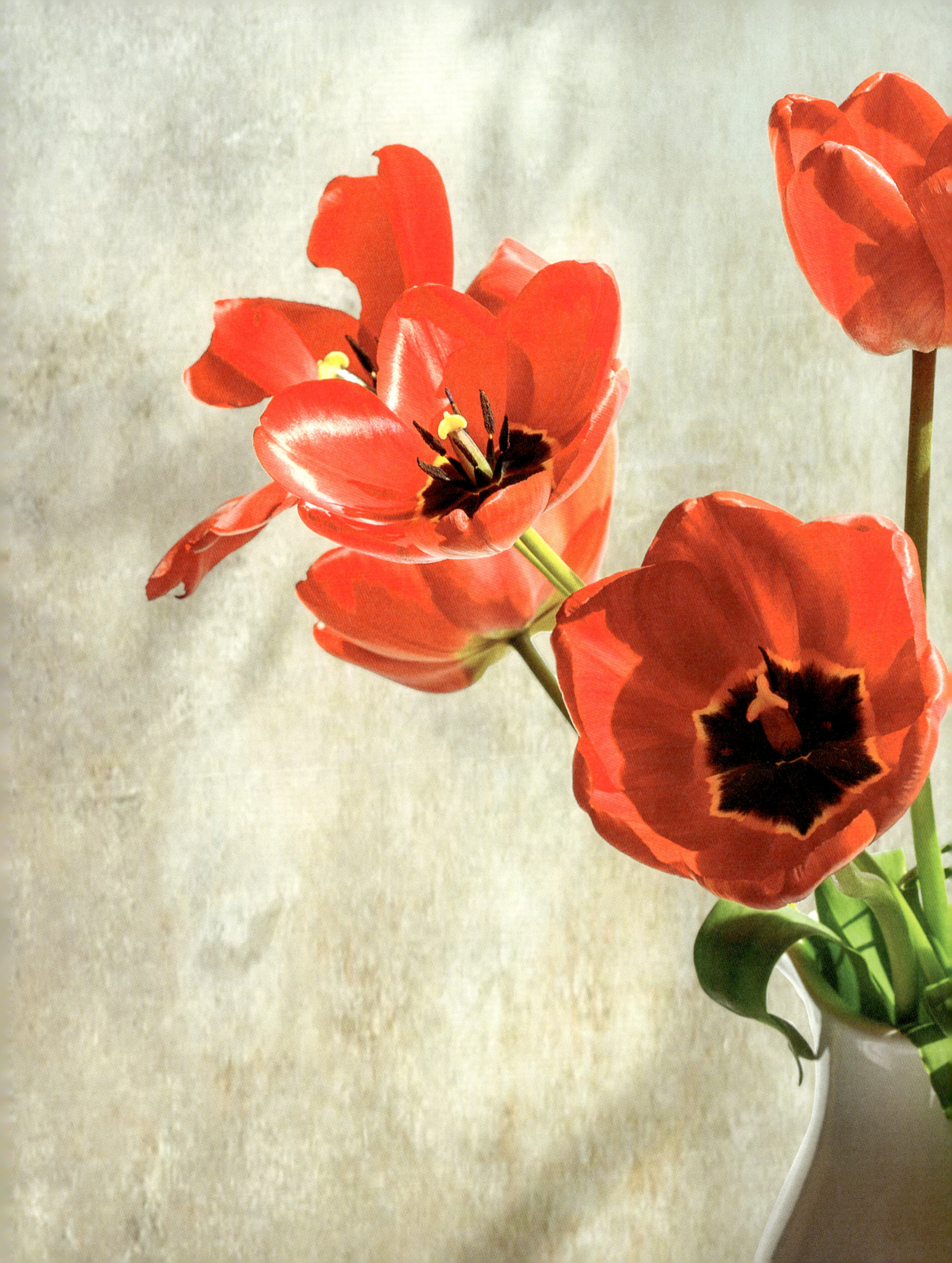

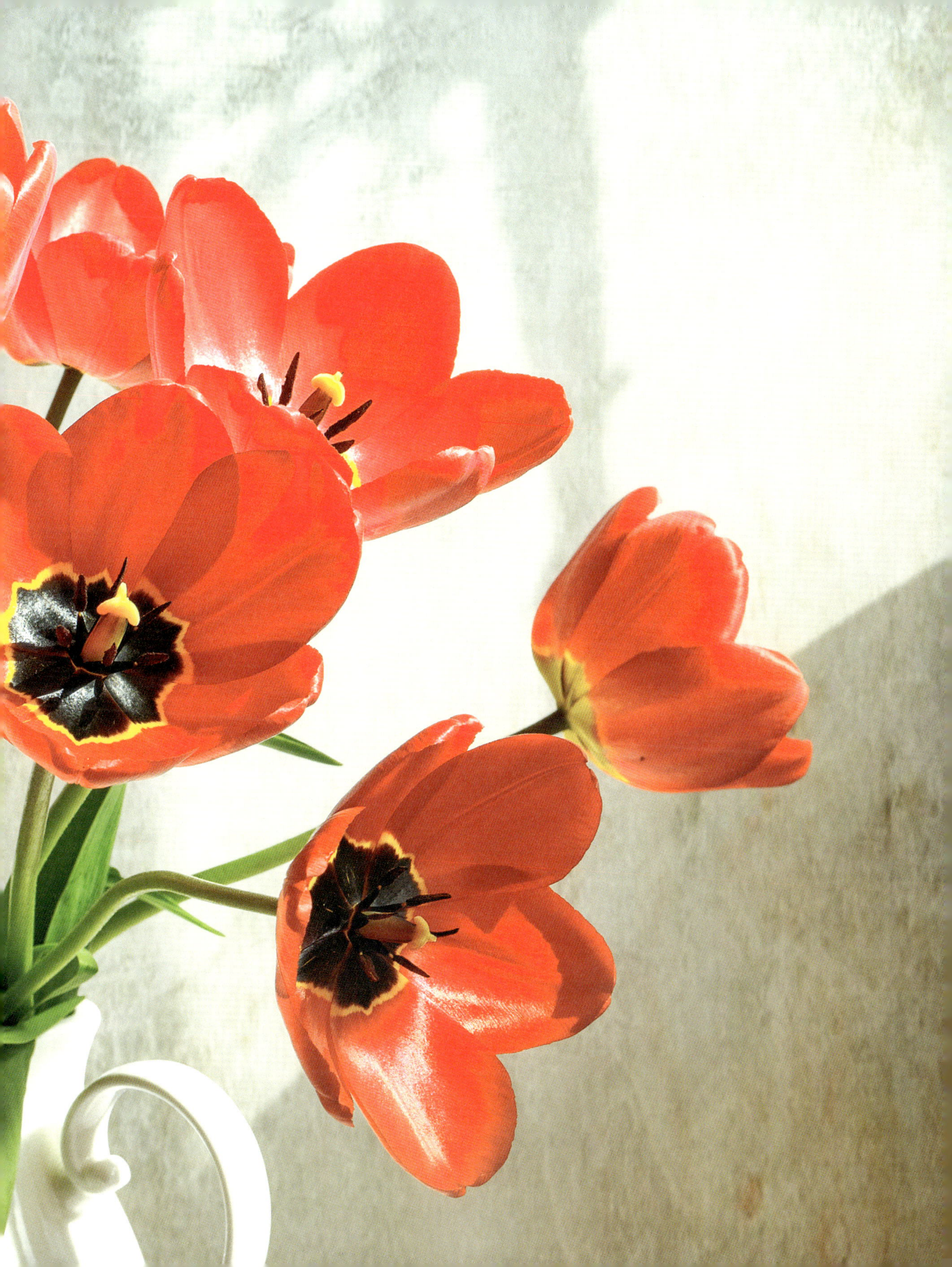

FLORA'S GIFTS

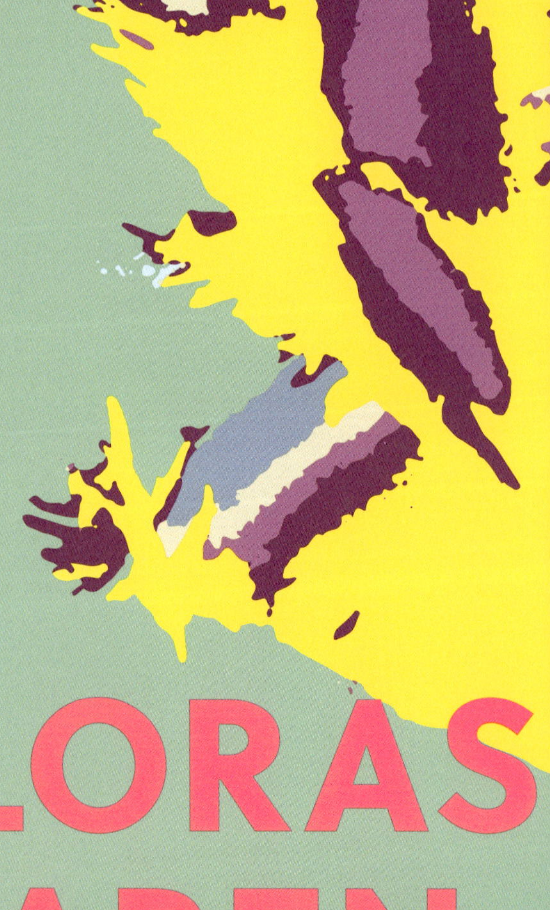

FLORAS GABEN

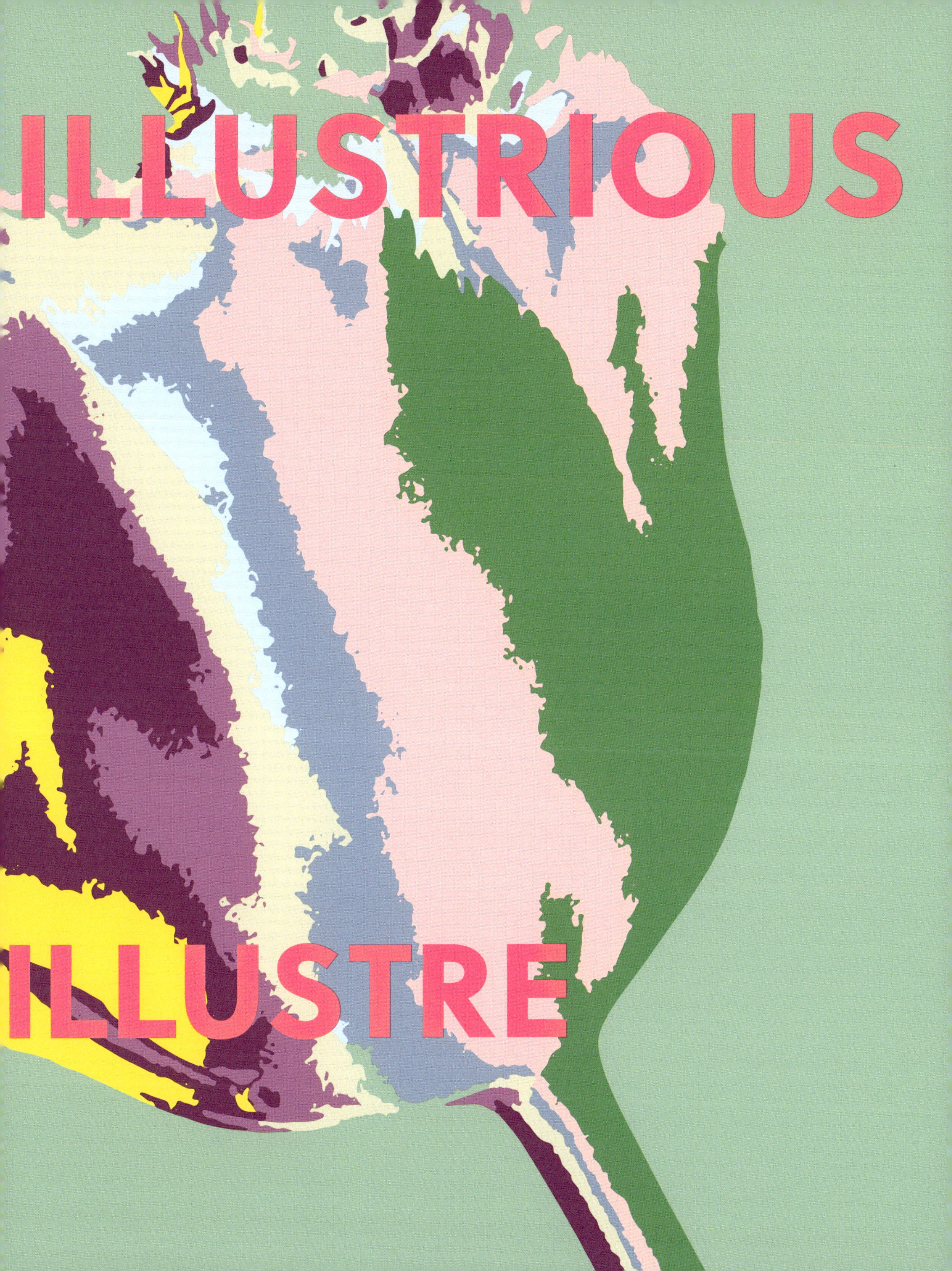

ILLUSTRIOUS
ILLUSTRE

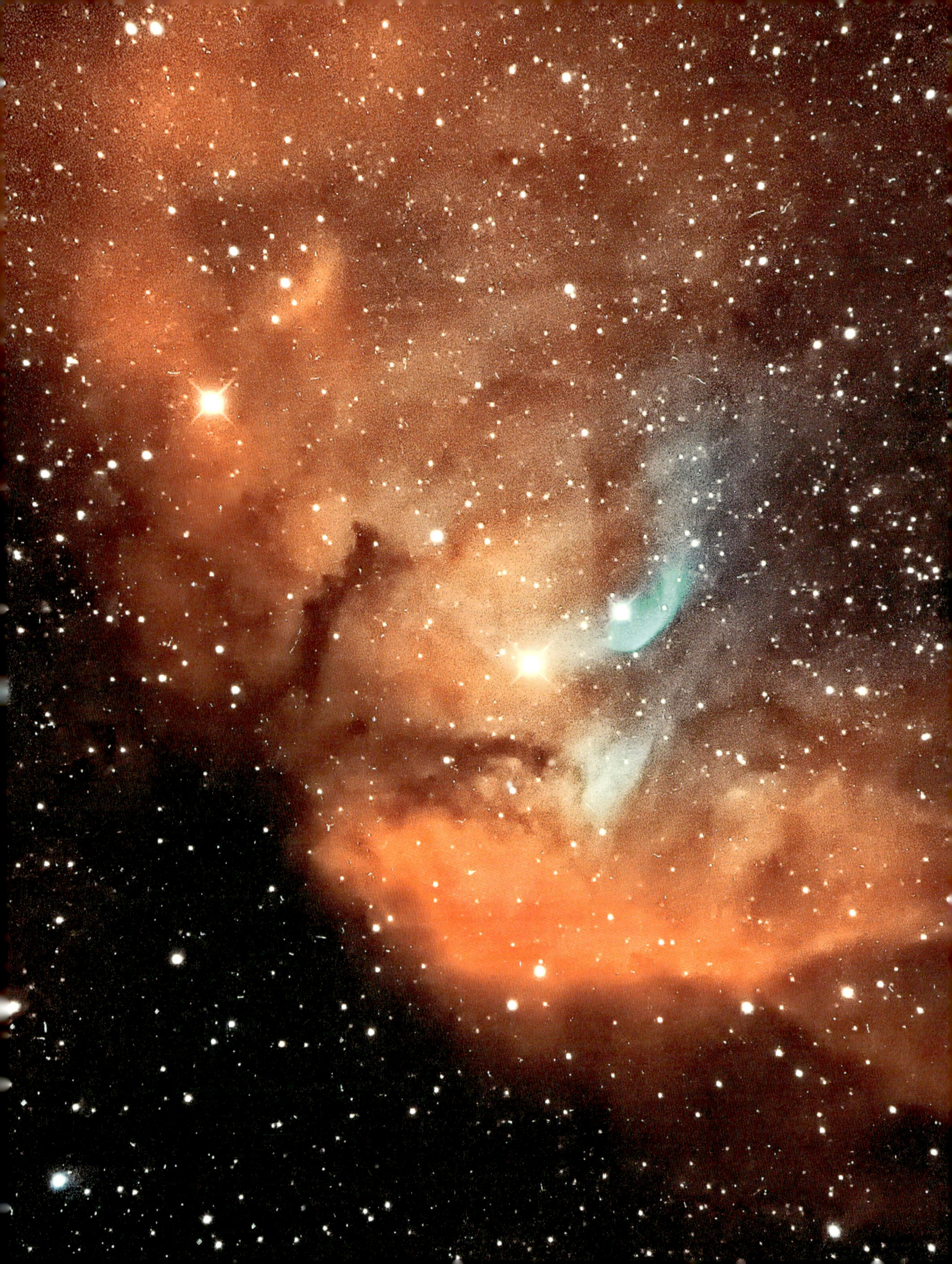

To infinity and beyond

HEAVENLY REALMS

THIS BLESSED FLOWER'S DIVINE SPLENDOR DAZZLES EVERYWHERE

Flora, the goddess of nature, brings flowers to life, and tulips open up as if Flora had touched them with a gentle finger. After all, according to Islamic belief, tulips are divine signs.

A cosmic tulip appears in the constellation of the Swan. The Tulip Nebula Sh2-101 shines from around 8,000 light years away, with a diameter of 70 light years. Is this a sacred blossom, created by higher powers and fallen from the sky only to shatter into thousands of tiny fragments on Earth?

Selbst im Weltall

HIMMLISCHE GEFILDE

DIE BLUMEN MIT GÖTTLICHEM GLANZ LASSEN SICH WIRKLICH ÜBERALL BESTAUNEN

Flora, die Göttin der Natur, erweckt die Blumen zum Leben. Auch Tulpen öffnen ihre Blüten, als hätte Flora sie mit den Fingern berührt. Immerhin sind Tulpen nach islamischem Glauben göttliche Zeichen.

Eine kosmische Tulpe zeigt sich im Sternbild des Schwans. Rund 8000 Lichtjahre entfernt, mit 70 Lichtjahren im Durchmesser, leuchtet der Tulpennebel Sh2-101. Eine sakrale Blüte, von höheren Mächten geschaffen und in zigtausend Splittern vom Himmel auf die Erde gefallen?

Bulbs

SUBTERRANEAN SUSTENANCE

TULIPS DRAW THEIR VITALITY AND STRONG GROWTH FROM THE DEPTH

A characteristic element of the tulip that has contributed to its success story as one of the most widespread and beloved flowers worldwide is hidden underground: the bulb.

It is a specialized storage organ. The bulb consists of thickened leaf bases tightly packed together to form a roundish, usually tapering body enclosed by a dry sheath, which stores sustenance reserves. This enables plants to survive difficult times (see also pages 124).

Tulips have always been easy to handle in the form of bulbs. Even in ancient times, transportation over thousands of kilometers posed no major problems; the plant was dormant, a Sleeping Beauty. Once it is inserted into the ground and given access to vital water, it awakens again. Sultans, kings, and botanists—all tulip enthusiasts received their first tulips in the form of bulbs. Yet these subterranean organs triggered fateful floral events not only in past centuries; bulbs still shape the value of tulips today.

A little anecdote: During tulip mania at the beginning of the 17th century, destroying a tulip bulb was a punishable criminal offense. A sailor ended up behind bars because he had eaten what he had assumed to be an onion. Unfortunately, it was a tulip bulb whose financial value would have been sufficient to feed an entire ship's crew for a year.

Zwiebeln

UNTERIRDISCH GEHALTVOLL

IHRE ÜBERLEBENSKRAFT UND WUCHSFREUDE SCHÖPFEN TULPEN AUS DER TIEFE

Ein charakteristisches Element der Tulpe, das zu ihrer Karriere als eine der am meisten verbreiteten und beliebtesten Blumen weltweit beigetragen hat, versteckt sich unter der Erde: die Zwiebel.

Ein sehr spezielles Pflanzenorgan! Fachsprachlich auch Bulbus genannt, besteht es aus verdickten Blattbasen, die dicht an dicht zusammengepackt einen rundlichen, meist spitz zulaufenden und von einer trockenen Hülle umschlossenen Körper bilden, in dem Reservestoffe gespeichert werden. Damit können Pflanzen schlechte Zeiten überdauern (siehe auch Seite 125).

In Form von Zwiebeln ließen sich Tulpen schon immer einfach handhaben. Ein Transport über tausende von Kilometern bereitete selbst in antiken Zeiten keine großen Probleme, die Gewächse sind wie in einen Dornröschenschlaf versunken. In die Erde gesteckt und mit lebensnotwendigem Nass versorgt, erwachen sie wieder. Ob Sultan, König oder Botaniker – alle bekamen die ersten Tulpen in Form von Zwiebeln in die Hände. Nicht nur in vergangenen Jahrhunderten sorgten diese unterirdischen Organe für schicksalhafte Begebenheiten, sie prägen bis heute den Wert der Tulpen.

Dazu eine kleine Anekdote: Während der Zeit der Tulpenhysterie zu Beginn des 17. Jahrhunderts war es bei Strafe verboten, eine Tulpenzwiebel zu zerstören. Ein Seemann kam hinter Gitter, weil er eine vermeintliche Gemüsezwiebel gegessen hatte. Es war jedoch eine Tulpenzwiebel, mit deren Gegenwert man eine Schiffsbesatzung ein ganzes Jahr lang hätte ernähren können.

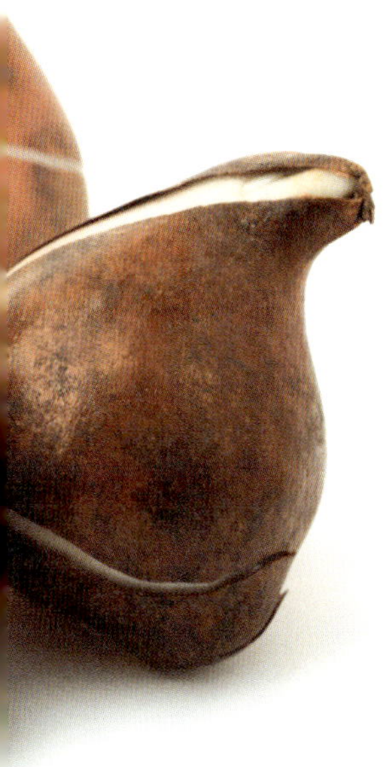

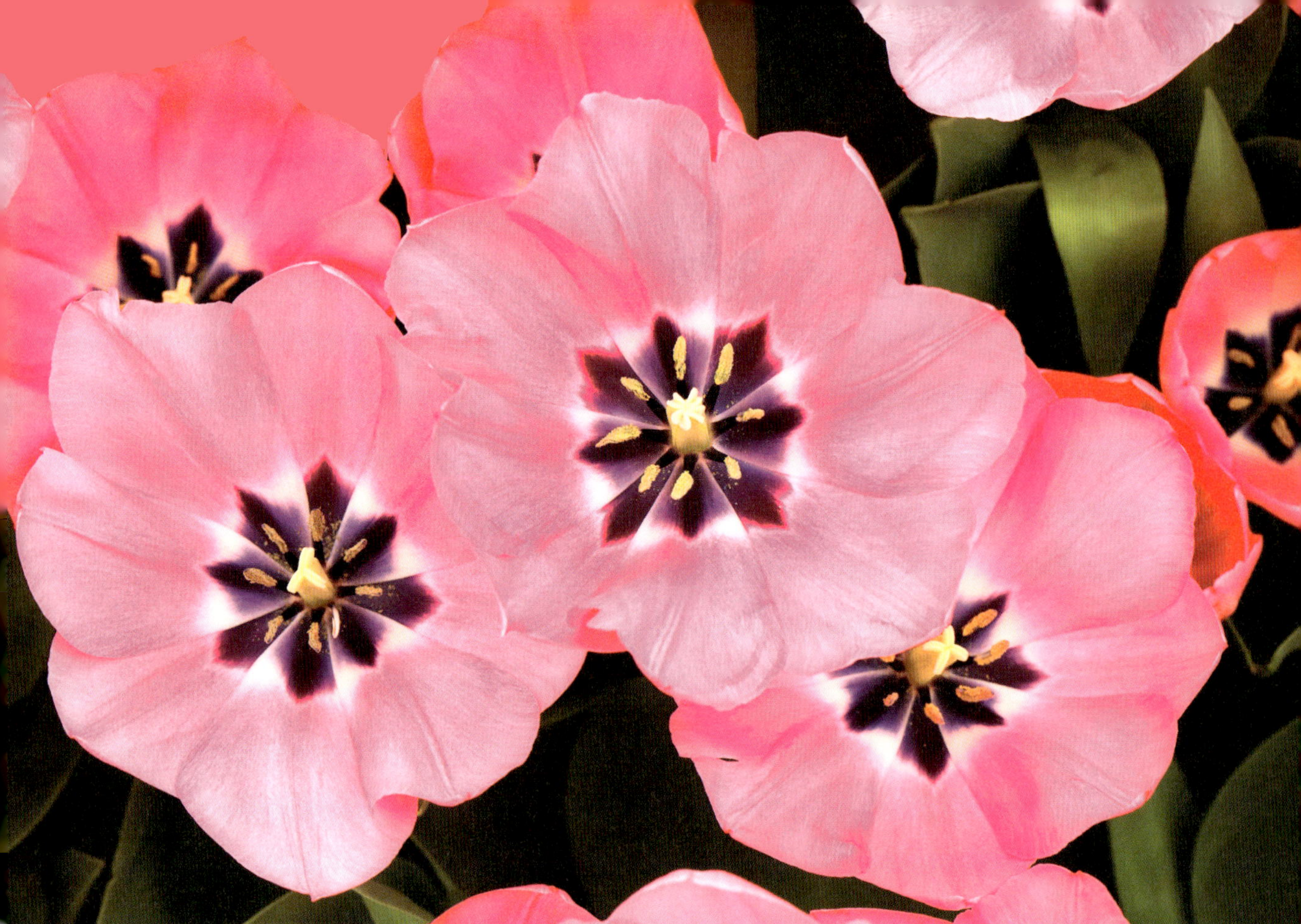

TERRANEAN TRICKS

TULIP FLOWERS IN BLOOM CATCH EVERYONE'S EYE

A tulip bears a homochlamydeous floral envelope, a simple perianth or perigone of six corollaceous tepals—as the seasoned botanist would say. What might sound incomprehensible at first is, in fact, quite obvious. Looking at tulip heads, we see that they consist of six very similar (homochlamydeous, meaning "same cloak"), large, and colorful crown-like (corollaceous, meaning "like a crown") leaves (the tepals). These form the envelope (the perianth) around the inner parts.

Inviting: Since tulips, in this case, the Fosteriana hybrid 'Janis Joplin', rarely have a fragrance, they have to rely on their looks to attract bees, bumblebees, and beetles.

Fascinating, right? Botanical pedantry should by no means diminish the tulip flower's visual delight but rather emphasize it. "Who shall presume to imitate the colors of the tulip, or to improve the proportions of the lily of the valley?" asked Edgar Allan Poe (1809–1849). Because of their splendor, tulips were also called Turkish lilies in the past, and lilies, after all, were considered the epitome of beauty.

Lilies and daffodils captivate with strikingly large blossoms in rich colors, and they exude a lavish fragrance. In terms of blossom size and color intensity, tulips can hold their own. They even surpass the other two with an unmatched color palette ranging from white through yellow and orange to red—only blue hues never appear because tulips lack the required genes. Most of them also lack any kind of floral scent.

Protected by the envelope, six stamens surround a pistil inside the flower; these are the plant's reproductive parts. Yet the tulip unabashedly displays all love affairs on an open stage rather than hiding them in secluded corners. Tulip blossoms open wide for the bridal show. With provocative color displays, they charm suitors such as bees, bumblebees, or even beetles, enticing them to play love messengers and carry pollen from one flower to the next.

When there are no potential partners out and about, such as at night or in bad weather, tulip blossoms close so that their vital parts are protected from harm. The opening and closing of the flowers can be observed both outdoors and indoors when tulips are in a vase. It occurs through growth, controlled by temperature. Warmth causes increased growth on the inside of the petals, and the petals open. In contrast, cold causes more growth on the outside of the petals, and the petals close—we can measure this phenomenon. A tulip head can double in size during its flowering period.

Blüten

ÜBERIRDISCH AUSGEKLÜGELT

TULPENBLÜTEN SIND EYECATCHER, WO IMMER SIE AUFBLÜHEN

Eine Tulpe trägt eine homoiochlamydeische Blütenhülle, ein einfaches Perianth oder Perigon aus sechs corolloiden Tepalen – würde der eingefleischte Botaniker sagen. Das klingt wie aus einem Buch mit sieben Siegeln, ist aber doch klar ersichtlich. Schaut man sich Tulpenblüten an, so setzen sie sich aus sechs gleichartigen (homoiochlamydeisch, bedeutet so viel wie „gleiches Kleid"), großen und farbenfrohen kronblattartigen (corolloiden, von lat. *corolla*, „kleine Krone") Blättern (den Tepalen) zusammen. Diese bilden die Hülle (das Perianth) um die inneren Teile.

Faszinierend, oder? Die botanische Schlaumeierei soll keinesfalls die Augenweide beeinträchtigen, die jede Tulpenblüte schlicht und ergreifend ist, sondern vielmehr unterstreichen. „Wer wollte sich anmaßen, die Farben der Tulpe nachzuahmen oder die Gestalt des Maiglöckchens zu verbessern?" meinte Edgar Allan Poe (1809–1849), wobei letzteres auf Englisch *lily of the valley* heißt, also etwa „Lilien im Talgrund". Wegen ihrer Pracht hat man Tulpen früher auch Türkische Lilien genannt, und immerhin galten Lilien als Inbegriff der Schönheit.

Lilien und Narzissen betören mit auffallend großen Blüten in satten Farben, dazu duften sie verschwenderisch. Bezüglich Blütendimension und Farbintensität können Tulpen problemlos mithalten. Sie übertreffen die beiden anderen Zwiebelgewächse sogar noch mit einer ungeahnten Farbpalette von Weiß über Gelb und Orange bis Rot – einzig blaue Farbtöne kommen niemals vor, weil den Tulpen die Gene dafür fehlen. Versagt bleibt ihnen auch das Blütenparfüm, jedenfalls den meisten.

Geborgen von der Hülle reihen sich im Inneren der Blüte sechs Staubblätter um einen Stempel, die geschlechtlichen Teile der Pflanze. Das

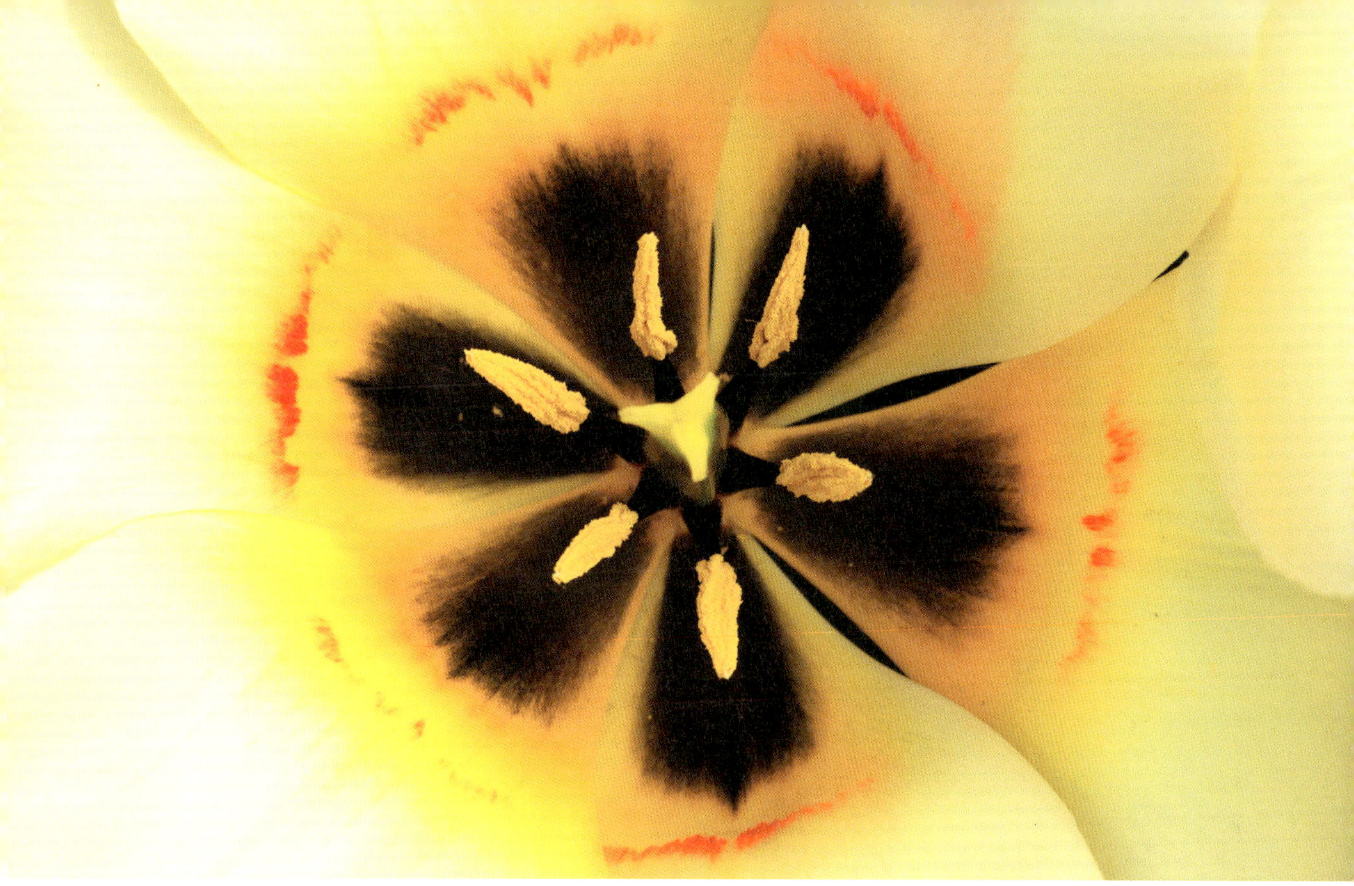

Einladend: Da Tulpen – hier die *Greigii*-Tulpe
'Diablo' – selten duften, locken sie Bienen, Hummeln
und Käfer mit einer attraktiven Optik an.

Liebesspiel der Tulpen findet aber keineswegs verborgen im Séparée statt, sondern offenherzig auf dem Präsentierteller. Tulpenblüten öffnen sich weit für die Brautschau. Mit provozierenden Farbspielen becircen sie Galane wie Bienen, Hummeln oder auch Käfer, damit diese als *postillons d'amour* Blütenstaub aus der einen zur nächsten Blüte bringen.

Sind die intimen Partner aber nicht unterwegs, also nachts oder bei schlechtem Wetter, schließen sich Tulpenblüten, damit ihre wertvollsten Teile keinen Schaden nehmen. Das Auf und Zu der Blüten lässt sich draußen ebenso verfolgen wie drinnen, wenn Tulpen in einer Vase stehen. Es erfolgt durch Wachstum, gesteuert von Temperatur. Wärme bewirkt ein verstärktes Wachstum an der Innenseite der Blütenblätter, die Blüten öffnen sich. Bei Kälte sprießt dagegen die Außenseite der Blütenblätter mehr, die Blüten gehen zu – das lässt sich eindeutig nachmessen. Eine Tulpenblüte kann sich in der Größe während ihrer Blütezeit durchaus verdoppeln.

Experiment

UNEXPECTED ULTRAMARINE

ASTONISHING EXPERIMENTS WITH TULIP BLOSSOMS

In this experiment, white tulips will not keep their snowy petals for long. Soon they will take on a blue hue in what appears to be magic but is in fact a simple trick that can be easily replicated at home with a few supplies. Place fresh tulips, preferably with white or light cream-colored blossoms, in dyed water. It is best to use ink diluted with water at a ratio of about 1:1. Position the tulips in a bright and warm location—then wait. After a few hours, you will see the first lines of color on the petals, usually at the tips. The next day, the petals are covered with blue stripes. There is quite a mundane reason for this mysterious process: tulips, like all plants, take in water through their roots, and in the vase, they absorb it directly through the cut stems. The water then travels through narrow channels to all parts of the plant, driven by evaporation. With clear water, there is, of course, no noticeable color change; however, with dyed water, the color particles travel upward with the water.

If you see blue tulips at a market, they have been artificially colored using exactly this method. Natural blue tulips do not yet exist.

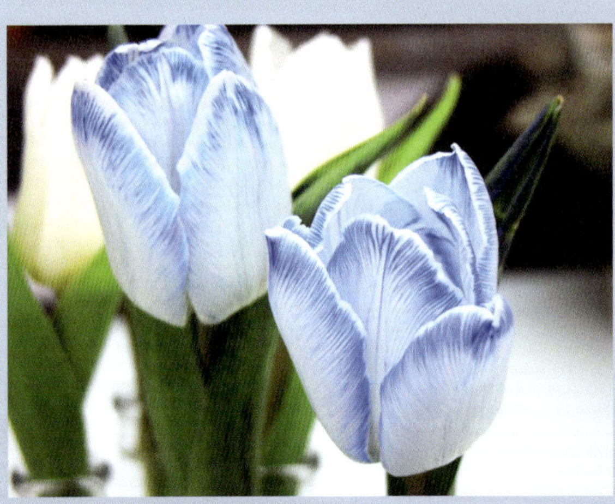

There are no blue tulips, but light-colored ones can be dyed blue with ink.

Blaue Tulpen gibt es nicht, helle Exemplare lassen sich aber mit Tinte blau färben.

Experiment

BLAUES WUNDER

EIN VERBLÜFFENDES EXPERIMENT MIT TULPENBLÜTEN

Weiße Tulpen. Nicht mehr lange, bald werden sie wie von Zauberhand blaue Farbe zeigen. Dank eines einfachen Tricks, den man mit wenigen Mitteln zu Hause ausführen kann. Frische Tulpen, vorzugsweise mit weißen oder hell cremefarbenen Blüten, werden in gefärbtes Wasser gestellt. Dafür nutzt man am besten Tinte, etwa 1:1 mit Wasser verdünnt. Tulpen möglichst hell und warm aufstellen – abwarten. Nach wenigen Stunden sieht man erste Farblinien auf den Blütenblättern, meist an den Spitzen. Am Tag darauf sind die Blüten von blauen Streifen durchzogen.

Hinter diesem rätselhaften Vorgang steckt ein ganz banaler Grund: Tulpen nehmen wie alle Pflanzen über Wurzeln Wasser auf, in der Vase über die Schnittstelle am Stängel. Das Wasser wird über feine Bahnen in alle Pflanzenteile geleitet, angetrieben von Verdunstung. Bei klarem Wasser ist selbstverständlich keine Farbveränderung zu bemerken, bei gefärbtem Wasser werden dagegen auch die Farbteilchen mit dem Wasser nach oben transportiert.

Falls im Handel blaue Tulpen angeboten werden, wurden sie mit genau dieser Methode künstlich gefärbt. Denn echte blaue Tulpen gibt es bis heute nicht.

Fruits

TIME CAPSULES FOR THE FUTURE

BLOSSOMS PRODUCE FRUITS WITH SEEDS

When insects transport a tulip's pollen onto another tulip's three-lobed stigma, pollination is accomplished. After this tender foreplay, the real action begins. Pollen grains germinate and send a long tube through the tissue into the interior of the ovary. Sperm cells carrying the male genetic information travel through this channel to the ovules in the ovary, where female egg cells are already waiting. This is the climax! Sperm cells unite with egg cells, and fertilization occurs.

Humans are blind witnesses, reduced to the sidelines; the tulip's fertilization takes place unnoticed. The consequences of these events are only visible when the flower head becomes pregnant, so to speak, meaning the ovary swells noticeably. A cylindrical to spindle-shaped, leathery fruit capsule develops.

When the round, flat seed—the tulip's "baby"—is ripe, the three chambers of the capsule split along the longitudinal seams and release it. It really is almost like a birth …

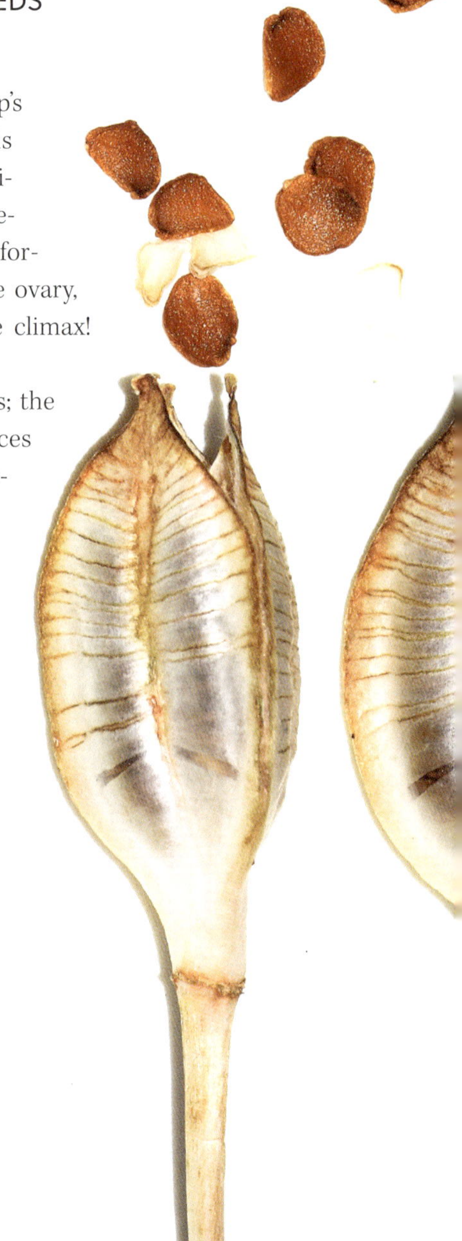

Früchte

KAPSELN FÜR DIE ZUKUNFT

AUS BLÜTEN ENTWICKELN SICH FRÜCHTE MIT SAMEN

Gelangt Blütenstaub einer Tulpe mittels Insekten auf die dreilappige Narbe einer anderen Tulpenblüte, ist die Bestäubung ausgeführt. Nach diesem Vorspiel geht es mit dem Sex aber erst richtig zur Sache. Pollenkörner keimen aus und schicken einen langen Schlauch durchs Gewebe ins Innere des Fruchtknotens. Spermazellen mit den männlichen Erbinformationen gelangen durch diesen Kanal bis zu den Samenanlagen im Fruchtknoten, in denen die weiblichen Eizellen schon warten. Höhepunkt! Spermazellen vereinigen sich mit den Eizellen, die Befruchtung ist erfolgt.

Der Mensch bleibt staunend außen vor, die Befruchtung der Tulpen vollzieht sich unbemerkt. Wahrgenommen werden erst die Folgen dieser Geschehnisse, wenn die Blüte gleichsam schwanger wird, d. h. der Fruchtknoten deutlich anschwillt. Es entwickelt sich eine walzen- bis spindelförmige, ledrige Kapselfrucht.

Sind die rundlichen, flachen Samen – die „Babys" der Tulpen – reif, reißen die drei Kammern der Kapsel entlang der Längsnähte auf und geben sie frei. Fast wie bei einer Geburt …

Leaves

FOLIAGE FOR LIFE

MUCH MORE THAN JUST DECORATIVE ACCESSORIES

What would tulips be without their foliage? The proud flower heads demand appropriate subjects; even as cut flowers, tulips need subservient but flattering companions. Johann Wolfgang von Goethe (1749–1832) expressed in his poems on the "Four Seasons": "Tulips, you are scolded by sentimental connoisseurs; But a cheerful mind also wishes for a cheerful leaf."

A tulip's leaves really can be quite cheerful. Not all varieties bear the traditionally plain gray to dark green, elongated leaves. Some tulips, especially wild species like the Greigii tulips *(Tulipa greigii)*, display attractive foliage with patterns of reddish stripes, spots, or dots. In cultivated forms, specific varieties boast variegated leaves, ranging from white to yellow-patterned. An uneven, curling leaf edge also adds a decorative touch, as seen, for example, in *Tulipa undulatifolia.*

Beauty aside, green leaves are essential for life. It is where photosynthesis, a unique process that only occurs in plants, takes place. Here, sunlight is converted into biochemical energy, combining carbon dioxide and water to produce sugar and release oxygen. This nourishes every plant, shapes each tulip's entire appearance, and, last but not least, helps produce its dazzling flowers.

NEXT PAGE | Beautiful even before they bloom—tulips with colorfully patterned leaves are particularly pretty.

RIGHT PAGE | In early-blooming Kaufmanniana tulips, e.g. the 'Glück' variety pictured here, patterned leaves complement the spectacle of multicolored flowers in a particularly attractive way.

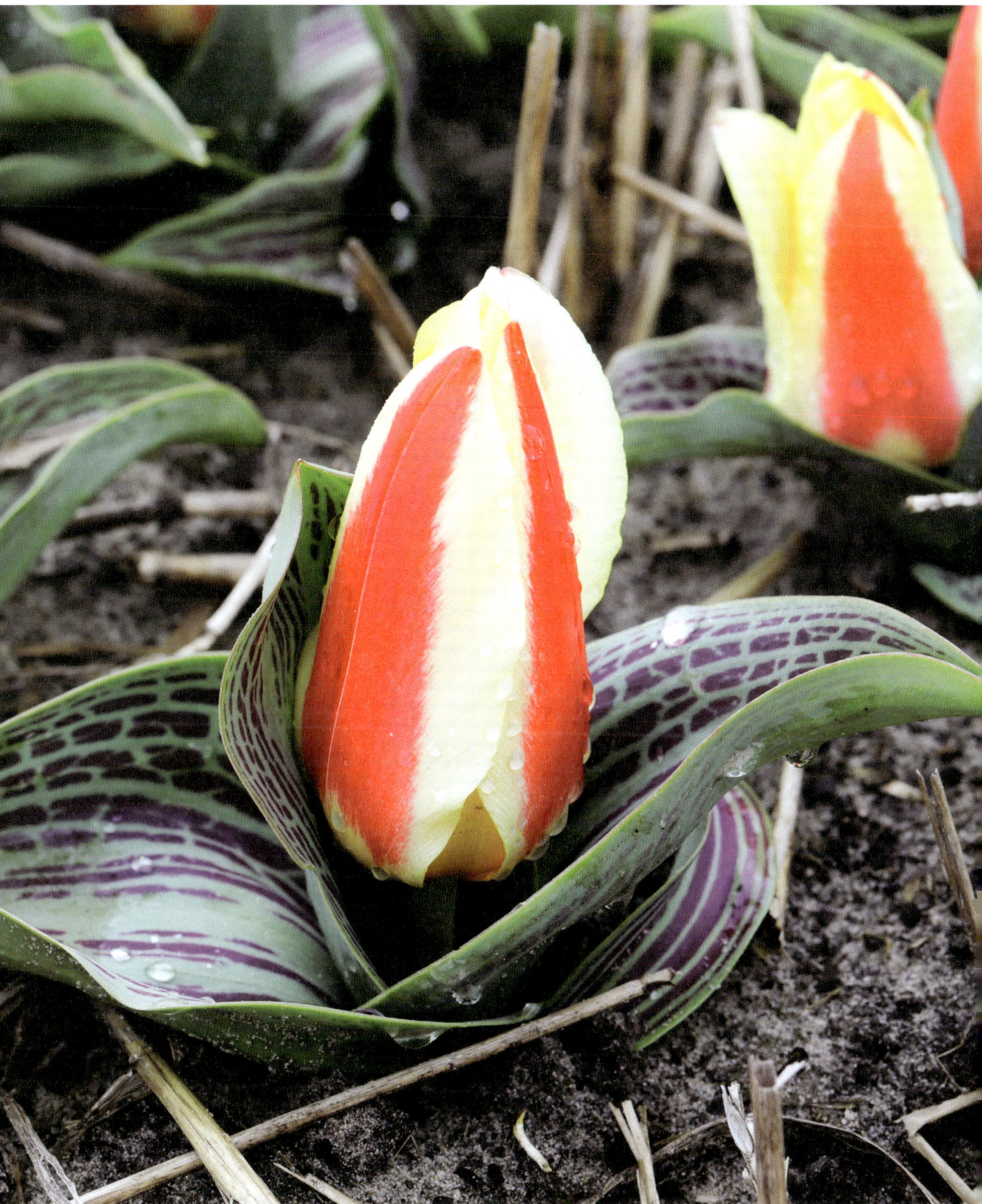

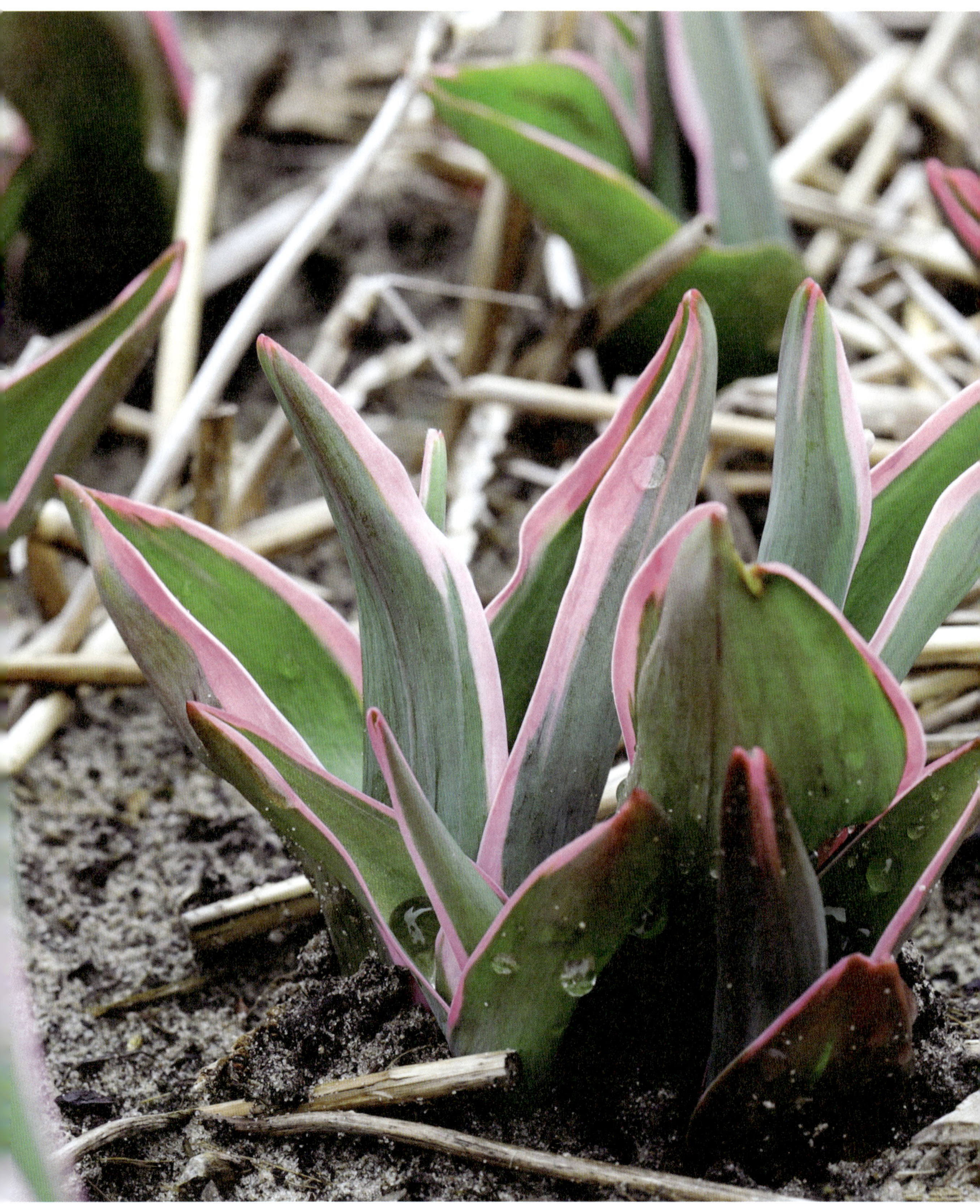

Blätter

GRÜNES FÜRS LEBEN

VIEL MEHR ALS NUR SCHMÜCKENDES BEIWERK

Was wären Tulpen ohne ihre Laubblätter. Den aristokratisch aufragenden Blüten fehlte eine angemessene Untermalung, selbst als Schnittblumen brauchen Tulpen untertänige, aber schmeichelnde Begleitung. Johann Wolfgang von Goethe (1749–1832) meinte in seinen Gedichten der „Vier Jahreszeiten": „Tulpen, ihr werdet gescholten von sentimentalischen Kennern; Aber ein lustiger Sinn wünscht auch ein lustiges Blatt."

Lustige Blätter haben Tulpen durchaus zu bieten. Nicht bei allen Arten und Sorten bleiben die ungestielten, lang ausgezogenen Laubblätter schlicht grau- bis dunkelgrün, bisweilen kommen sie bemerkenswert vielfältig daher. Einige Tulpen, vor allem Wildarten wie Greig-Tulpen *(Tulipa greigii)* tragen schmuckes Laub mit Mustern aus rötlichen Streifen, Flecken oder Tupfen. Bei Zuchtformen warten spezielle Sorten mit panaschierten, also weiß- bis gelbbunt zonierten Blättern auf. Auch ein gewellter Blattrand wirkt dekorativ, zu bewundern beispielsweise bei *Tulipa undulatifolia.*

Grüne Blätter sind aber schlichtweg lebenswichtig. In ihnen findet die Photosynthese statt, dieser einzigartige Prozess, den nur Pflanzen beherrschen. Hier wird Sonnenlicht in biochemische Energie umgewandelt, Kohlendioxid und Wasser damit zu Zucker verbunden und Sauerstoff freigesetzt. So ernährt sich jede Pflanze, bringt jede Tulpe ihre gesamte Gestalt und nicht zuletzt auch ihre phantastischen Blüten hervor.

LINKE SEITE | Schon vor der Blüte schön – Tulpen mit farbig gemustertem Blattwerk wirken besonders anziehend.

VORIGE SEITE | Bei den früh blühenden *Kaufmanniana*-Tulpen, hier die Sorte 'Glück', ergänzen gemusterte Blätter das Schauspiel der mehrfarbigen Blüten auf besonders attraktive Weise.

Well adapted

THE TULIP'S BIOGRAPHY

PERFECTLY ADAPTED TO ADVERSE CONDITIONS

It may be hard to believe, but tulips are perennial plants that can live for many years, even decades. Wild tulips, in particular, often reach a ripe old age. They repeatedly and persistently shoot up, but most of the time, they lead an underground life—trying to conserve their energy. The vigorous, growth-intensive phases only occur during short periods when the climate and conditions around them allow it.

The tulip's original native habitat is marked by challenging, almost inhospitable conditions. Long and icy winters, dry and hot summers, with only brief periods of slightly more agreeable weather. Tulips have adapted to this. During unfavorable times, they endure underground, only to then seize the more favorable intervals.

The bulbs make this adaptation possible. The technical term for these underground storage organs is geophytes. Thanks to them and their stored energy reserves, tulips can grow extraordinarily fast. They begin this process in the moderate fall to avoid losing precious time in spring. Another specialty ensures their survival: contractile roots. By contracting their older root sections, they can pull their own bulbs to an ideal depth.

NEXT PAGE | Tulip bulbs can tolerate various conditions, including sandy soil near the sea.

Gut angepasst

AUS DER BIOGRAFIE DER TULPEN

PERFEKT AUF WIDRIGE LEBENSUMSTÄNDE ABGESTIMMT

Man mag es kaum glauben, aber Tulpen sind ausdauernde Pflanzen, die viele Jahre, sogar Jahrzehnte alt werden können. Vor allem wilde Tulpen erreichen oft ein hohes Alter. Beharrlich treiben sie immer wieder aus, führen die meiste Zeit jedoch ein unterirdisches Leben – und das überwiegend auf Sparflamme. Die ungestümen, wachstumsintensiven Lebensabschnitte konzentrieren sich auf die kurzen Phasen, in denen die Umstände ihrer Heimat es zulassen.

In ihren Ursprungsgebieten herrschen beschwerliche, fast lebensfeindliche Bedingungen. Lange und eisige Winter, trockene und heiße Sommer, und nur kurze Abschnitte mit etwas weniger unbarmherzigen Verhältnissen. Genau daran haben sich Tulpen angepasst. Während der ungünstigen Zeitspannen harren sie unterirdisch aus, die günstigen Intervalle nutzen sie.

Dabei helfen ihnen ihre Zwiebeln. Botanisch nennt man sie Zwiebel-Geophyten oder Erdpflanzen. Dank der angelegten Speicher können Tulpen außerordentlich schnell wachsen. Sie beginnen damit schon im gemäßigten Herbst, um im Frühling nur ja keine kostbare Zeit zu verlieren. Noch eine Spezialität sichert ihr Überleben: Zugwurzeln. Indem sich ihre älteren Wurzelabschnitte kontrahieren, ziehen sie die Zwiebeln in die jeweils optimale Tiefe.

NÄCHSTE SEITE | Tulpenzwiebeln kommen mit allen möglichen Bedingungen zurecht, auch mit sandigen Böden in der Nähe des Meers.

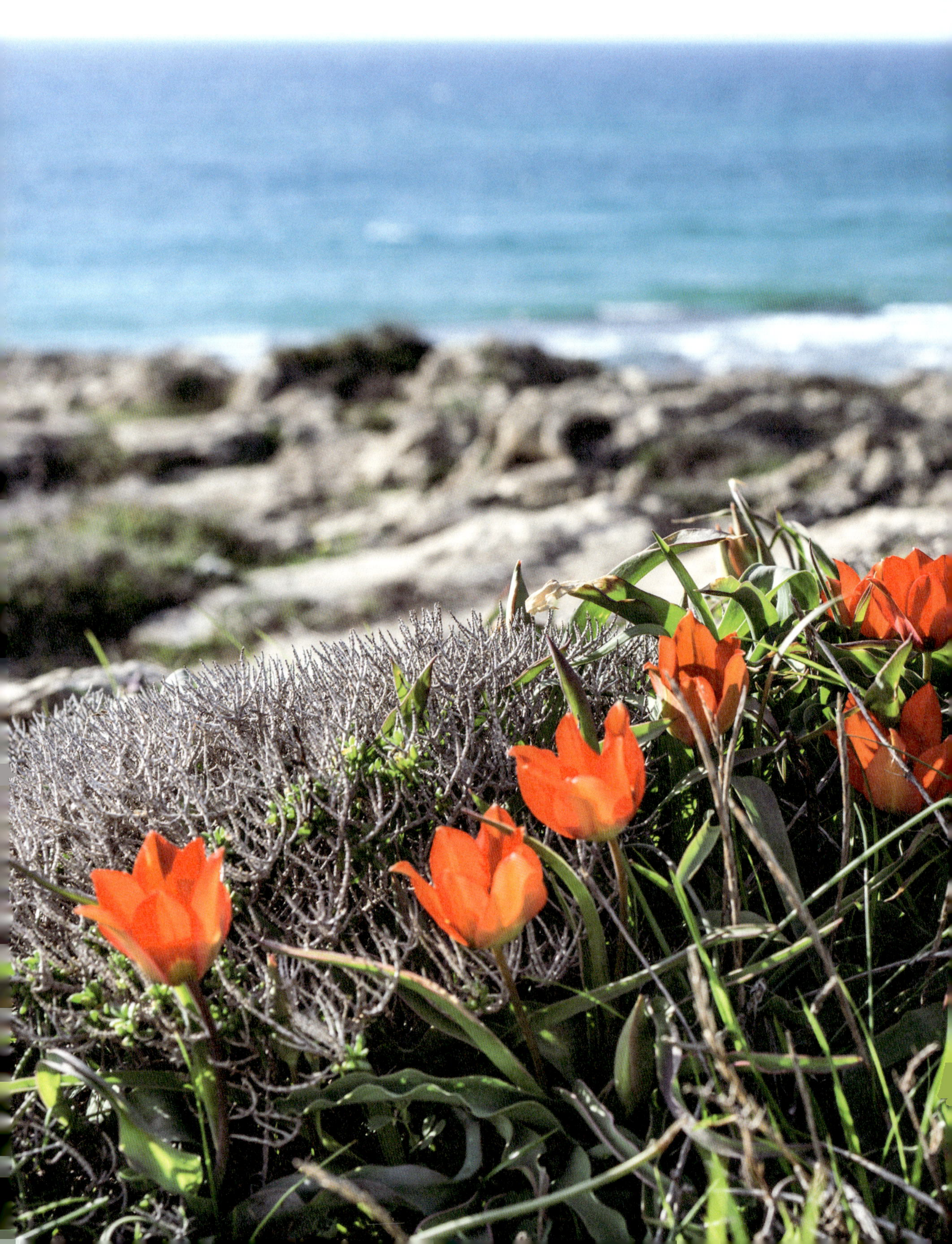

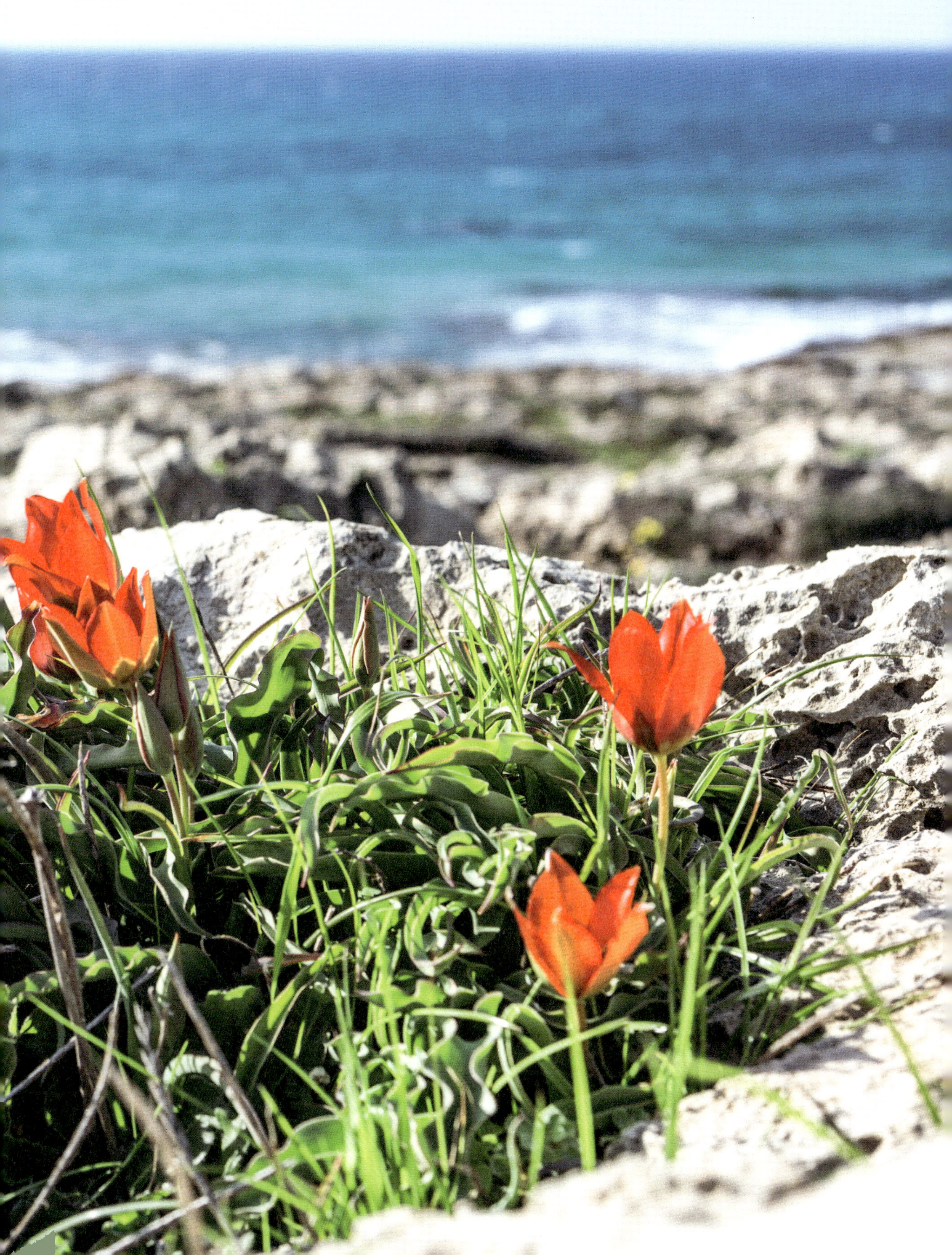

Vegetative reproduction

ALL FOR PROGENY

A MOTHER BEGETS MANY DAUGHTERS

Due to the challenging conditions in their native habitat, tulips rely on specific methods to preserve their species. They cannot depend on pollinating insects, which are scarce in high-altitude areas with late spring frosts, nor can they rely on the soil staying moist long enough before everything dries up in summer. Therefore, tulips choose the path of least resistance, which is vegetative reproduction: they form daughter bulbs.

A bulb contains enough energy for at least one set of strong leaves and flowers to sprout. Compared to the bulb, the actual plant that is visible above the ground seems incredibly large. Producing and ripening fruit consumes a lot of energy. Often, a tulip dies afterward, both the aboveground plant and the bulb.

Yet there are buds between the bulb's layers, some of which develop into new bulbs, the daughter bulbs. The tulip's final effort is to utilize its green leaves, its solar panels, so to speak, to nurture the daughter bulbs, ensuring the future and continuity of the species. The following year, the daughter bulbs produce new tulips; since no exchange or mix of genetic information occurs in this method of reproduction, they are identical to the mother.

Vegetative Vermehrung

ALLES FÜR DEN NACHWUCHS

EINE MUTTER BEKOMMT VIELE TÖCHTER

Aufgrund der schwierigen Lebensumstände in ihrer Urheimat sind Tulpen darauf angewiesen, spezielle Methoden für die Erhaltung ihrer Art zu entwickeln. Sie können sich weder auf bestäubende Insekten verlassen, die es in den hochgelegenen Gebieten mit Wintereinbrüchen bis ins späte Frühjahr gibt, noch darauf, dass der Boden lange genug feucht bleibt, bevor im Sommer alles austrocknet. Also wählen Tulpen den Weg der vegetativen Vermehrung: Sie bilden Tochterzwiebeln.

In einer Zwiebel steckt ausreichend Kraft, dass aus ihr mindestens einmal starke Blätter samt Blüten sprießen. Im Vergleich zur Zwiebel erscheint es fast unwirklich, welche Größe die oberirdischen Teile erreichen. Eine besondere Anstrengung bedeutet es, Früchte zur Reife zu bringen. Das zehrt gewaltig. Oft stirbt eine Tulpe anschließend, mit den oberirdischen Teilen auch die Zwiebel.

Doch zwischen den Zwiebelschuppen gibt es Knospen, von denen sich einige zu neuen Zwiebeln entwickeln, den Tochterzwiebeln. Das letzte Bestreben der Tulpe liegt darin, ihre Solaranlagen, die grünen Blätter zu nutzen. Mit denen werden die Tochterzwiebeln aufgepäppelt, um die Zukunft, den Fortbestand der Art zu sichern. Aus den Tochterzwiebeln wachsen im nächsten oder übernächsten Jahr Tulpen, die der Mutter aufs Haar gleichen, sie sind genetisch identisch – denn ein Austausch von Erbinformationen hat bei dieser Art der Vermehrung nicht stattgefunden.

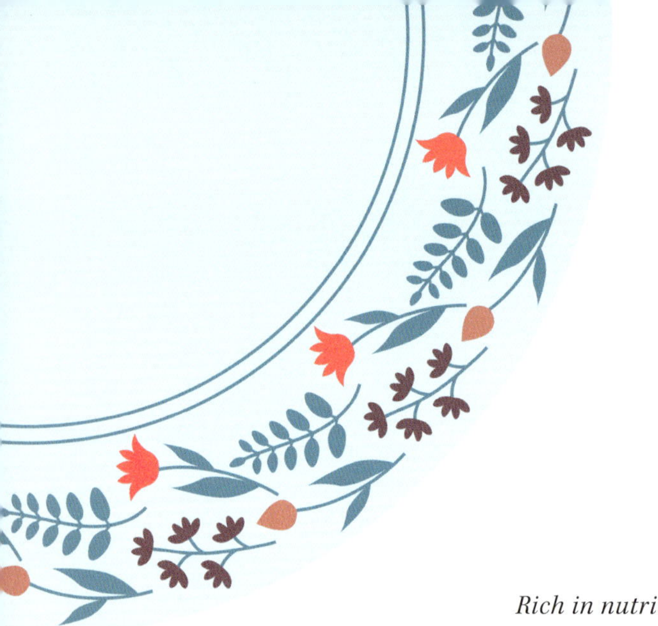

TULIP CHEMISTRY

TRAGIC-COMICAL STORIES OF THE TULIP'S ALMOST ALCHEMICAL ARTISTRY

Towards the end of the Second World War, the Netherlands faced a catastrophic famine. Out of desperation, anything that seemed nutritious was consumed, including starchy tulip bulbs. If prepared correctly, three to four bulbs per day were considered safe to consume, though we can assume that they would have tasted horrible. When the Allies carried out the supply flights for operations "Manna" and "Chowhound" in late April 1945, the Dutch waved at the planes with tulips in bloom.

That being said, all parts of the tulip are now considered toxic. They contain tulipalins and tuliposides, with the latter substance responsible for the flowers' vibrant colors. These substances can cause nausea, vomiting, stomach cramps, and even respiratory failure. On the skin, they cause tulip dermatitis, an itchy and painful rash. "Tulip fingers" is the term for an allergy that primarily affects people who handle tulip bulbs frequently and come into contact with tulipalin A in the bulb sap. This condition is even recognized as an occupational disease.

Yet for the vast majority of people, tulips remain harmless. Eating a tulip flower or bulb is considered to be relatively safe. However, there are plenty of other flowers and bulbs that are much better suited for culinary purposes. Also entirely safe: tulip ornaments on crockery and cutlery.

Gehaltvoll und giftig

TULPEN-CHEMIE

TRAGISCH-KURIOSE GESCHICHTEN VON DEN FAST SCHON ALCHEMISTISCHEN KÜNSTEN DER TULPE

Gegen Ende des Zweiten Weltkriegs waren die Niederlande von katastrophaler Hungersnot betroffen. Aus Verzweiflung wurde alles verzehrt, was irgendwie nahrhaft erschien – auch stärkehaltige Tulpenzwiebeln. Drei bis vier Stück pro Tag, entsprechend zubereitet, hielt man für zumutbar. Doch geschmeckt hat es sicher nicht. Als die Alliierten Ende April 1945 bei den Operationen „Manna" und „Chowhound" Versorgungsflüge unternahmen, winkte die Bevölkerung dankend den Flugzeugen mit blühenden Tulpen zu.

Aber: Tulpen gelten in allen Teilen als giftig. Sie enthalten Tulipanide und Tuliposid, wobei letzterer Stoff mit für die leuchtenden Farben der Blüten verantwortlich ist. Diese Stoffe können Übelkeit, Erbrechen, Magenkrämpfe, sogar Atemstillstand hervorrufen. Auf der Haut verursachen sie Tulpenkrätze, einen juckenden und schmerzhaften Ausschlag.

Tulpenfinger nennt man eine Allergie, die vor allem Menschen betrifft, die viel mit Tulpenzwiebeln umgehen und mit dem Tulipalin A im Zwiebelsaft in Kontakt kommen. Dieses Leiden ist sogar als Berufskrankheit anerkannt.

Doch für die allermeisten Menschen bleiben Tulpen harmlos. Selbst der Verzehr einer Tulpenblüte oder einer Zwiebel wird als vertretbar eingeschätzt. Es gibt jedoch eine Fülle anderer Blumen und Zwiebeln, die ungleich besser für kulinarische Zwecke geeignet sind. Ebenfalls völlig risikolos: Geschirr mit Tulpenmotiven.

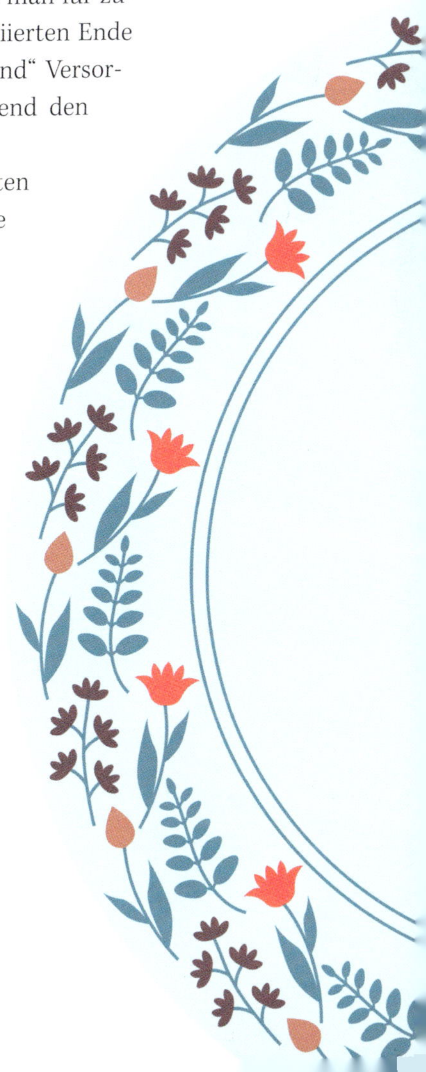

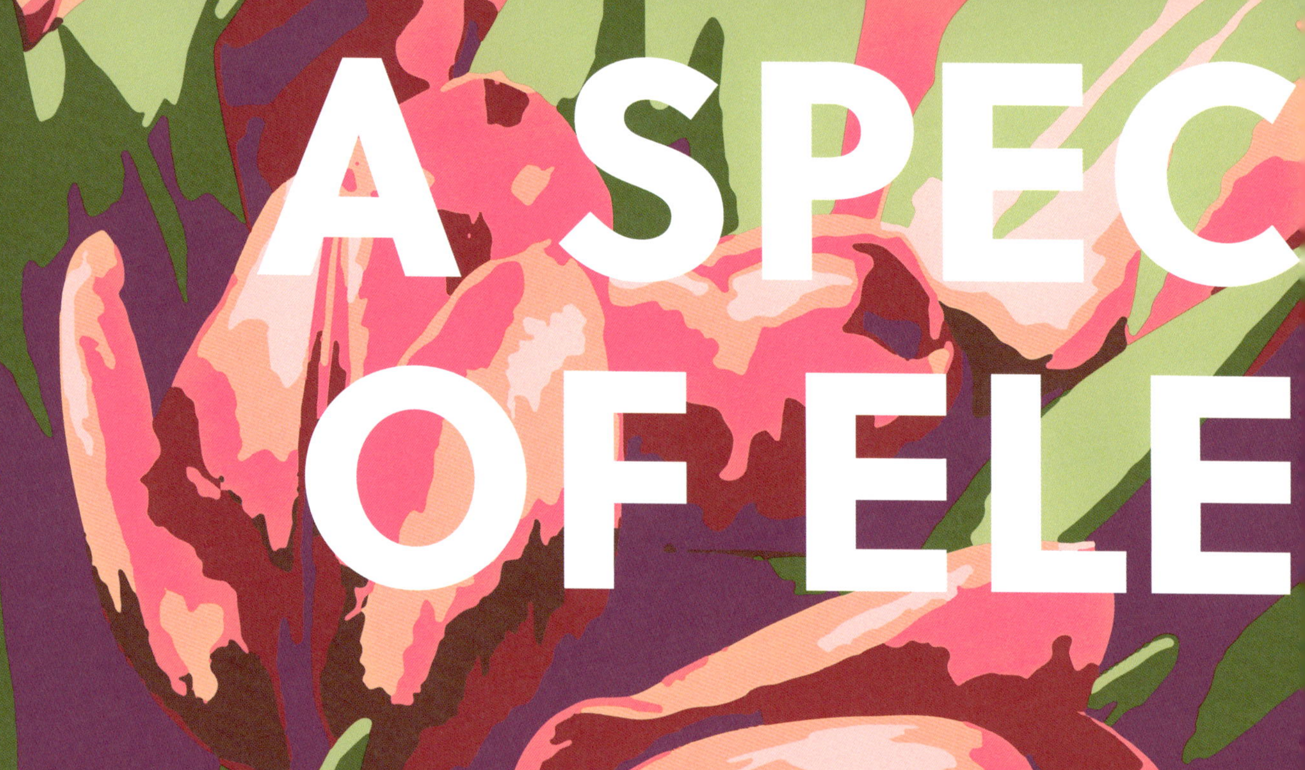
A SPEC
OF ELE

SPEKTRUM
DER ELEGANZ

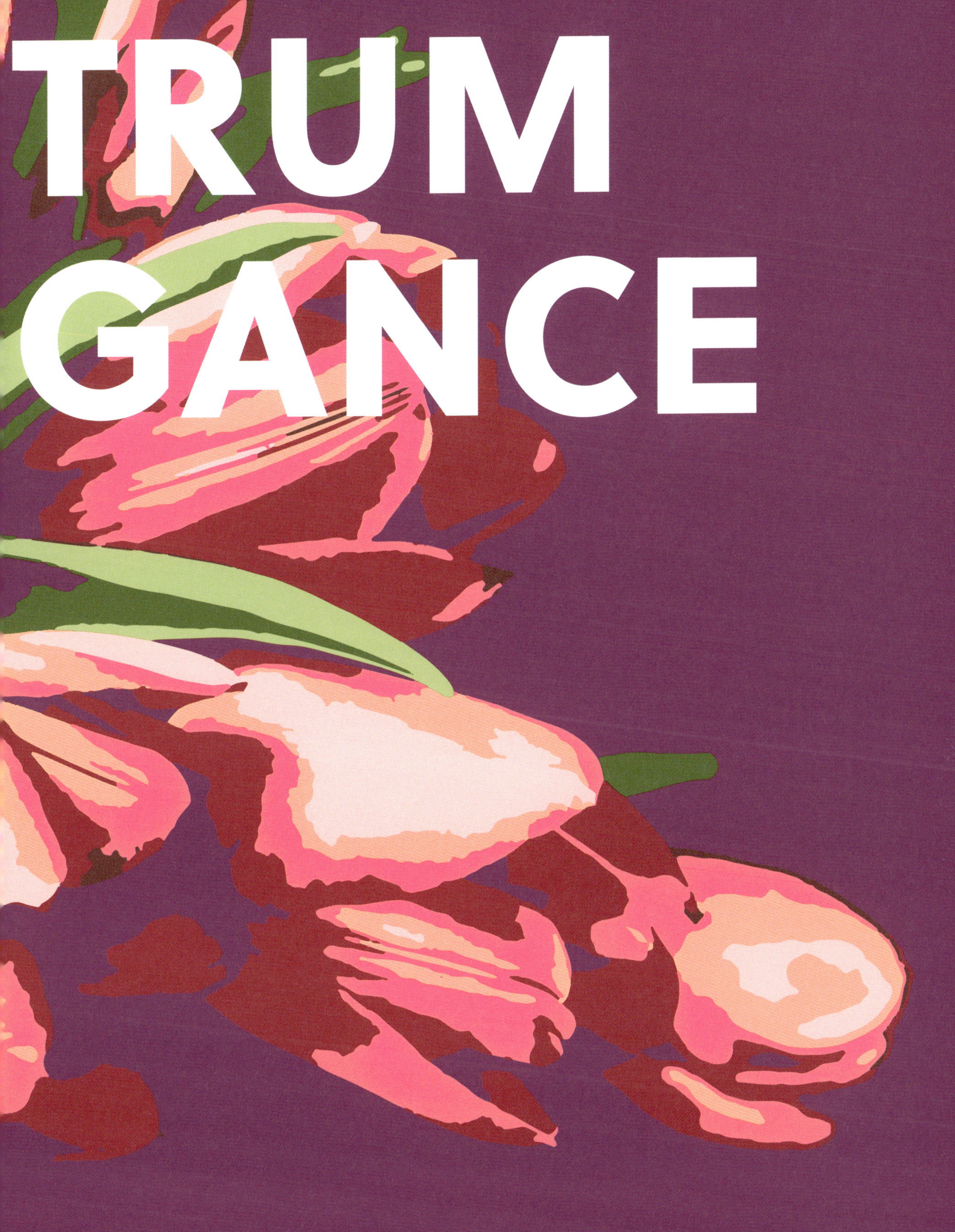

TRUM
GANCE

Taxonomy

TULIPS IN THE BOTANICAL SYSTEM

TULIPS ARE CLASSIFIED BASED ON THEIR RELATIVES IN THE PLANT KINGDOM

What do tulips have in common with orchids, palms, and grasses? At first glance, not much. All these angiosperms, commonly referred to as flowering plants, belong to the monocotyledons, also known as monocots. To locate tulips in the botanical family tree, we must first branch into the *Liliales* order. The *Liliales* in turn count ten families: these include *Colchicaceae, Melanthiaceae*, and, notably, our now familiar *Liliaceae*, or lily family. This family's 16 genera include trout lilies, giant lilies, mariposas, yellow star-of-Bethlehems, fritillaries, and, of course, tulips. All of these family members share the bulb which acts as a perennial organ, as well as parallel-veined and simple leaves with smooth edges.

In Europe, before tulips had a uniform name, they were compared not only to lilies but also to daffodils. *Lilionarcissus* was once the term used in scholarly circles for tulips before *Tulipa* prevailed. Finally, Carl Linnaeus (1707–1778), the Swedish naturalist and founder of scientific nomenclature, introduced the botanical term *Tulipa* in 1753—a term that has endured to this day.

Systematik

TULPEN IM BOTANISCHEN SYSTEM

TULPEN WERDEN NACH VERWANDTSCHAFTLICHEN BEZIEHUNGEN IM PFLANZENREICH EINGEORDNET

Was haben Tulpen mit Orchideen, Palmen und Gräsern gemeinsam? Auf den ersten Blick nicht viel. All diese Bedecktsamer, im Sprachgebrauch als Blütenpflanzen benannt, gehören zu den einkeimblättrigen Pflanzen, den Monokotyledonen. Um im botanischen Stammbaum zur Gattung der Tulpen zu gelangen, müssen wir zunächst bei den Ordnungen in den Ast der *Liliales* abbiegen. Zehn Familien wiederum gehören zu den Lilienartigen, darunter die Zeitlosengewächse, die Germergewächse und insbesondere auch die uns wohlvertrauten Liliengewächse: Kröten-, Zahn-, Riesenlilien, Gelbsterne, Fritillarien und eben auch unsere Tulpen zählen zu dieser Familie, um nur einige der 16 Gattungen zu nennen. Alle Familienmitglieder eint, dass sie immer eine Zwiebel als Überdauerungsorgan sowie parallelnervige und einfache Laubblätter mit einem glatten Rand besitzen.

Als man in Europa noch keinen einheitlichen Namen für Tulpen hatte, verglich man sie nicht nur mit Lilien, sondern auch mit Narzissen. *Lilionarcissus* lautete einst in Gelehrtenkreisen die Bezeichnung für Tulpen, bevor *Tulipa* sich durchsetzte. Schließlich gab Carl von Linné (1707–1778), schwedischer Naturforscher und Begründer der wissenschaftlichen Nomenklatur, im Jahr 1753 den botanischen Terminus *Tulipa* vor – was sich bis heute etabliert hat.

Wild tulip species

NATURAL ORIGINS

GARDEN TULIPS' CHARMING WILD ANCESTORS

Icy cold winters, scorching heat, and agonizing aridity in summer—wild tulips from the steppes and mountain regions of West and Central Asia are accustomed to these conditions. North Africa and southern Europe are home to other wild species. Despite their small size, these delicate beauties have accomplished great things: as ancestors of our present-day garden tulips, they provided breeders with a rich buffet of diverse traits. Unsurprisingly, scientists and collectors commissioned by breeding nurseries went wild in the 19th century, traveling to Central Asia to discover new forms and shapes of tulips.

The exact number of wild tulip species is difficult to determine. Tulips have always been masters of transformation. Morphological features such as colors and lengths can vary considerably within a species. Moreover, many studies are based on herbarium material, where some details found in wild specimens may no longer be clearly visible, or tulip collections from altered habits. The World Checklist of Selected Plant Families recognizes 94 species of the genus *Tulipa*. It would be a shame to think of "tulips" only in terms of robust, cultivated tulips. Why not enrich rock gardens or barren roadside areas with these exotic wild species?

NEXT PAGE | Wild tulips from Central Asia thrive in rock gardens, where they find conditions similar to those in their native regions.

Tulpen-Wildarten

URSPRÜNGLICH NATÜRLICH

DIE WILDEN VORFAHREN DER HEUTIGEN GARTENTULPEN HABEN IHRE EIGENEN REIZE

Eisige Kälte im Winter, sengende Hitze und qualvolle Trockenheit im Sommer – daran sind die wilden Tulpen aus den Steppen und Bergregionen West- und Zentralasiens gewöhnt. Weitere Wildarten stammen aus Nordafrika und Südeuropa. Ungeachtet ihrer geringen Größe leisteten diese filigranen Schönheiten Großes: Als Vorfahren unserer heutigen Gartentulpen stellten sie den Züchtern ein reichhaltiges Büfett mit unterschiedlichsten Eigenschaften bereit. So verwundert es nicht, dass sich Wissenschaftler und von Zuchtgärtnereien beauftragte Sammler im 19. Jahrhundert wie wild auf den Weg nach Zentralasien machten, um neue Formen zu entdecken.

Wie viele Tulpenwildarten es wirklich gibt, lässt sich nicht mit Sicherheit sagen. Seit jeher zeigten sich Tulpen als Verwandlungskünstlerinnen. Morphologische Merkmale wie Farben und Längen können innerhalb einer Art beträchtlich variieren. Zudem basieren viele Studien auf Herbarmaterial mit nicht sichtbaren Details oder Tulpensammlungen mit verändertem Habitus. Anerkannt sind nach der World Checklist of Selected Plant Families 94 Arten der Gattung *Tulipa*. Es wäre wirklich schade, beim Stichwort „Tulpe" nur an die kräftigen Zucht-Tulpen zu denken. Wie wäre es, Steingärten oder karge Wegränder mit diesen fremdartigen Wildarten zu bereichern?

NÄCHSTE SEITE | Wildtulpen aus Zentralasien wachsen im Steingarten gut, wo sie Bedingungen ähnlich wie in ihrer Heimat vorfinden.

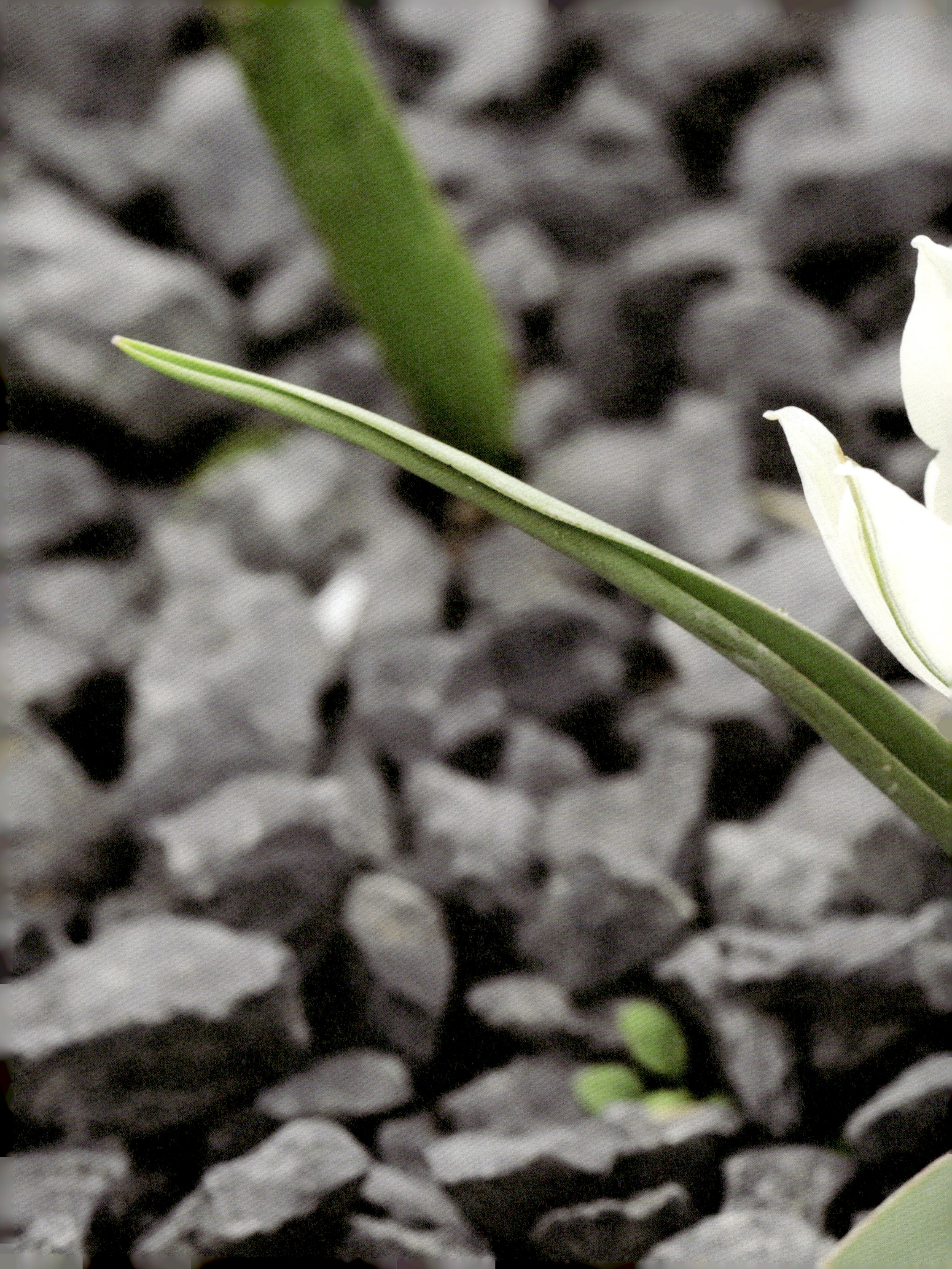

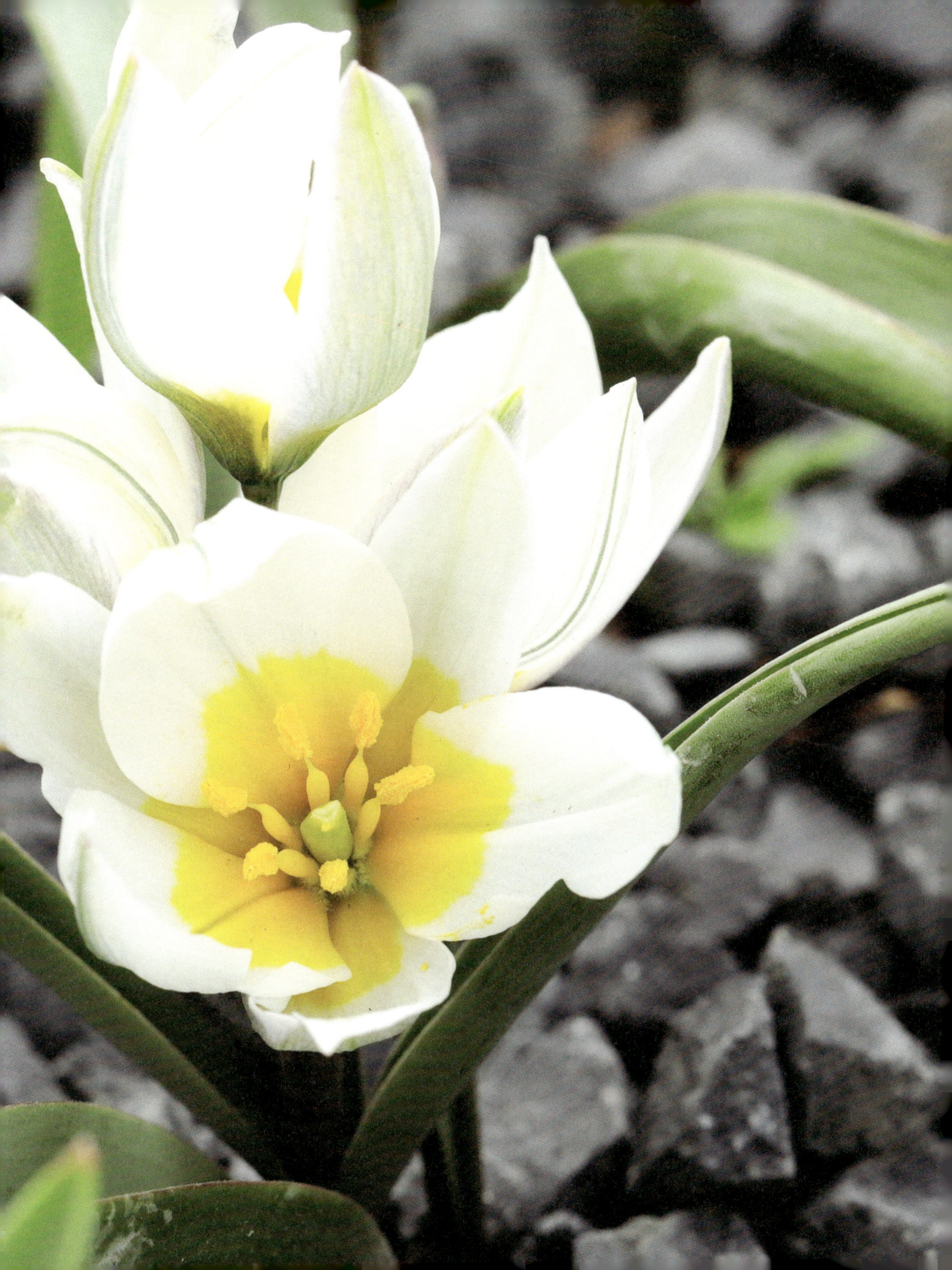

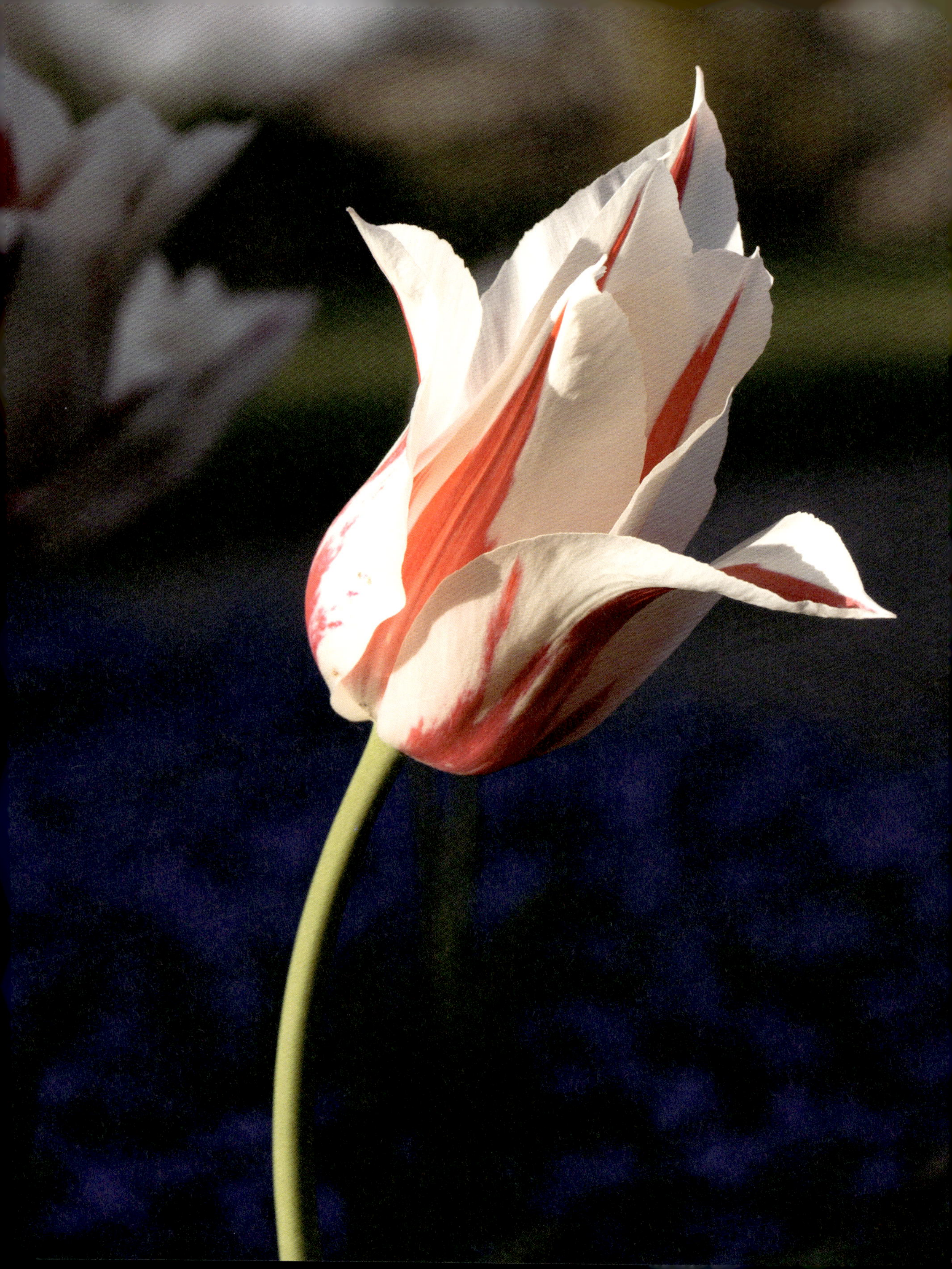

Tulipa clusiana

LADY TULIP

ATTRACTIVE, YET NEVER ARROGANT

Slim, attractive, elegant—these adjectives to describe the lady tulip, one of the noblest wild tulip species, are all truly ladylike. It was already known by this name in the time of Carolus Clusius (see page 40). In his honor, the species received its botanical epithet. The English botanist John Parkinson (1567–1659) referred to it as the Persian tulip.

DAMEN-TULPE

APART, ABER KEINESFALLS ARROGANT

Schlank, attraktiv, elegant, eine der edelsten Wildtulpenarten – wahrlich *ladylike* klingen die Beschreibungen der Damen-Tulpe. Unter diesem Namen kannte man sie bereits zu Zeiten von Carolus Clusius (siehe Seite 43). Ihm zu Ehren bekam die Art ihren botanischen Artzusatz. Der englische Botaniker John Parkinson (1567–1659) beschrieb sie als Persische Tulpe.

Tulipa turkestanica, Tulipa tarda, Tulipa dasystemon

GNOME AND STAR TULIPS

MINISCULE YET MAGNIFICENT

Frost-resistant, undemanding, and small—these multi-flowered wild tulips, which thrive on rocky ground in Central Asia, often at elevations of around 2,000 meters or higher, are a sight to behold. Imagine the enchanting view in the Tian Shan (Mountains of Heaven) when countless stars adorn the rocky slopes.

Starting in early March, the Turkestan tulip *(Tulipa turkestanica)* displays its numerous ivory-white flowers with a striking orange-yellow center. The green-tinged buds of the approximately 3.9 inches small late tulip *(Tulipa tarda)* open into golden-yellow star-shaped flowers with white edges in April and May. It is similar to *Tulipa dasystemon* whose flowers also resemble little stars.

NEXT PAGE | Tiny but tough: *Tulipa turkestanica* thrives on barren soil and enchants with its ivory-white flowers.

Tulipa turkestanica, Tulipa tarda, Tulipa dasystemon

GNOMEN- UND STERN-TULPEN

ZWERGENHAFT UND DOCH GRANDIOS

Unempfindlich gegen Frost, anspruchslos und klein – auf steinigem Boden in Zentralasien, nicht selten in Höhenlagen um 2000 m oder höher, gedeihen diese mehrblütigen Wildtulpen. Was muss das im Tian Shan (Himmelsgebirge) für ein reizvoller Anblick sein, wenn unzählige Sterne die felsigen Hänge zieren.

Ab Anfang März zeigt die Turkestanische oder Gnomen-Tulpe *(Tulipa turkestanica)* ihre zahlreichen elfenbeinweißen Blüten mit einer auffällig orange-gelben Mitte.

Grünlich angehauchte Knospen und goldgelbe, weiß berandete Blütensterne der etwa 10 cm kleinen (Zwerg-)Stern-Tulpe *(Tulipa tarda)* öffnen sich im April und Mai. Ihr ähnlich ist die Kleine Stern-Tulpe *(Tulipa dasystemon)*.

NÄCHSTE SEITE | Klein, aber wow: *Tulipa turkestanica* gedeiht auf kargen Böden und bezaubert mit ihren elfenbeinweißen Blüten.

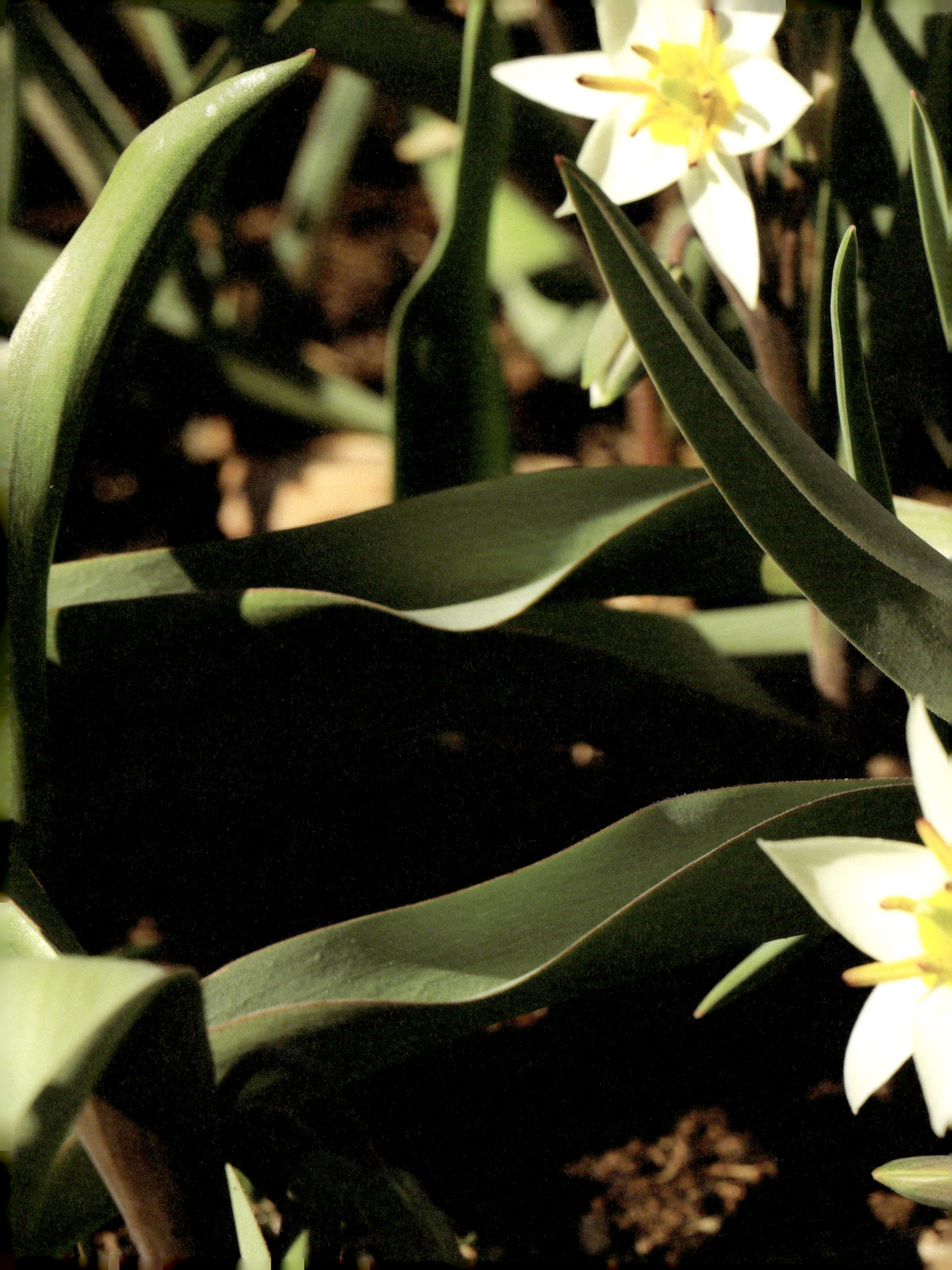

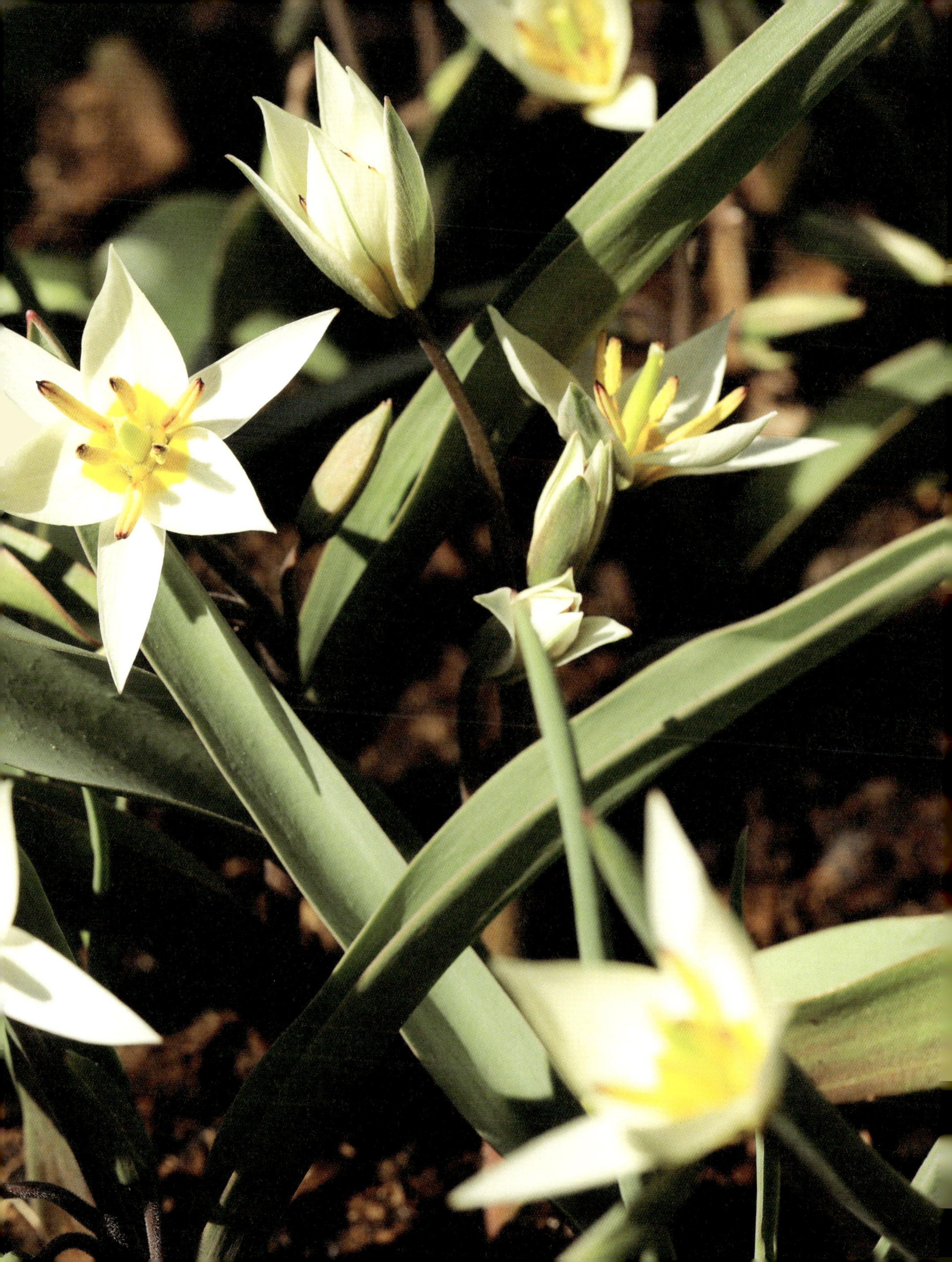

Tulipa sylvestris

WOODLAND TULIP

UNWANTED WEED, ENDANGERED CULTIVATED PLANT, ROBUST SURVIVALIST

For centuries, it has been native to Germany and is the only wild tulip species here. It comes as no surprise then that, after all this time, no one remembers the original home of *Tulipa sylvestris*. Its native range now extends across Eurasia and North Africa.

Possibly starting in Bologna, it embarked on its journey from the warm regions of the Mediterranean northwards over the Alps in the second half of the 16th century. As an ornamental plant, it adorned the parks of the aristocracy as well as castle and monastery gardens. Yet the unruly tulip did not stay behind monastery walls for long; it made its way back into the wild. The sun-loving flower is now often found in vineyards, hence its German common name, "vineyard tulip".

Lightly nodding, greenish-yellow flower buds, delicately scented yellow star-shaped flowers—a feast for the eye in early spring when flowers are still sparse! J. C. Döll referred to it as a *mauvaise herbe* in 1857, but the prolific and "annoying weed" has been tamed in recent decades through adjustments in soil management.

Let us encourage and promote biological diversity in our cultural landscape so that more vineyards may transform into a colorful sea of deep blue grape hyacinths, shining white star-of-Bethlehems, and bright yellow wild tulips.

NEXT PAGE | The woodland tulip came to Central Europe as an ornamental plant but quickly naturalized itself.

Tulipa sylvestris

WEINBERG-TULPE

UNLIEBSAMES UNKRAUT, GEFÄHRDETE KULTURPFLANZE, ROBUSTE ÜBERLEBENSKÜNSTLERIN

Seit Jahrhunderten ist sie schon heimisch bei uns, die einzige wild wachsende Tulpenart in Deutschland. So lange, dass niemand mehr um die ursprüngliche Heimat von *Tulipa sylvestris* weiß. Ihr natürliches Verbreitungsgebiet erstreckt sich heute über Eurasien und Nordafrika.

Womöglich mit Start in Bologna hat sie in der zweiten Hälfte des 16. Jahrhunderts ihre Reise aus den warmen Gefilden des Mittelmeerraums nach Norden über die Alpen angetreten. Als Zierpflanze schmückte sie Parkanlagen von Adelshäusern sowie Schloss- und Klostergärten. Lange hielt es die Wilde nicht hinter Klostermauern, sie gelangte in die freie Natur. Die Sonnenliebhaberin gehört nun zur charakteristischen Weinbergsflora.

Leicht nickende, grünlich-gelbe Blütenknospen, zart duftende gelbe Blütensterne – im noch spärlich blühenden Frühjahr eine Freude für unsere Augen! Von J. C. Döll bereits 1857 als *mauvaise herbe* erwähnt, wurde das vermehrungsfreudige und „lästige Unkraut" in den letzten Jahrzehnten durch veränderte Bodenbewirtschaftung stark gezähmt.

Möge die biologische Vielfalt in unserer Kulturlandschaft mit allen Kräften gefördert werden, damit sich wieder mehr Weinberge in ein buntes Farbenmeer aus tief blauen Traubenhyazinthen, weiß strahlenden Milchsternen und leuchtend gelben Wildtulpen verwandeln.

NÄCHSTE SEITE | Die Weinberg-Tulpe kam als Zierpflanze nach Mitteleuropa, wilderte sich jedoch rasch selbst aus.

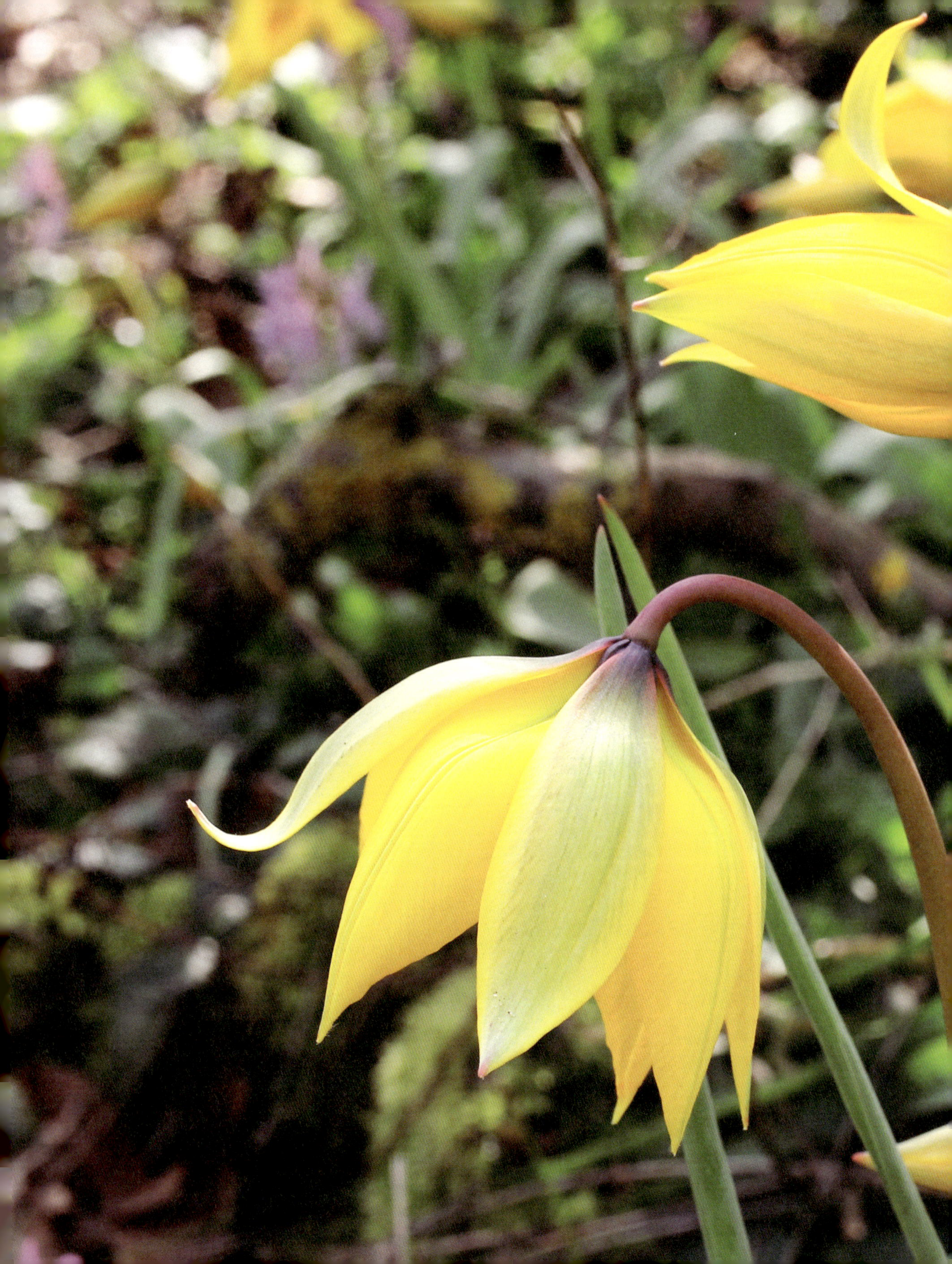

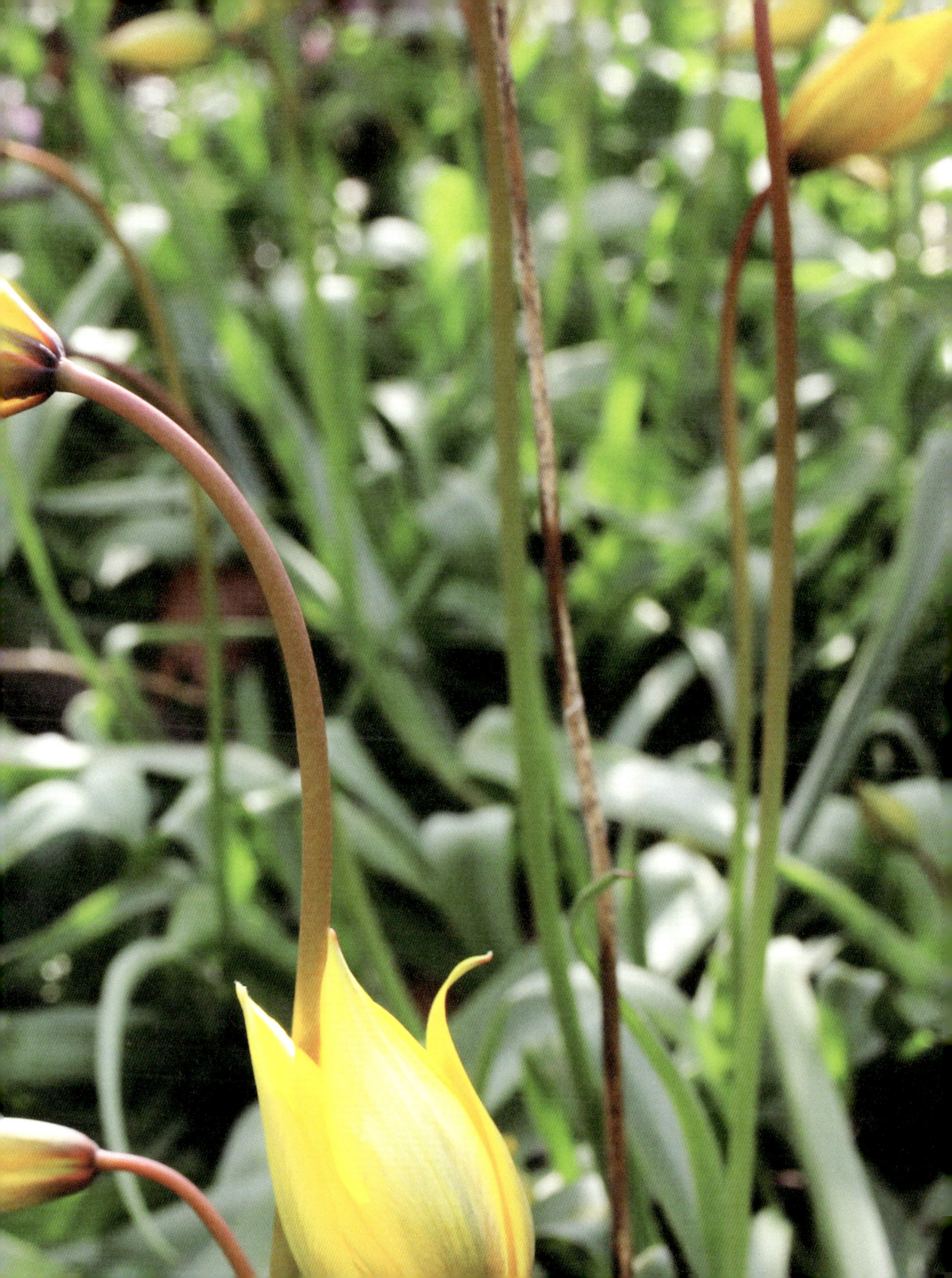

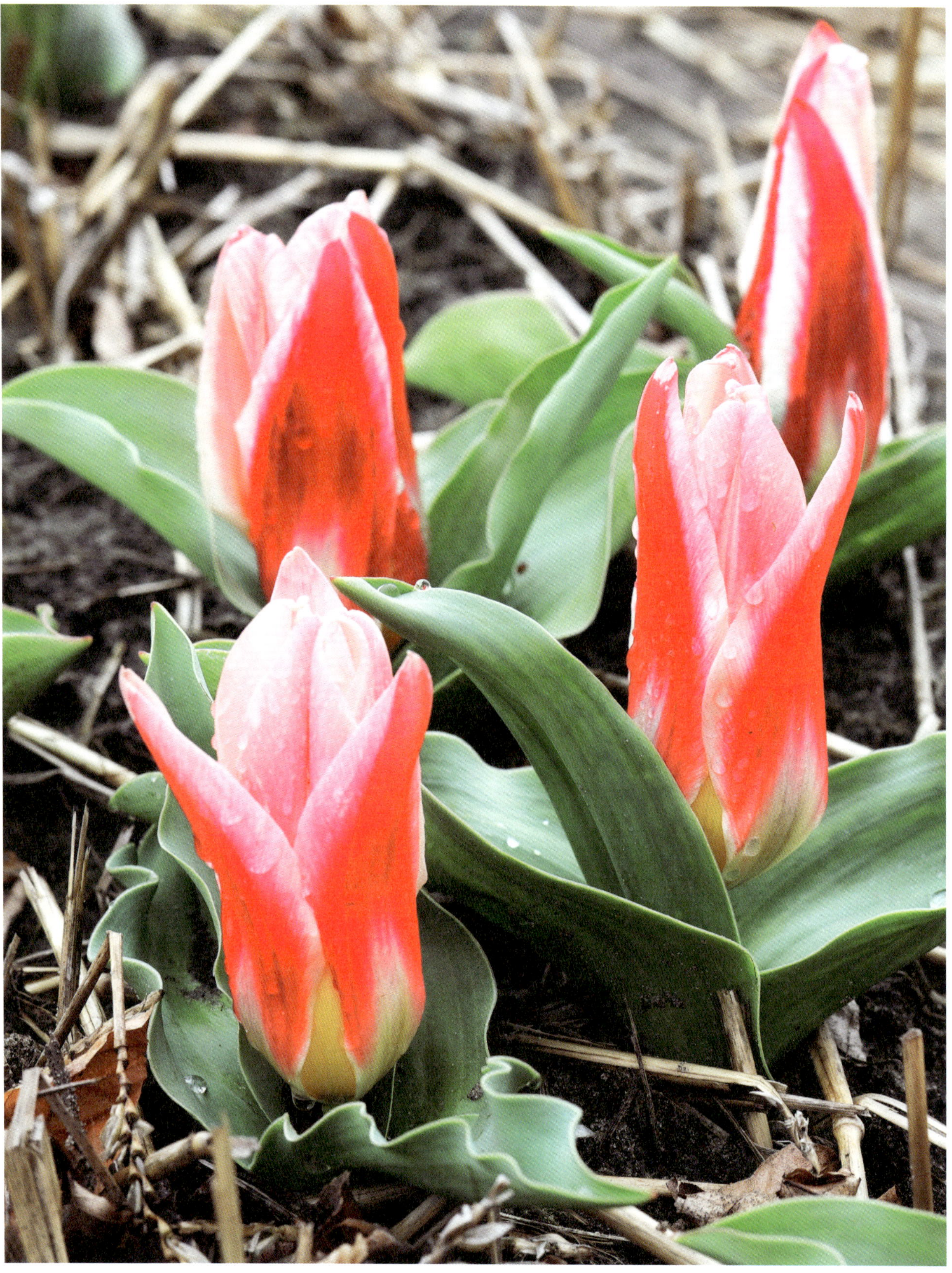

Botanical tulips, wild tulips, and hybrids

WILD BLOOD

BOTANICAL TULIPS AS A LINK BETWEEN WILD SPECIES AND CULTIVATED VARIETIES

Botanical tulips? Are not all tulips, in a way, botanical? This term refers to wild tulip hybrids, especially Kaufmanniana, Fosteriana, and Greigii tulips. These three species of wild tulips, *Tulipa kaufmanniana* (see left side), *Tulipa fosteriana*, and *Tulipa greigii*, hybridized either naturally in the wild or were extensively crossed through horticultural finesse and selected for their suitability as garden flowers—the origin story for countless varieties of our modern garden tulips.

Botanische Tulpen, Wildtulpen und Hybriden

MIT WILDEM BLUT

BOTANISCHE TULPEN STELLEN EINE VERBINDUNG ZWISCHEN WILDARTEN UND KULTURSORTEN DAR

Botanische Tulpen? Sind nicht alle Tulpen gewissermaßen botanisch? Gemeint sind Wildtulpen-Hybriden, insbesondere *Kaufmanniana-*, *Fosteriana-* und *Greigii*-Tulpen. Die drei gleichnamigen Arten der Wildtulpen *Tulipa kaufmanniana* (siehe linke Seite), *Tulipa fosteriana* und *Tulipa greigii* hybridisierten bereits in der freien Natur oder wurden durch gärtnerische Finesse vielfach miteinander gekreuzt und für den Garten geeignet ausgewählt – daraus sind unzählige Sorten unserer modernen Gartentulpen erwachsen.

Tulipa kaufmanniana, Tulipa greigii and hybrids

KAUFMANNIANA AND GREIGII TULIPS

THEIR FLOWERS WERE COMPARED TO WATER LILIES AND PEACOCKS

In 1878, Albert Regel, a doctor in East Turkestan, encountered the wild species *Tulipa kaufmanniana* (see previous page). The distinctive flowers are of an unusual shape: the rounded petals bend far outward and open into a flat star, resembling a water lily. A few years later, a man traveled through the Central Asian steppe, scanning the hilly landscape, looking to collect and deliver numerous color variants of these tulips. This man was P. L. Graeber, a German national living in Tashkent. He was commissioned by Johannes Marius Cornelis Hoog of the bulb company Van Tubergen to search for tulips described by A. Regel in the valleys of the Tien Shan Mountains, with the aim of cultivating them.

Graeber and his people also collected a selection of *Tulipa greigii* varieties and sent them back to Europe. In 1871, Albert Regel had already sent bulbs to St. Petersburg. His father, Dr. E. Regel, named this wild species after Samuel Greig, the president of the Russian Horticultural Association. Greigii tulips were one of the first wild tulip species introduced to the market. They stand out due to the brown-striped pattern on their gray-green foliage.

NEXT PAGE | The 'Quebec' variety belongs to the Greigii tulips and has short, sturdy stems.

Tulipa kaufmanniana, Tulipa greigii und Hybriden

KAUFMANN- UND GREIGII-TULPEN

SIE TRAGEN BLÜTEN, DIE MAN MIT SEEROSEN UND PFAUEN VERGLEICHT

Es war das Jahr 1878, in dem Albert Regel, als Arzt im Osten Turkestans lebend, der Wildart *Tulipa kaufmanniana* (siehe vorige Seite) begegnete. Ungewöhnlich sind die markanten Blüten geformt: die abgerundeten Blütenblätter biegen sich weit nach außen und öffnen sich zu einem flachen Stern, einer Seerose gleichend. Gesammelt und verschickt wurden etliche Farbvarianten dieser Tulpen wenige Jahre später von einem Mann, der durch die zentralasiatische Steppe zog und die hügelige Landschaft mit seinen Augen scannte: Es war P. L. Graeber, ein in Taschkent lebender Deutscher. Beauftragt von Johannes Marius Cornelis Hoog von der Blumenzwiebelfirma Van Tubergen, sollte er in den Tälern des Tian-Shan-Gebirges nach Tulpen suchen, die zuvor von A. Regel beschrieben worden waren, um sie zur Zucht einzuführen.

Ebenfalls von Graeber und seinen Leuten wurde eine Vielzahl von *Tulipa greigii* ausgegraben und nach Europa entsendet. Bereits im Jahr 1871 hatte Albert Regel Zwiebeln nach St. Petersburg geschickt. Sein Vater, Dr. E. Regel, benannte diese Wildart nach Samuel Greig, dem Präsidenten der Russischen Gartenbauvereinigung. Bei den *Greigii*-Tulpen handelt es sich um eine der ersten in den Handel gebrachten Wildtulpenart, die aufgrund des braunen Streifenmusters auf ihrem graugrünen Laub besonders auffällt.

NÄCHSTE SEITE | Die Sorte 'Quebec' gehört zu den *Greigii*-Tulpen und besitzt kurze kräftige Stiele.

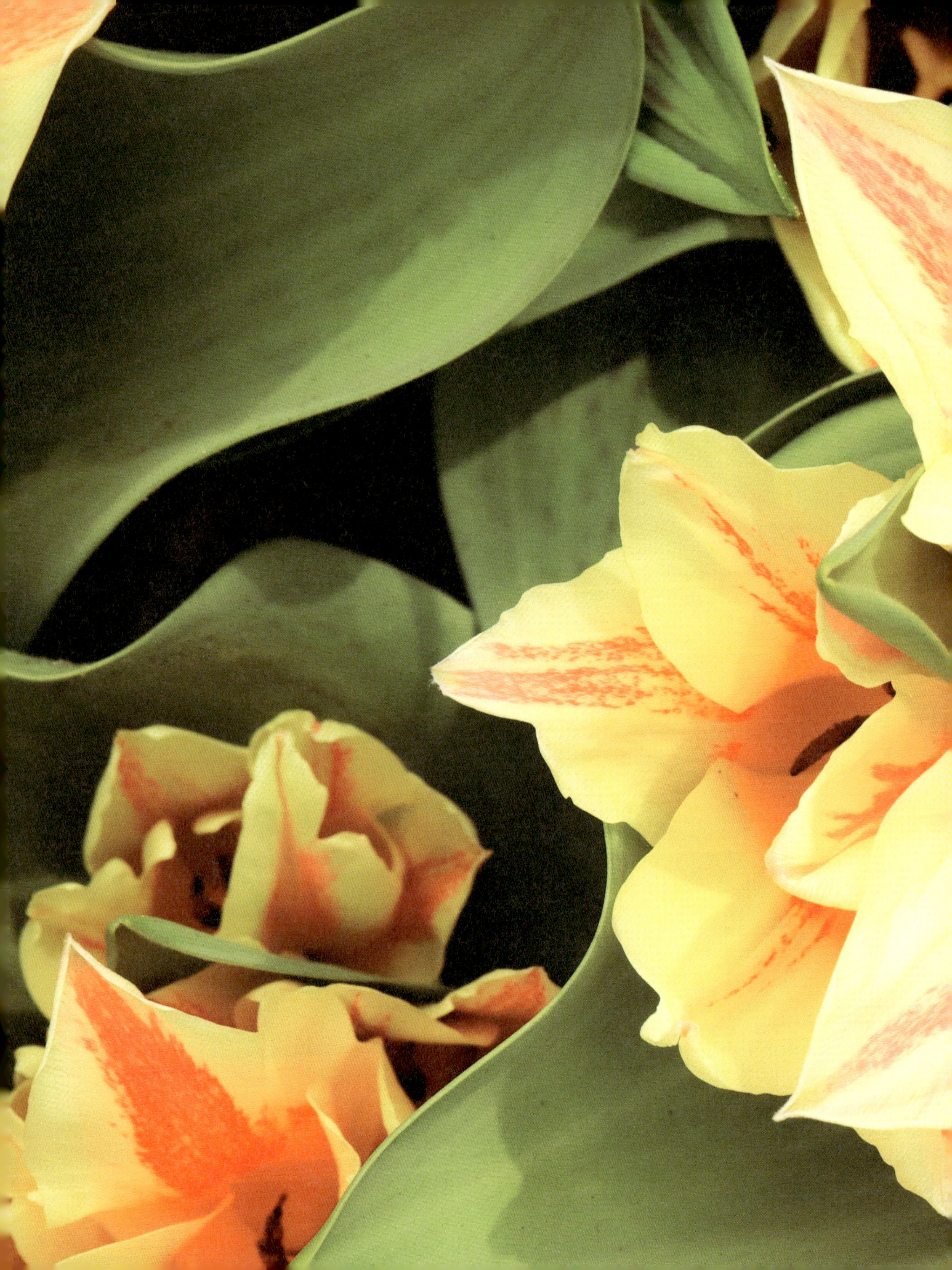

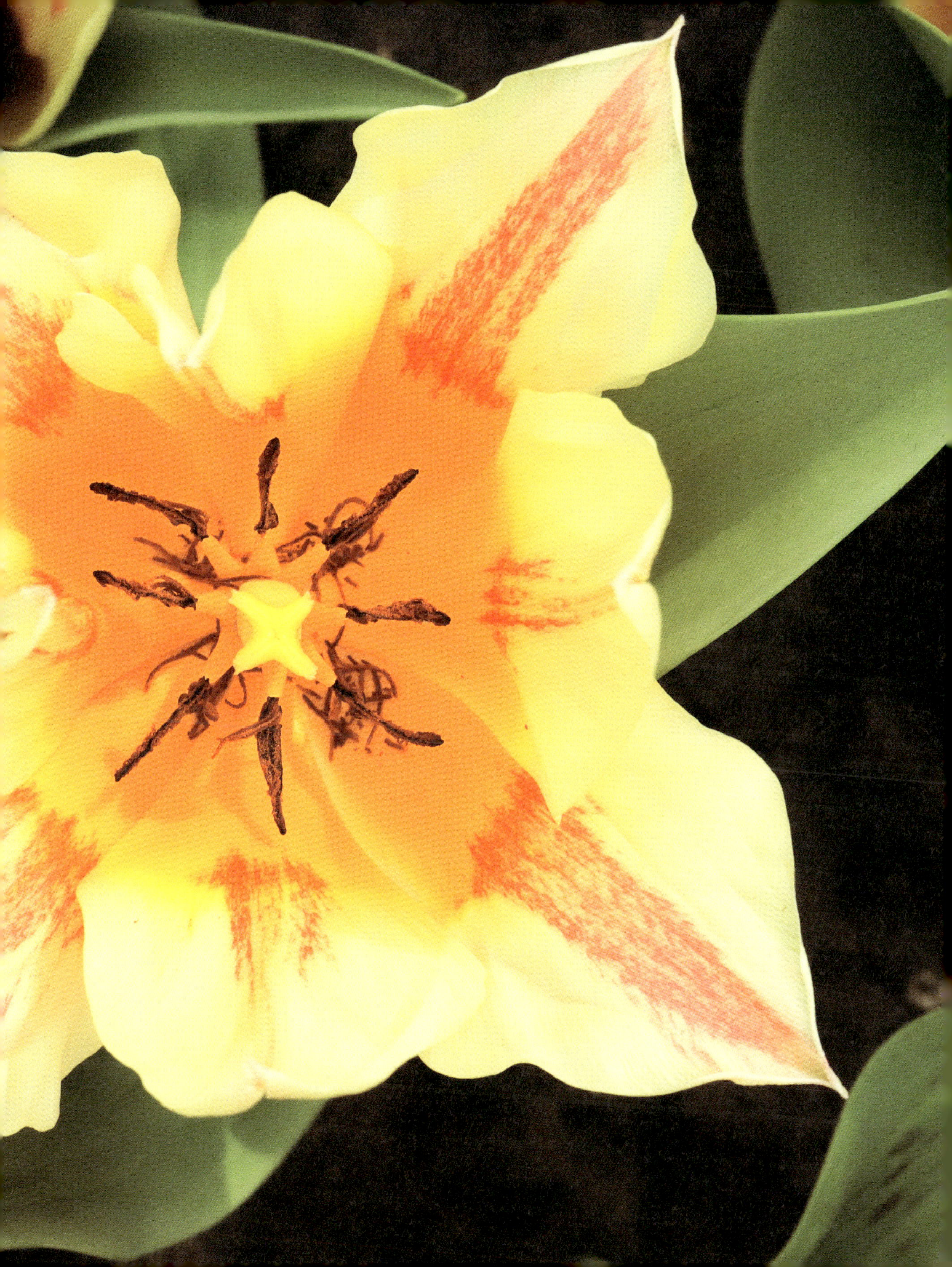

Tulipa fosteriana and hybrids

FOSTERIANA TULIPS

THE 'EMPEROR' TULIPS BOASTING STRIKINGLY LARGE FLOWERS

A large flower in vibrant red with a black base spot, a yellow border, and broad, fine foliage—this is the wild tulip *Tulipa fosteriana*. Its name is attributed to Sir Michael Foster, a British iris expert. This wild species' rise to popularity began in 1904 when Joseph Haberbauer, a tulip collector from the Van Tubergen company, sent two large shipments from the mountainous region south of Samarkand to Johannes Marius Cornelis Hoog. Among them was a magnificent variety, which Hoog named 'Red Emperor.' Dirk W. Lefeber continued breeding this royal tulip and renamed it 'Madame Lefeber,' achieving great crosses with Darwin tulips, thus adding new varieties in the yellow-orange-red color range to the Darwin Hybrid tulip group.

Moreover, *Tulipa fosteriana* possesses immunity against the dreaded tulip virus. This resistance can be passed on, to the delight of every breeder, to other Fosteriana tulips such as 'Cantata' (Van Tubergen, 1942) or 'Princeps.' Is this not every breeder's dream come true?

NEXT PAGE | Award-winning and widely planted: The Fosteriana tulip 'Orange Emperor', bred in 1962 by the Segers brothers, impresses with long-lasting flowers on sturdy stems.

RIGHT PAGE | In 1942, van Tubergen succeeded in breeding the outstanding Fosteriana tulip 'Cantata' in vivid scarlet.

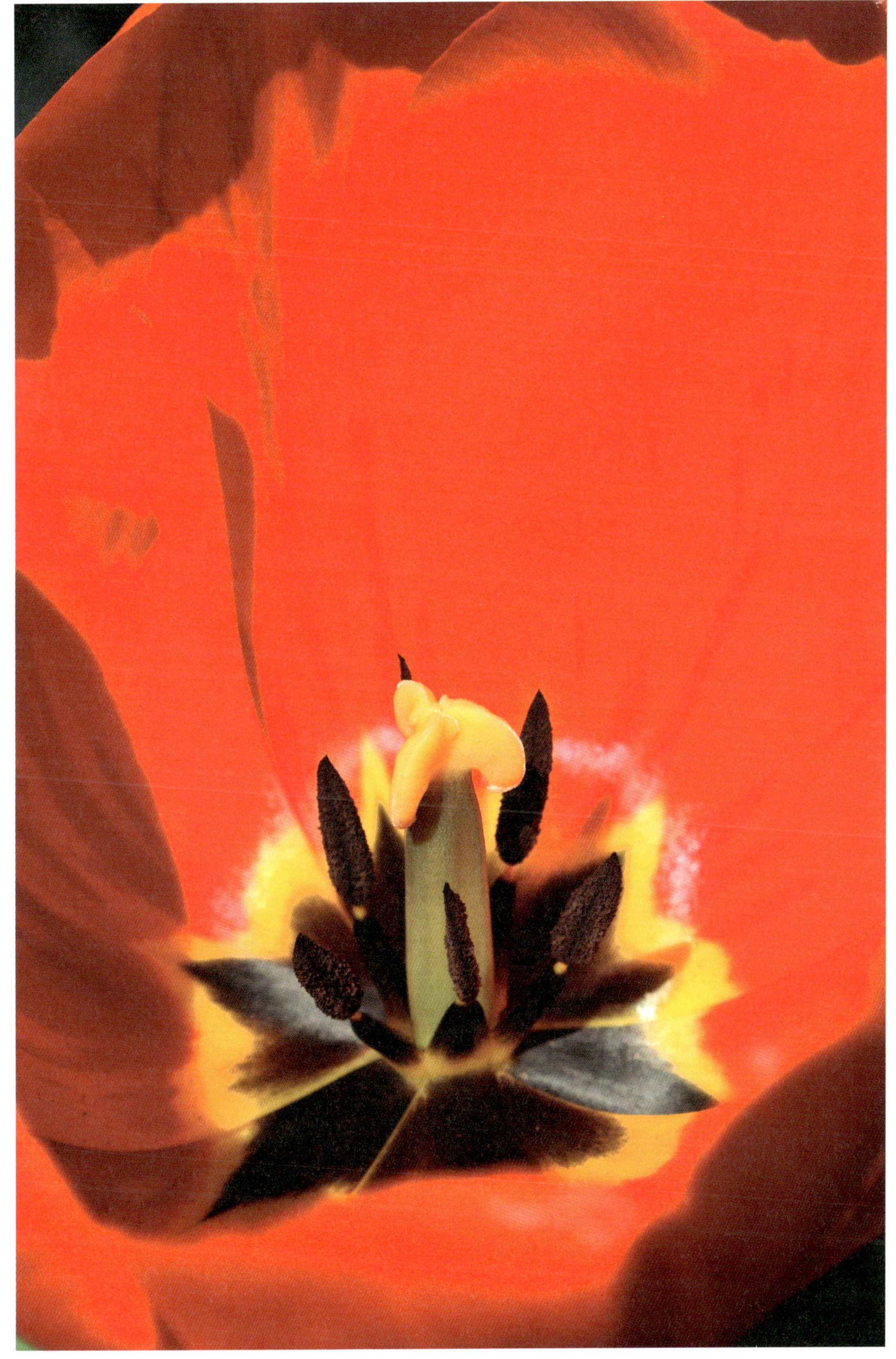

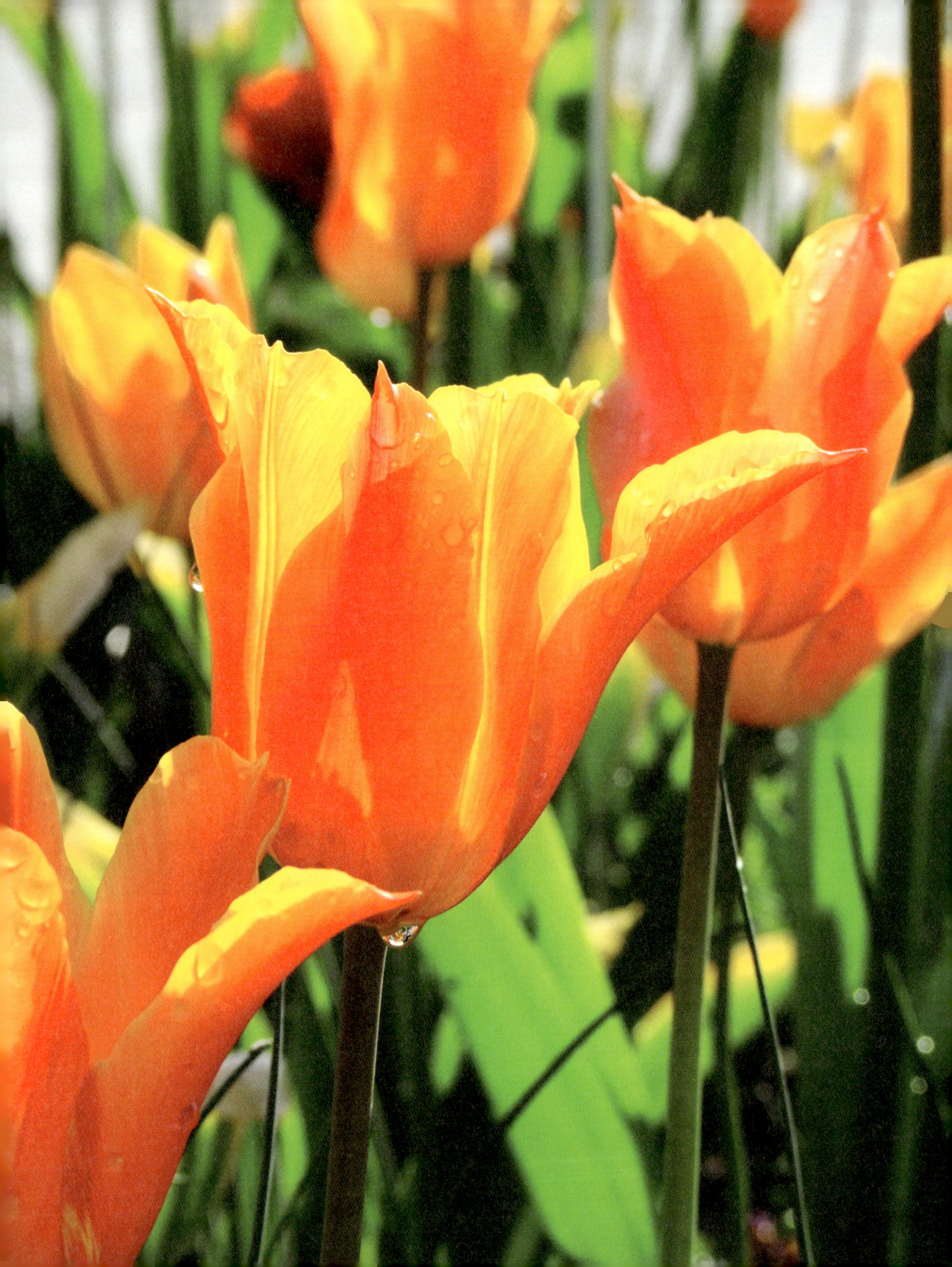

Tulipa fosteriana und Hybriden

FOSTER-TULPEN

WEGEN IHRER AUFFALLEND GROSSEN BLÜTEN WERDEN SIE AUCH KAISER-TULPEN GENANNT

Eine große Blüte in lebhaftem Rot mit einem schwarzen, kräftig gelb umrandeten Grundfleck sowie einem breiten, feinen Blattwerk – so tritt die Wildtulpe *Tulipa fosteriana* in Erscheinung. Ihr Name geht auf Sir Michael Foster, einen britischen Iris-Experten, zurück. Die Karriere dieser Wildart begann im Jahr 1904, als Joseph Haberbauer, Tulpensammler der Firma Van Tubergen, zwei große Lieferungen aus der Bergregion südlich von Samarkand an Johannes Marius Cornelis Hoog schickte. Darunter befand sich eine prächtige Varietät, die von Hoog den Namen 'Red Emperor' bekam. Weiter gezüchtet und umbenannt zu 'Madame Lefeber' gelangen Dirk W. Lefeber mit dieser kaiserlichen Tulpe großartige Kreuzungen mit Darwin-Tulpen, woraufhin sich die Gruppe der Darwin-Hybrid-Tulpen zusehends mit neuen Sorten im gelb-orange-roten Farbbereich füllte.

Und ganz nebenbei besitzt *Tulipa fosteriana* eine Immunität gegen das gefürchtete Tulpenvirus. Diese Resistenz konnte zur Freude jedes Züchters an andere *Fosteriana*-Tulpen wie 'Cantata' (Van Tubergen, 1942) oder 'Princeps' weitergegeben werden. Züchterherz, was begehrst du mehr?

LINKE SEITE | Preisgekrönt und viel gepflanzt: Mit langlebigen Blüten auf stabilen Stielen besticht die 1962 von den Gebrüdern Segers gezüchtete Foster-Tulpe 'Orange Emperor'.

VORIGE SEITE | 1942 gelang van Tubergen diese herausragende, lebhaft scharlachrote Foster-Tulpe 'Cantata'.

Neo-Tulipae

ESCAPED FROM GARDENS?

TULIPS THAT SUDDENLY APPEAR IN EUROPE, SEEMINGLY OUT OF NOWHERE

Taking a closer look at *neo-tulipae*, which is to say, new tulips, opens up a world of mystery. Since the 19th century, up to 16 new species have spontaneously popped up in botanically explored areas. The areas in question are in Italy, France, and Switzerland, near Florence, Saint-Jean-de-Maurienne, and Sion. The discoveries led to animated discussions, and to this day, the origins of these seemingly wild and non-native tulips are a mystery. The suggestion that they are garden escapees seems unsatisfying.

It was impossible to identify plausible parent species for most of these new tulips, despite modern genetic analyses. Swiss botanist Émile Levier (1839–1911) speculated that several newly introduced species had adapted to the climate and, after numerous crosses, eventually spread through seeds. An experiment by the Englishman Henry John Elwes (1846–1922) made an astonishing finding: a once large garden tulip became unrecognizable when planted in nutrient-poor soil. It resembled a small, Central Asian wild species.

Today, the tulip guild in the Swiss village of Grengiols fights for the preservation of its endemic new tulip: *Tulipa grengiolensis* blooms in the second half of May alongside other field weeds in rye fields. In order to protect these tulips, rye cultivation is now largely natural, using traditional methods.

NEXT PAGE | *Tulipa grengiolensis* blooms in the Swiss village of Grengiols, along with other weeds in the fields.

RIGHT PAGE | *Tulipa marjoletti* was widely known in the 19th century, yet until the 1970s, it was believed to be extinct. Today, it thrives in the Savoy Alps—where and how it survived remains unclear.

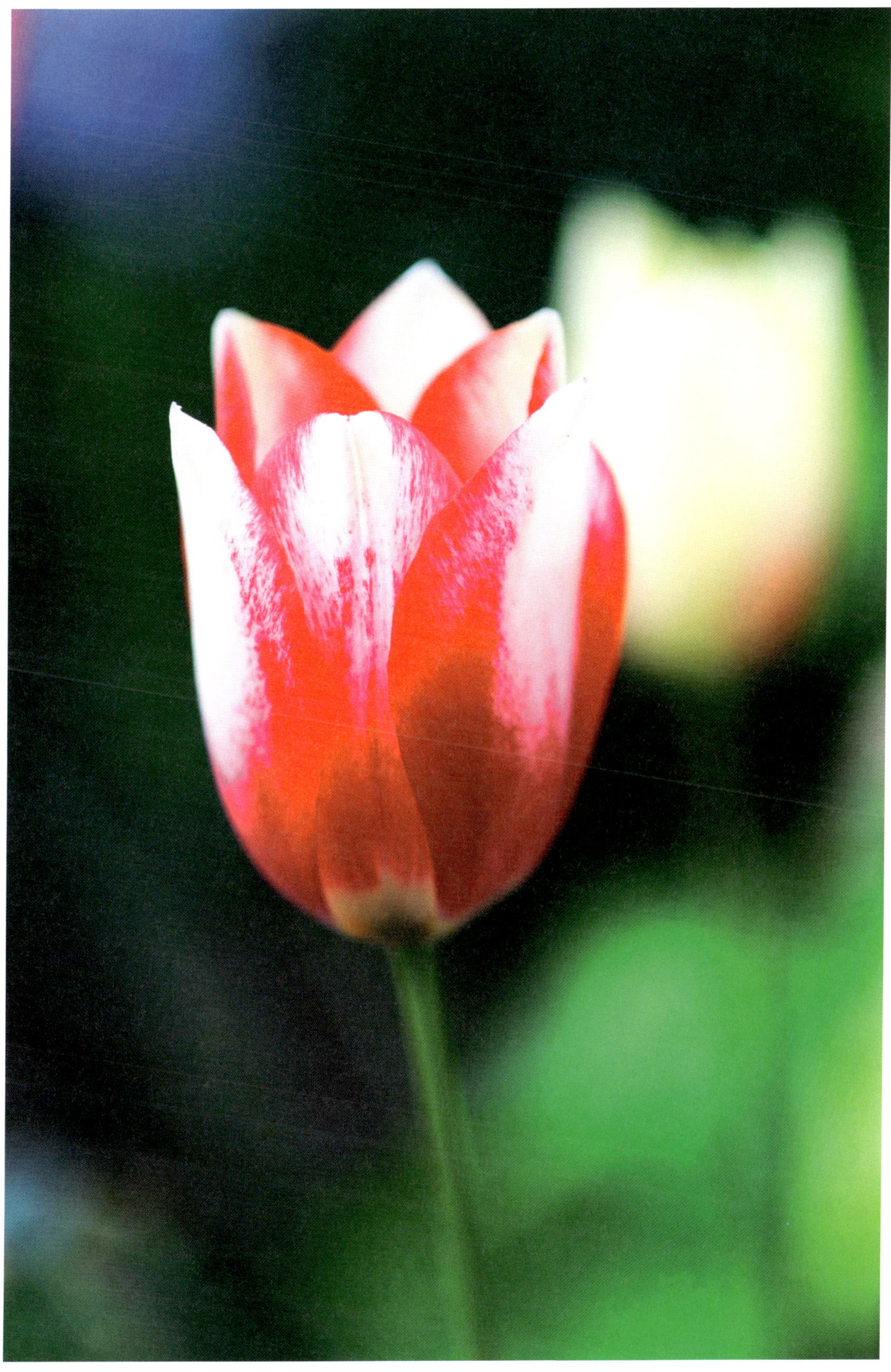

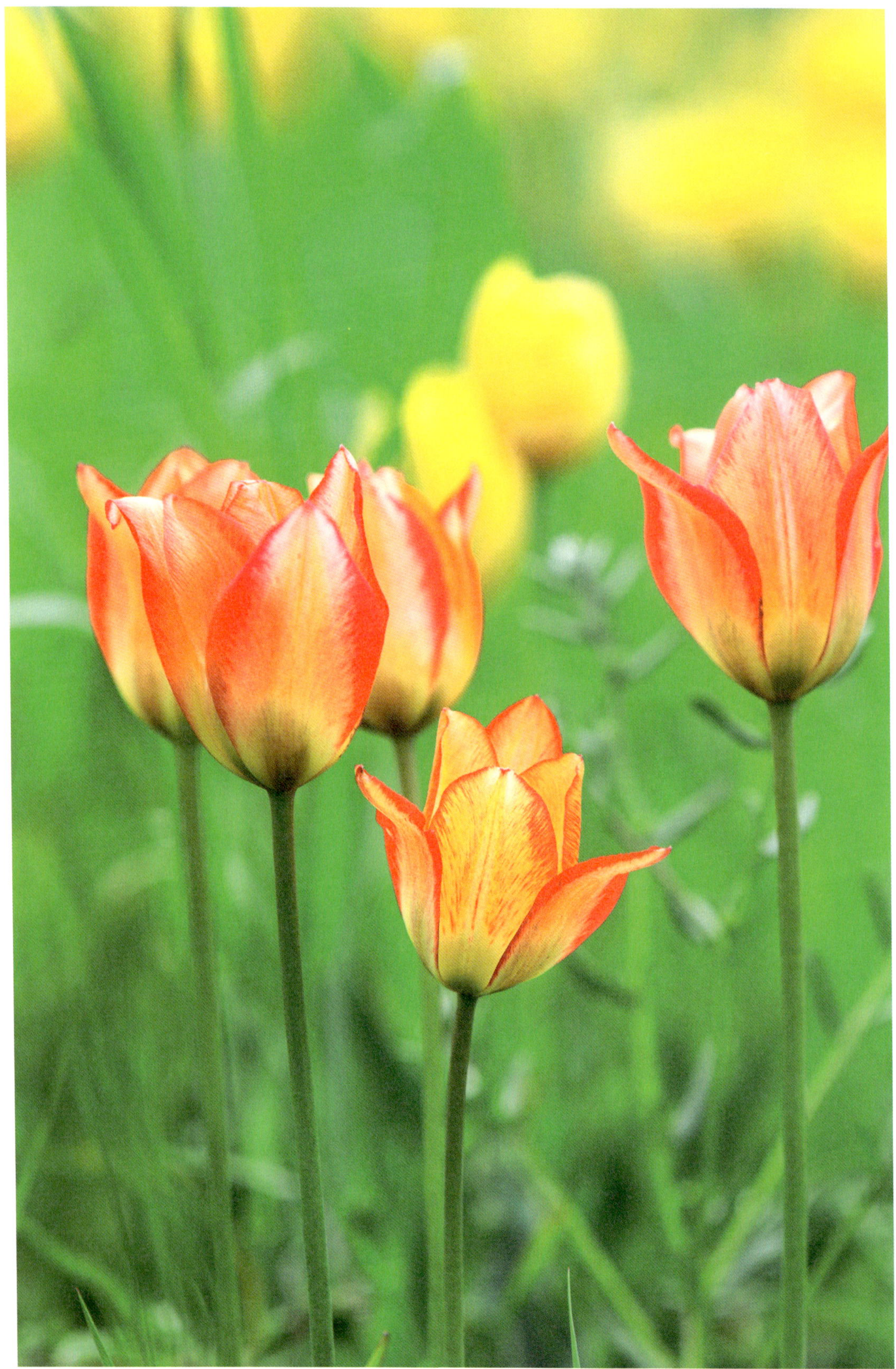

Neo-Tulipae

AUS GÄRTEN ENTFLOHEN?

VIELE GEHEIMNISSE UMWITTERN TULPEN, DIE SCHIER AUS DEM NICHTS IN EUROPA AUFTAUCHTEN

Mysteriös wird es, wenn man sich den *Neo-Tulipae*, den Neu-Tulpen, zuwendet. Bis zu 16 Arten sind seit dem 19. Jahrhundert plötzlich in botanisch erschlossenen Gebieten erschienen. Die Schauorte liegen in Italien, Frankreich und der Schweiz, etwa in der Nähe von Florenz, Saint-Jean-de-Maurienne und Sion. Damals wilde Diskussionen entfachend scheint es bis heute rätselhaft, woher diese offenbar verwilderten und nicht einheimischen Tulpen plötzlich stammten. Unzureichend waren die Erklärungsversuche, es handle sich um Gartenflüchtlinge.

Für kaum eine Form konnten plausible Elternarten ermittelt werden, nicht einmal mittels moderner Genanalysen. Der Schweizer Botaniker Émile Levier (1839–1911) vermutete, die ursprünglich eingeführten Arten hätten sich klimatisch angepasst und nach unzähligen Kreuzungen schließlich durch Samen ausgebreitet. Erstaunliches verriet ein Experiment des Engländers Henry John Elwes (1846–1922): Eine ehemals große Gartentulpe war in nährstoffarmer Erde nicht mehr wiederzuerkennen. Sie ähnelte den kleinen, zentralasiatischen Wildarten.

Heute kämpft die Tulpenzunft im Schweizer Ort Grengiols um den Erhalt ihrer endemischen Neu-Tulpe: *Tulipa grengiolensis* blüht in der zweiten Maihälfte zusammen mit anderen Ackerunkräutern inmitten von Roggen, der zum Schutz der Tulpen natürlich nach traditioneller Methode angebaut wird.

LINKE SEITE | *Tulipa grengiolensis* blüht im Schweizer Ort Grengiols zusammen mit Unkräutern auf dem Acker.

VORIGE SEITE | Ursprünglich war *Tulipa marjoletti* schon im 19. Jahrhundert bekannt, man hielt sie bis in die 1970er-Jahre für ausgestorben. Heute gedeiht sie in den Savoyer Alpen – unklar ist, wo sie „überlebt" hat.

Cultivated tulips

HOW TO COUNT THE SHAPES AND COLORS?

GROUPS MAKE THIS ABUNDANCE MORE MANAGEABLE

If you could plant only one tulip, which would it be? What an agonizing choice. Would you dismiss wild species and opt for a cultivated variety? Should it be a specific color or perhaps multicolored? Should patterns adorn it like blazing flames? Or would you prefer simple elegance? No? Do you want petals that are fringed, curled, or lily-shaped? A single or a double-flowered tulip? An early, mid, or late flowering variety?

Over the centuries of tulip breeding, an endless variety of cultivars have emerged. Due to completely inconsistent naming, many tulip varieties were once traded under several different names. After 1917, this confusion of names was finally brought into order, and synonyms were eliminated. Lists for scientific classification were published, constantly expanded, and adjusted according to breeding successes and trade demands.

The Dutch Koninklijke Algemeene Vereeniging voor Bloembollencultuur (Royal General Bulb Growers' Association) is the globally recognized institution cataloging and registering the flood of cultivars. Currently, it lists nearly 6,000 cultivated varieties. These are classified into 15 groups based on their flowering time, the shape of their flower heads, and their height. Wild tulips and their hybrids are listed in groups 12 to 15.

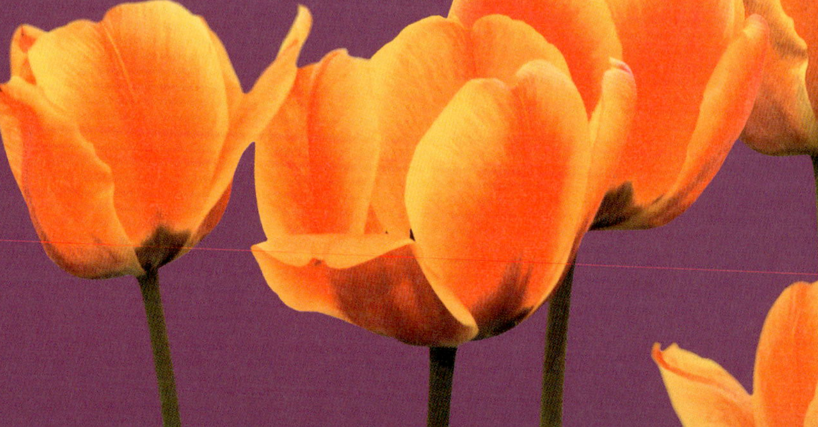

Zucht-Tulpen

WER ZÄHLT DIE FORMEN, WER DIE FARBEN?

UM IHRE FÜLLE ÜBERSCHAUBARER ZU MACHEN, GRUPPIERT MAN SIE IN KLASSEN

Wenn Sie die Qual der Wahl hätten und nur eine einzige Tulpe pflanzen dürften, welche sollte es dann sein? Keine Wildart, sondern eine Zucht-Tulpe? In einer bestimmten Farbe oder gar mehrfarbig? Von lodernden Flammen gezeichnet? Oder klassisch in schlichter Eleganz? Nein? Doch lieber gefranst, gekräuselt oder mit lilienförmigen Blütenblättern? Besser einfach als doppelt gefüllt? Früh, mittel oder spät blühend?

Über die Jahrhunderte der Tulpenzucht ist eine unendliche Fülle an Sorten entstanden. Einer völlig regellosen Namensgebung geschuldet, wurde so manch eine Tulpensorte einst unter mehreren verschiedenen Bezeichnungen gehandelt. Ab 1917 brachte man Licht ins Dunkel der Namenswirrnis und beseitigte Synonyme. Klassifizierungslisten wurden publiziert, stetig erweitert und entsprechend der Züchtungserfolge und des Handels angepasst.

Die niederländische Koninklijke Algemeene Vereeniging voor Bloembollencultuur (Royal General Bulb Growers' Association) ist die weltweit anerkannte Institution, welche die Flut von Züchtungen katalogisiert und registriert. Dort gelistet sind heute knapp 6000 Zuchtsorten. Sie werden nach ihrer Blütezeit, Blütenform und Wuchshöhe in fünfzehn Sortengruppen eingeteilt. Wildtulpen und ihre Hybriden sind den Gruppen 12 bis 15 zugeordnet.

Group 1 and 2

EARLY TULIPS

SINGLE EARLY AND DOUBLE EARLY VARIETIES

The term "Single Early tulip" by no means designates a plain or inconspicuous plant. On the contrary, at this early time of year, from late March to early April, tulips, which are all early bloomers, stand out especially well with their colorful display. This group includes all unfilled varieties that do not belong to any other group.

Short, robust stems allow these hardy plants to withstand rain and spring storms. 'Lac van Rijn,' the oldest variety in this group (1620), and 'Keizerskroon' (1750) are among the heirloom varieties. 'Generaal de Wet,' according to Sir Alfred Daniel Hall, the "most beautiful of all early tulips", enchants with a sweet fragrance and orange flowers shaded in a darker hue. The historically significant 'Duc van Tol' tulips, which are the oldest cultivated tulips and formerly popular Christmas tulips, are also listed in this group.

The flowers of Double Early tulips are large and very densely filled. The 'Murillo' and its relatives are at the heart of this colorful group. On similarly robust stems, these compact varieties bring a lot of color to the gray of the fading winter. Double Early tulips are highly popular plants for containers and balcony boxes, ideally with minimal exposure to wind and rain to protect their heavy flowers.

NEXT PAGE | Historical varieties in this group:
'Keizerskroon' (left) and 'Lac van Rijn' (right)

Gruppe 1 und 2

FRÜHE TULPEN

UNTER IHNEN GIBT ES EINFACHE FRÜHE UND GEFÜLLTE FRÜHE SORTEN

Unter „Einfachen Tulpen" sollte man keineswegs schlichte oder gar unauffällige Pflanzen verstehen. Denn die Tulpen, die notabene Frühblüher sind, fallen gerade zu dieser frühen Zeit ab Ende März/Anfang April mit ihrer Farbenfreude besonders auf. Ihnen gehören alle ungefüllten Sorten an, die keiner anderen Gruppe zuzuordnen sind.

Kurze, kräftige Stängel ermöglichen es den Hartgesottenen, dem Regen und den Frühjahrsstürmen zu trotzen. 'Lac van Rijn', ältester Vertreter dieser Gruppe aus dem Jahr 1620, und 'Keizerskroon' (1750) zählen zu den historischen Sorten. 'Generaal de Wet', laut Sir Alfred Daniel Hall die „schönste aller Frühtulpen", verzaubert mit süßem Duft und orangefarbenen, von dunklerer Schattierung überzogenen Blüten. Dieser Gruppe wurden auch die historisch bedeutenden Duc van Tol-Tulpen zugeordnet, mit die ältesten kultivierten Tulpen und einst berühmte Weihnachtstulpen.

Groß und sehr dicht gefüllt sind die Blüten der Gefüllten Frühen Tulpen. 'Murillo' und ihre Verwandten stehen im Zentrum dieser farbenreichen Gruppe. Auf ebenfalls kräftigen Stängeln bringen die kompakten Sorten viel Farbe ins Grau des ausklingenden Winters. Sehr beliebt sind die Gefüllten daher für die Bepflanzung von Gefäßen und Balkonkästen, optimalerweise wegen der schweren Blüten gut geschützt vor Wind und Regen.

NÄCHSTE SEITE | Historische Sorten aus dieser Gruppe: 'Keizerskroon' (links) und 'Lac van Rijn' (rechts)

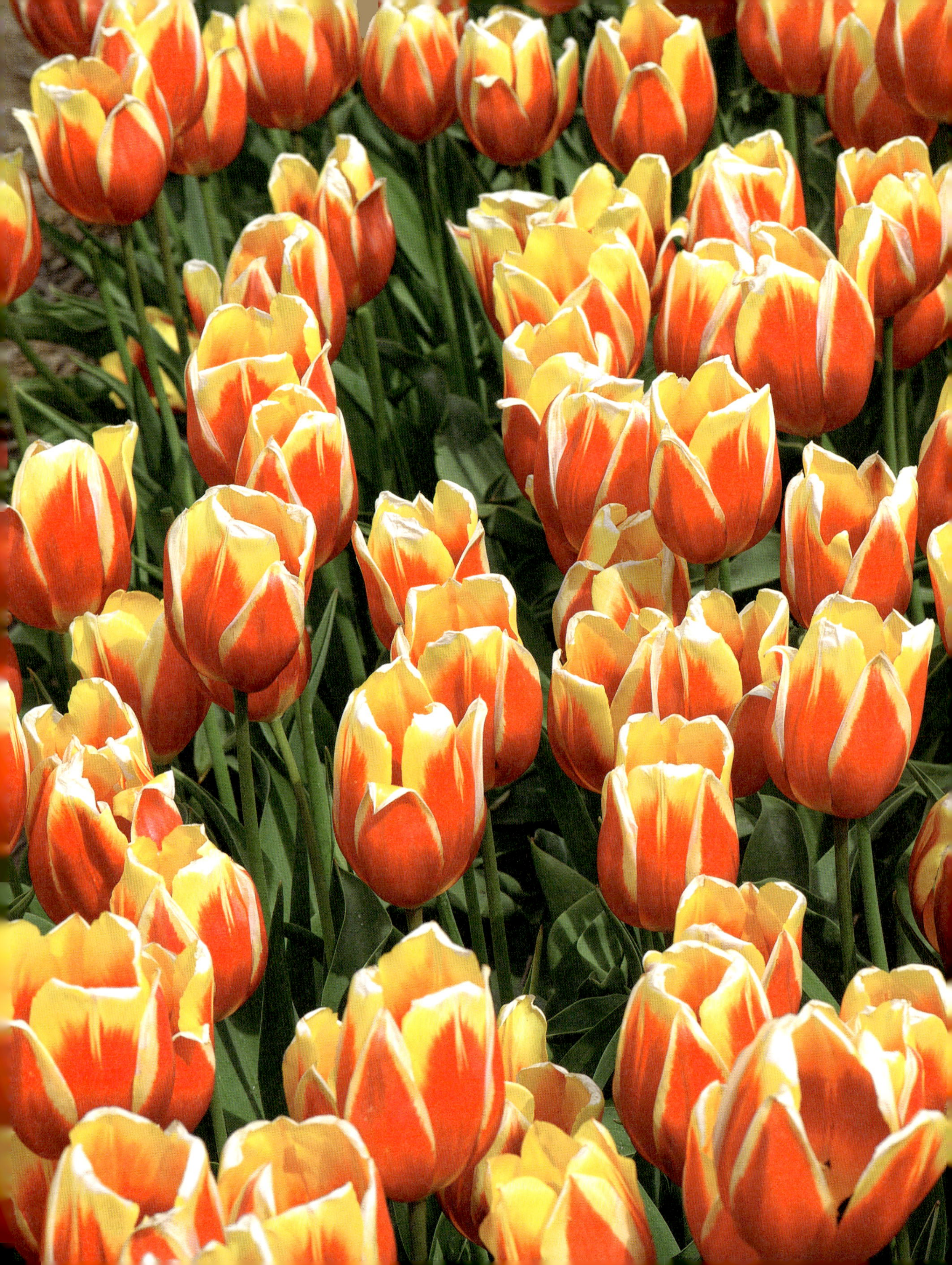

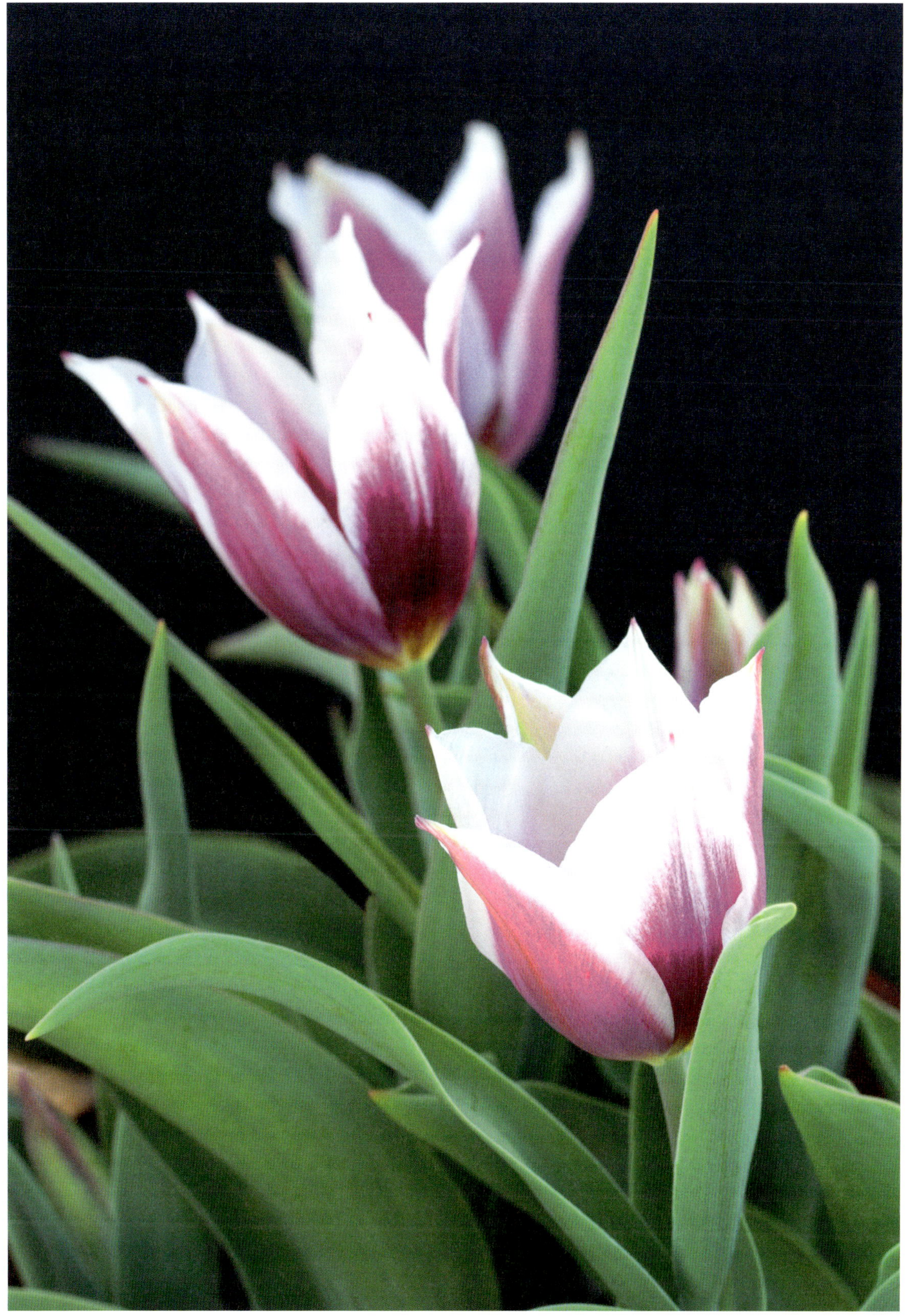

Group 3

TRIUMPH TULIPS

GREATEST VARIETY AND COLOR PALETTE

The Dutch tulip breeder N. Zandbergen must have felt incredibly lucky and experienced a deep sense of satisfaction in 1923 when his tulips, grown from seeds, bloomed with splendor and glory—truly a triumph. Initially, these tulips were also called Zandbergen tulips, but after other breeders brought similar varieties to the market by crossing Single Early and Darwin tulips, the classification of Triumph tulips was established. Only a few varieties of the first generation can still be admired at the Hortus Bulborum in Limmen, Netherlands.

With a height of 15–24 inches and robust stems, Triumph tulips make excellent cut flowers. Unsurprisingly, this group boasts the greatest number of varieties, their petals shining in a broad palette of colors: sometimes solid in white, yellow, orange, red, pink to violet, or even multicolored, patterned, or flamed. These beautiful cut flowers are easily propagated through daughter bulbs and are essential for forcing. They can be easily pre-grown from January 1st onwards. In the garden, these fragrant sun worshippers are low-maintenance. Even in stronger winds, they do not easily bend, and they shine in colorful attire from mid-April.

NEXT PAGE | Red is the ultimate tulip color, and Triumph tulips feature many varieties in various shades of red.

RIGHT PAGE | Triumph tulips: proud specimens with a classic flower shape on strong stems

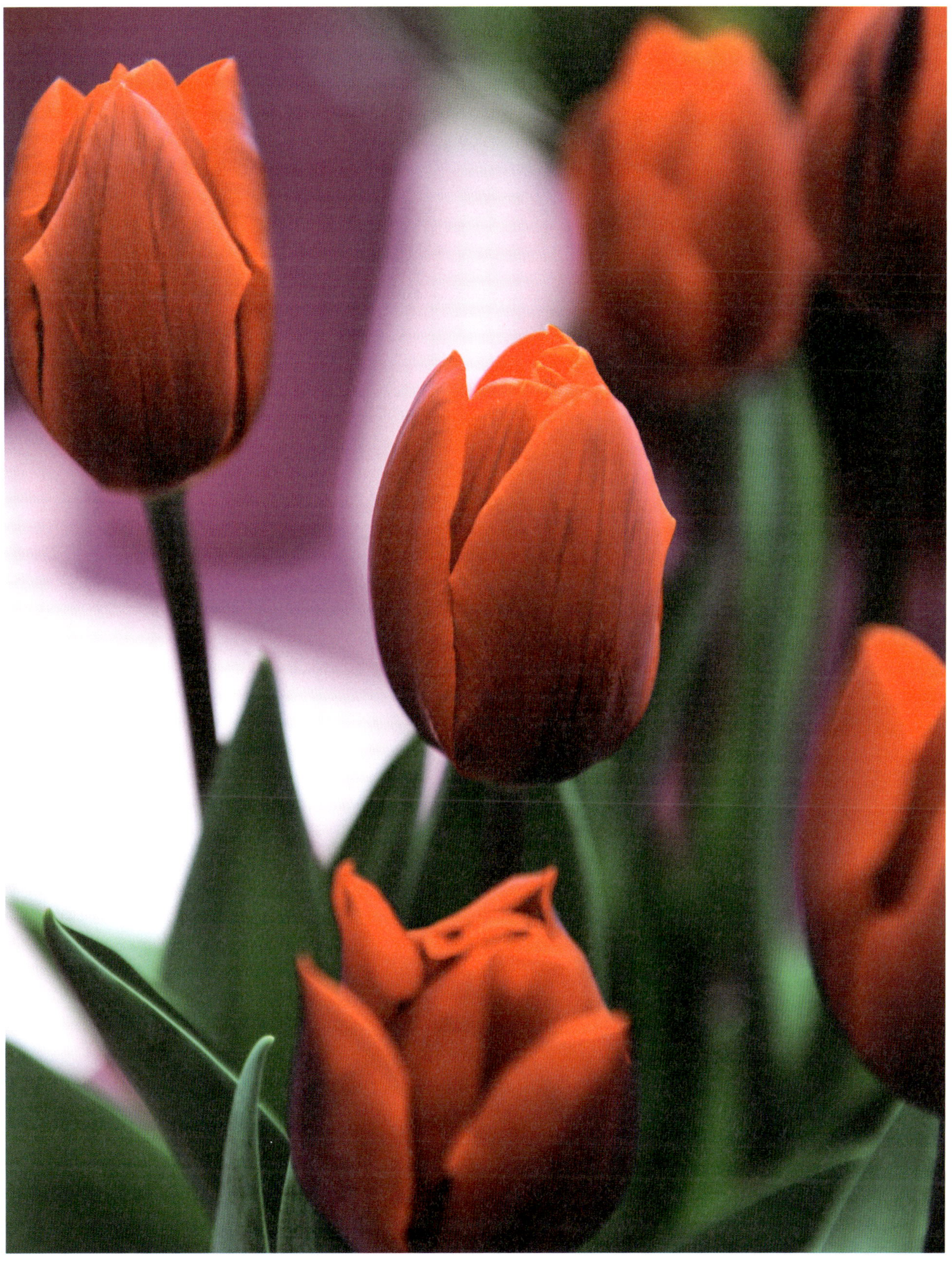

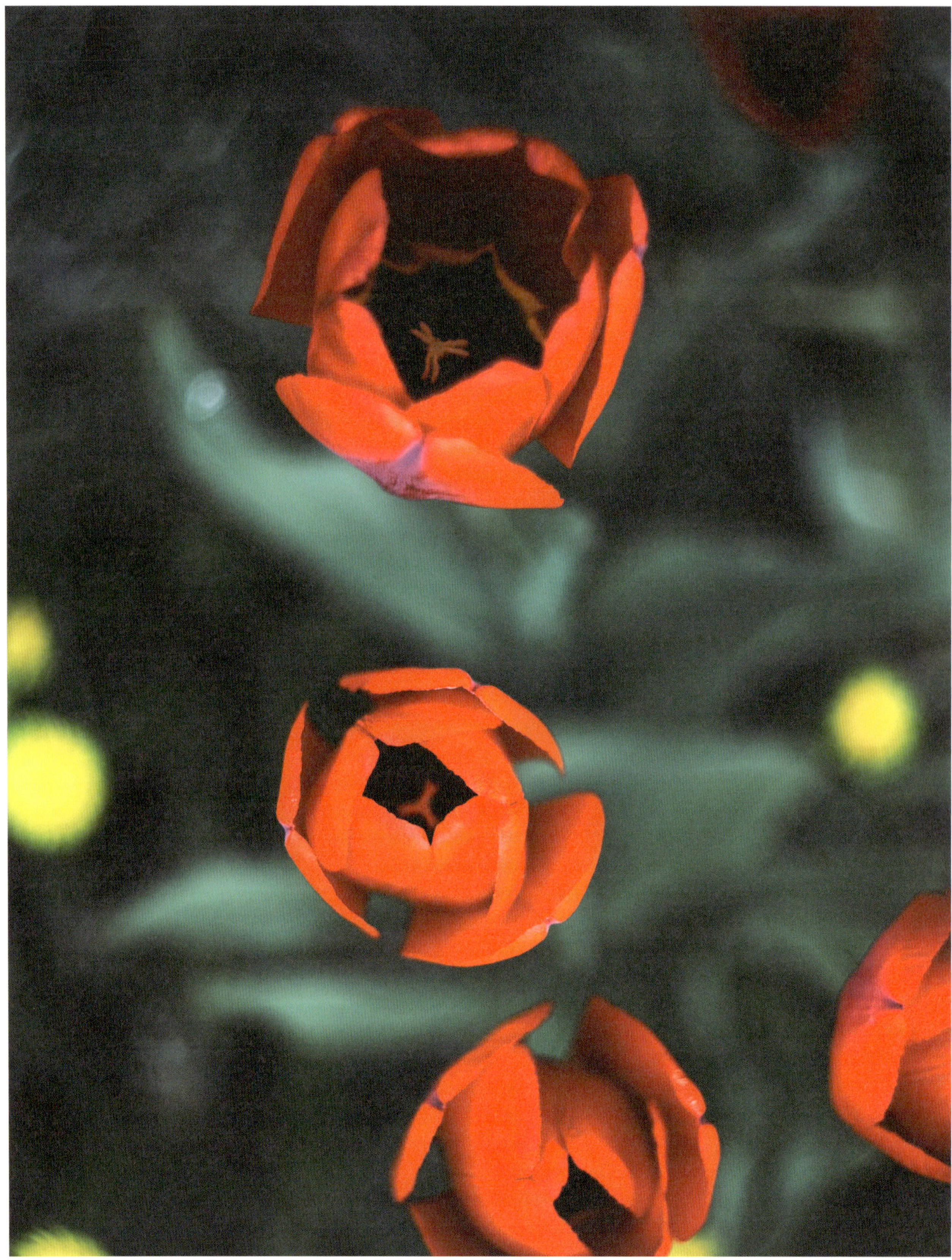

Gruppe 3

TRIUMPH-TULPEN

GRÖSSTE SORTENVIELFALT UND FARBPALETTE

Welch ein Glücksgefühl, welche Genugtuung muss der holländische Tulpenzüchter N. Zandbergen 1923 verspürt haben, als seine aus Samen gezogenen Tulpen mit Glanz und Gloria aufblühten. Wahrlich ein Triumph. Anfangs wurden diese Tulpen auch Zandbergen-Tulpen genannt. Erst nachdem andere Züchter ähnliche Sorten durch Kreuzung von Einfachen Frühen und Darwin-Tulpen auf den Markt brachten, etablierte sich die Klassifizierung namens Triumph-Tulpen. Von der ersten Generation können nur noch wenige Sorten im Hortus Bulborum im niederländischen Limmen bewundert werten.

Mit 40–60 cm Wuchshöhe und kräftigen Stielen sind die Triumph-Tulpen hervorragende Schnittblumen. Nicht verwunderlich, dass die Sortenvielfalt in dieser Gruppe am größten ist und sämtliche Blütenfarben auf ihrer Palette zu finden sind: manchmal einfarbig in Weiß, Gelb, Orange, Rot, Rosa bis Violett, oder auch mehrfarbig gemustert oder geflammt. Die Vasenschönheiten lassen sich leicht über Tochterzwiebeln vermehren und sind unverzichtbar für die Treiberei. Ab dem 1. Januar können sie sehr gut vorgezogen werden. Im Garten erweisen sich die duftenden Sonnenanbeterinnen als pflegeleicht. Selbst bei stärkerem Wind knicken sie nicht leicht um und erstrahlen ab Mitte April in farbenfrohem Gewand.

LINKE SEITE | Rot gilt als DIE Blütenfarbe der Tulpen schlechthin, auch unter den Triumph-Tulpen gibt es viele Sorten in den unterschiedlichsten Rottönen.

VORIGE SEITE | Triumph-Tulpen: stolze Exemplare mit klassischer Blütenform auf starken Stielen

Group 4

DARWIN HYBRID TULIPS

LARGE-FLOWERED, LONG-STEMMED, INTENSELY COLORED—IDEAL FOR FLOWER BEDS AND VASES

Nomen est omen: The famous British naturalist Charles Darwin (1809–1882), a pioneer of the theory of evolution and one of the most influential scientists in history, lends his name to this group of tulips. The nursery E. H. Krelage & Son in Haarlem introduced new, particularly color-intensive tulips to the market in 1889, causing a sensation at the World Exhibition in Paris. These tulips were named in honor of Darwin, to whom the breeder Jakob Heinrich Krelage felt indebted for all his new knowledge about tulip breeding. Krelage himself received the honorary title "Tulip King."

Large, simple blossoms with a roundish shape at the base are a typical feature of Darwin Hybrid tulips. Vivid shades of red, yellow, and orange dominate the limited color spectrum. With long, sturdy stems up to 27 inches high, these eye-catching plants make for impressive garden flowers as well as excellent cut flowers. They bloom in May and can return for many years.

The large-flowered Darwin Hybrid tulips trace back to Dirk Lefeber, a famous breeder from Lisse, Netherlands. Between 1940 and 1950, he succeeded in crossing Darwin tulips with a selection of the wild species *Tulipa fosteriana*. The most famous tulip in this group is probably the 'Apeldoorn' and its variations.

NEXT PAGE | Darwin hybrids 'Banja Luka' (left) and 'Apeldoorn' (right)

Gruppe 4

DARWIN-HYBRID-TULPEN

GROSSBLUMIG, LANGSTIELIG, FARBINTENSIV – IDEAL FÜR BEET UND VASE

Nomen est omen: Der berühmte britische Naturforscher Charles Darwin (1809–1882), der als Begründer der Evolutionstheorie zu den einflussreichsten Wissenschaftlern der Geschichte zählt, steht mit seinem Namen Pate für diese Tulpengruppe. Die Handelsgärtnerei E. H. Krelage & Sohn in Haarlem brachte 1889 neue, besonders farbintensive Tulpen auf den Markt, die auf der Weltausstellung in Paris für Furore sorgten. Zu Ehren Darwins, dem der Züchter Jakob Heinrich Krelage viel neues Wissen um die Tulpenzucht verdankte, wurden diese Tulpen dann benannt. Krelage selbst erhielt den Ehrentitel „Tulpenkönig".

Sehr große, einfache Blüten mit einer am Grunde rundlichen Form kennzeichnen die Darwin-Hybrid-Tulpen. Lebendige Farbtöne in kräftigem Rot, Gelb und Orange dominieren das begrenzte Farbspektrum. Lange, kräftige Stiele machen die im Mai und über viele Jahre hinweg blühenden, bis zu 70 cm hohen Blickfänger zu eindrucksvollen Gartenpflanzen und hervorragenden Schnittblumen.

Die großblumigen Darwin-Hybrid-Tulpen gehen auf Dirk Lefeber, einen berühmten Züchter aus dem holländischen Lisse, zurück. Zwischen 1940 und 1950 gelang ihm das Kreuzen von Darwin-Tulpen mit einer Auswahl der wilden Sorte *Tulipa fosteriana*. Die berühmteste Tulpe dieser Gruppe ist wohl 'Apeldoorn' samt ihrer Spielarten.

NÄCHSTE SEITE | Darwin-Hybriden 'Banja Luka' (links) und 'Apeldoorn' (rechts)

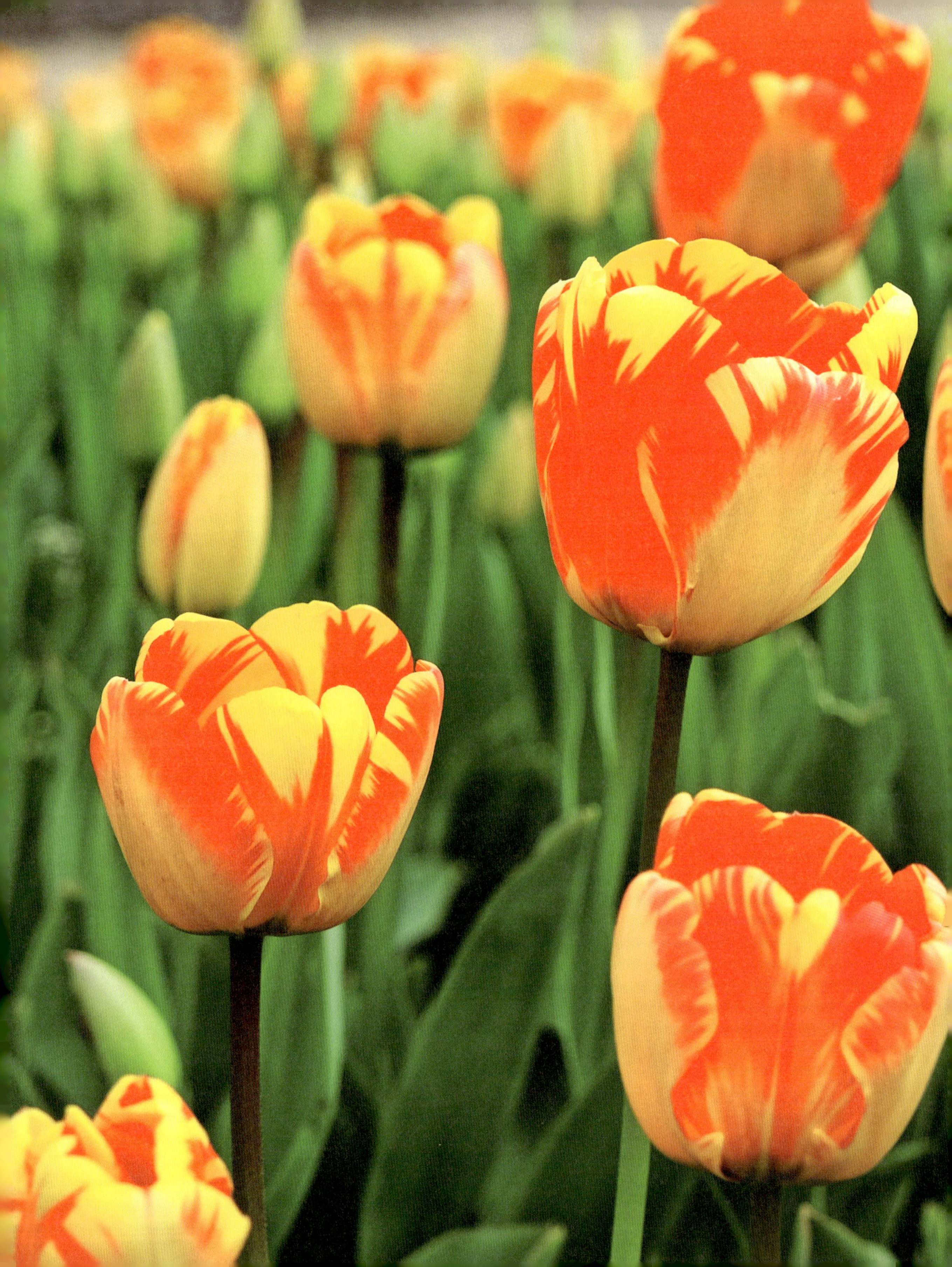

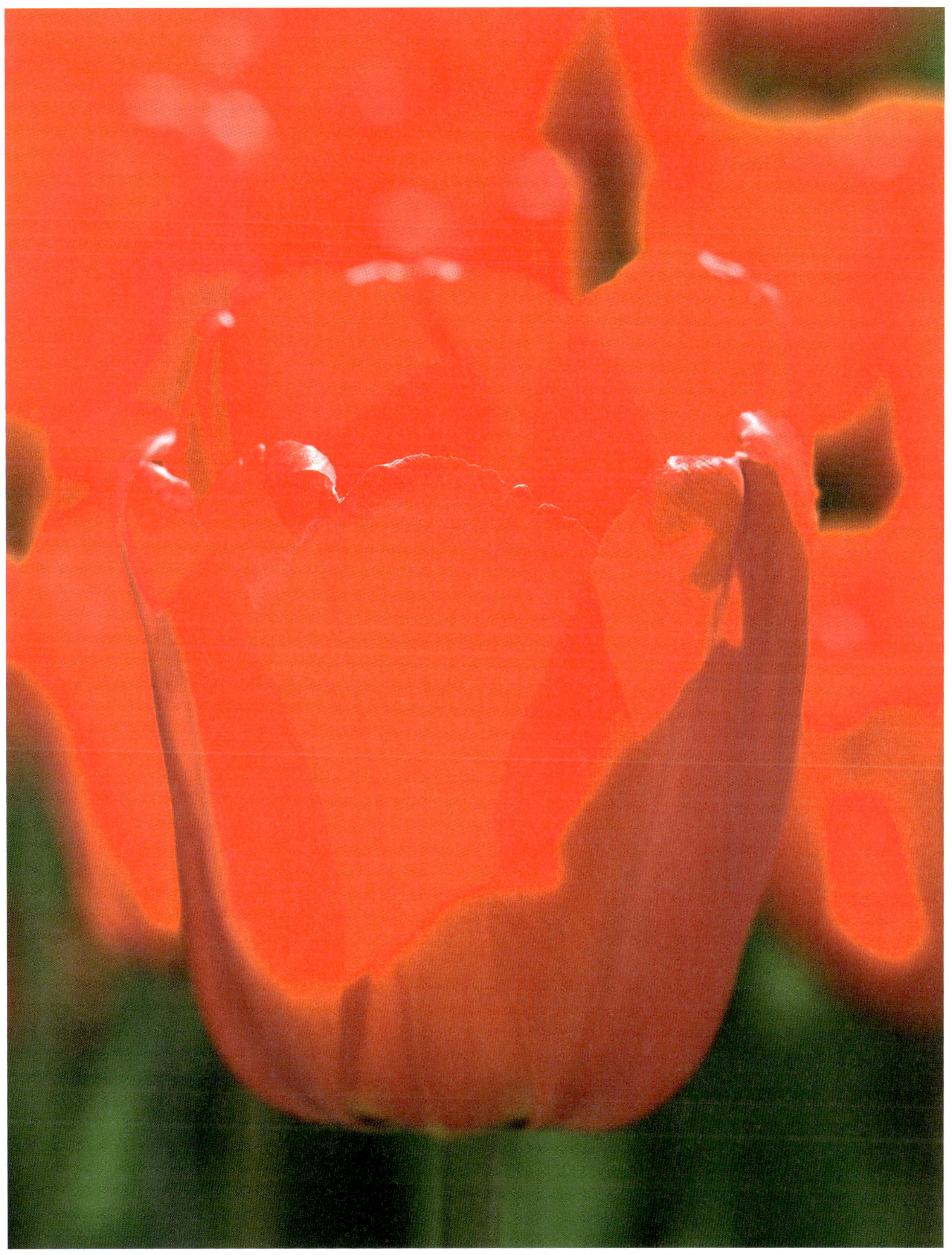

Group 5

SINGLE LATE TULIPS

UNFILLED MIRACLE FLOWERS TO PROLONG SPRING, ANYONE?

Tulip varieties from the Single Late group are perfect for parks and gardens to extend the tulip season. These classic, medium-sized flowers appear in May, when some early-blooming varieties have already dried up. With a height of 19–27 inches and robust growth, tulips in this group also make excellent cut flowers.

Single Late tulips include both Darwin tulips and Cottage tulips. The former can be traced back to the breeding successes of the Dutchman Ernst Heinrich Krelage who introduced them in 1886. One of the most notable and simultaneously one of the darkest varieties is the chestnut-brown, almost-black 'Queen of Night'. The outstanding 'Mrs. John T. Scheepers' gained increasing significance after the Second World War and was often used in crosses.

NEXT PAGE | This group includes robust varieties that look beautiful both in the garden and in vases.

Gruppe 5

EINFACHE SPÄTE TULPEN

UNGEFÜLLTE BLÜHWUNDER ZUR VERLÄNGERUNG DES FRÜHLINGS GEFÄLLIG?

Sorten aus der Gruppe der Einfachen Späten Tulpen sind genau das Richtige für Park- und Gartenanlagen, um die Tulpensaison auszudehnen. Die klassischen, mittelgroßen Blüten erscheinen erst im Mai, wenn manche frühblühenden Sorten schon längst ihre Blätter eintrocknen lassen. Mit 50–70 cm Wuchshöhe und einem kräftigen Charakter sind Tulpen dieser Gruppe außerdem sehr gute Schnittblumen.

Zu den Einfachen Späten Tulpen gehören sowohl Darwin-Tulpen als auch die englischen Cottage-Tulpen. Erstere gehen auf die Zuchterfolge des Niederländers Ernst Heinrich Krelage zurück und wurden im Jahr 1886 zum ersten Mal vorgestellt. Eine der namhaftesten und gleichzeitig eine der dunkelsten Sorten ist die kastanienbraun-schwarze 'Queen of Night'. Die herausragende 'Mrs. John T. Scheepers' gewann nach dem zweiten Weltkrieg zunehmend an Bedeutung und wurde oft bei Kreuzungen verwendet.

NÄCHSTE SEITE | In dieser Gruppe finden sich robuste Sorten, die im Beet wie in der Vase eine Zierde sind.

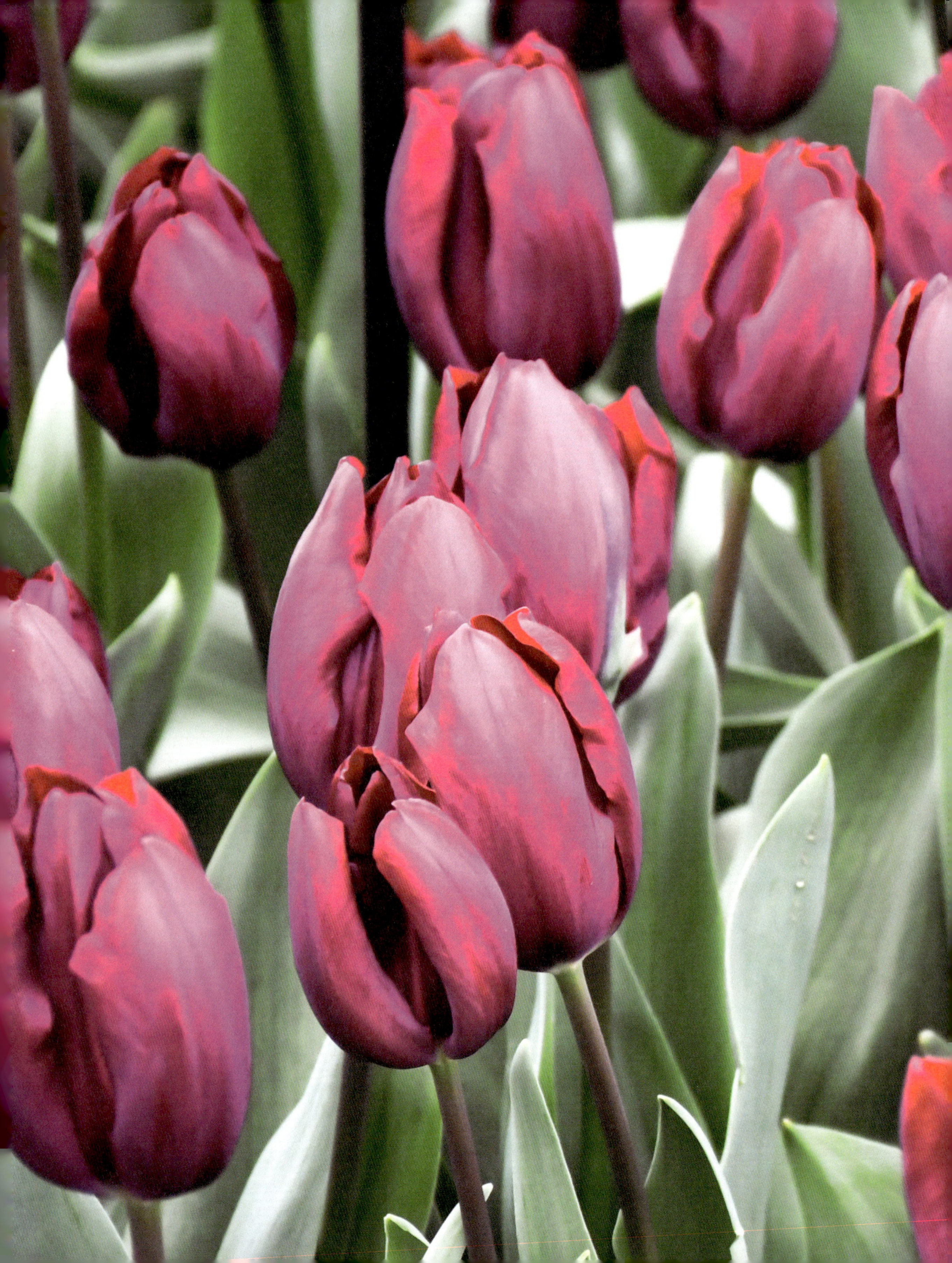

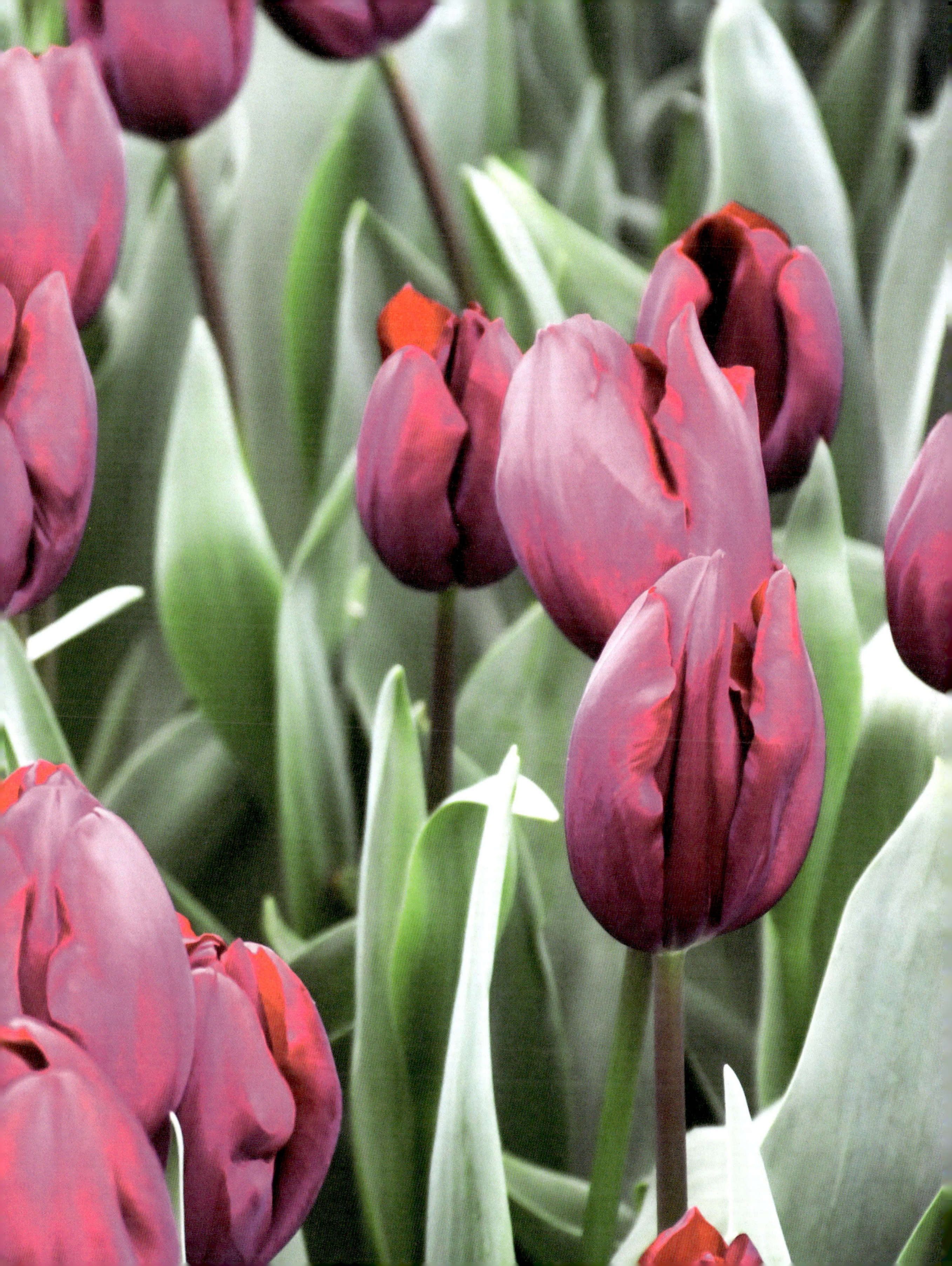

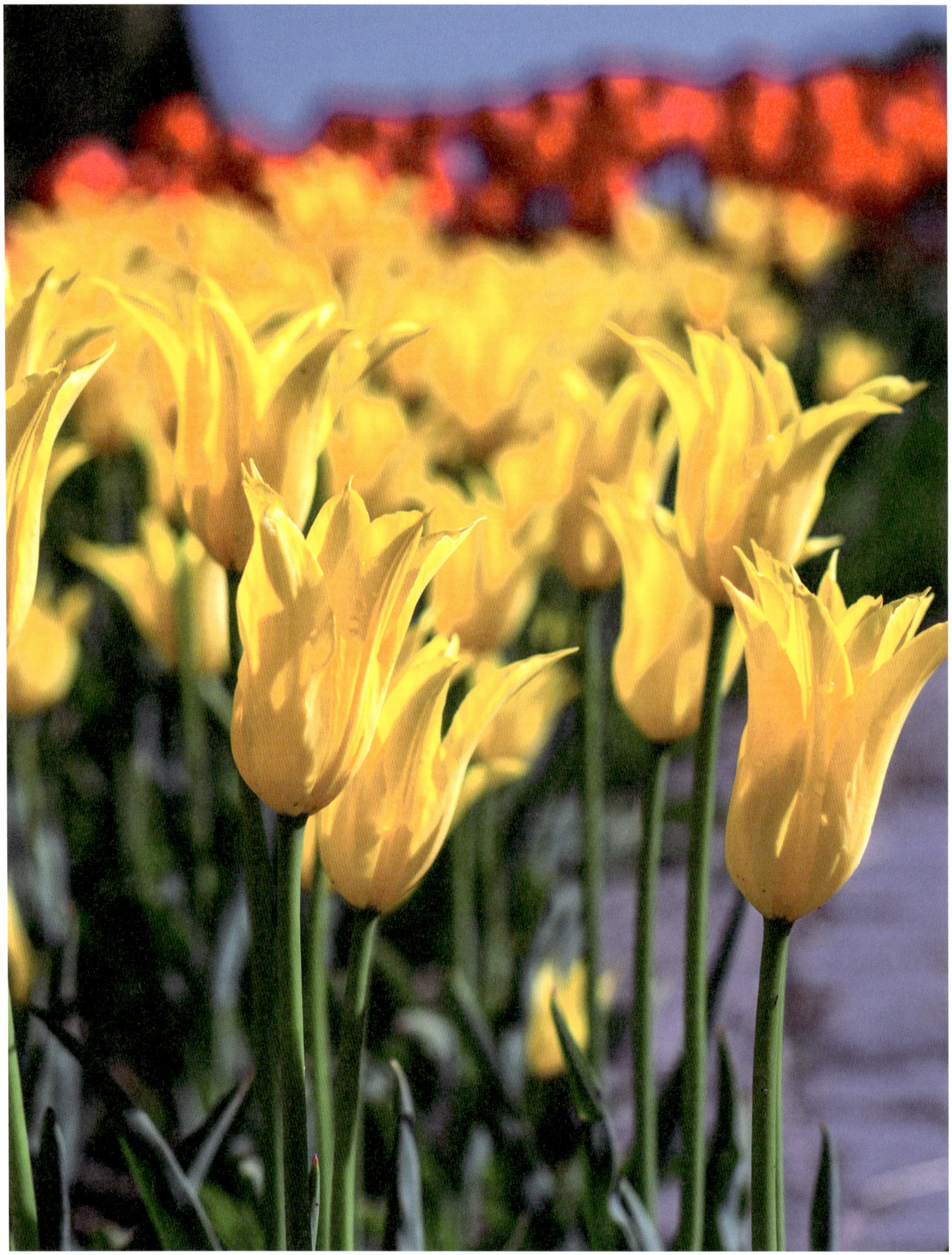

Group 6

LILY-FLOWERED TULIPS

LIVING UP TO THEIR NAME WITH ELEGANCE AND GRACE

With their characteristic flower shape, Lily-flowered tulips evoke the original beauty ideals of Turkish tulips. They originated from a cross between *Tulipa retroflexa* and late-blooming Darwin tulips. The most well-known tulip with a lily-shaped flower is the award-winning old variety 'West Point' (see left page). Its gracefully curved petals' bright yellow seems to try and outshine the sun.

Gruppe 6

LILIENBLÜTIGE TULPEN

ELEGANT UND GRAZIL, MACHEN SIE IHREM NAMEN ALLE EHRE

Mit ihrer charakteristischen Blütenform erinnern die Lilienblütigen Tulpen an das damalige Schönheitsideal türkischer Tulpen. Entstanden sind sie aus einer Kreuzung zwischen *Tulipa retroflexa* und den spät blühenden Darwin-Tulpen. Die bekannteste Tulpe mit Lilienblüte ist die preisgekrönte alte Sorte 'West Point' (Bild links). Ihre edel geschwungenen Blütenblätter strahlen mit dem leuchtenden Gelb der Sonne um die Wette.

Group 7

FRINGED TULIPS

AS IF STYLED BY A HAIRDRESSER OR DECORATED BY A PASTRY CHEF

A tulip can mutate not only in color but also in form. It was only in 1981 that mutations with finely fringed edges along the full length of all petals were categorized in this relatively young group we now know as Fringed tulips. For example, the scarlet 'Arma' is a mutation of the heirloom Triumph tulip 'Couleur Cardinal.'

Tulip enthusiasts may know these types of extravagant tulips as "Crispa". They look charming, as if rimmed with winter frost or adorned with sugar crystals. Each petal looks like a well-crafted masterpiece. The petals' delicate fringe can match the flower color, as seen, for example, in the pale yellow 'Maja,' or it can appear in a different color, as in the case of 'Burgundy Lace'. One of the most popular Fringed tulips was introduced by the Segers brothers in Lisse: the pale pink 'Fancy Frills' features a wide ivory base and an irregular white fringe.

NEXT PAGE | The rather aptly-named 'Fancy Frills' variety is part of the Fringed tulip group.

Gruppe 7

GEFRANSTE TULPEN

WIE VOM COIFFEUR GESTYLT ODER VOM ZUCKERBÄCKER VERZIERT

Eine Tulpe kann nicht nur in ihrer Farbe, sondern auch in ihrer Form mutieren. Erst im Jahr 1981 wurden Mutationen, deren Blütenblattränder in ihrer vollen Länge fein eingeschnitten sind, zu dieser relativ jungen Gruppe der Gefransten Tulpen zusammengefasst. Beispielsweise ist die scharlachrote 'Arma' durch Mutation der historischen Triumph-Tulpe 'Couleur Cardinal' entstanden.

Einem Tulpenfreund mögen diese extravaganten Tulpen auch unter dem Namen „Crispa" geläufig sein. Reizvoll sehen sie aus, wie von winterlichem Raureif gesäumt oder von Zuckerkristallen berandet. Jedes einzelne Blütenblatt gleicht einem Stück Handwerkskunst. Wie bei der blassgelben 'Maja' können die zarten Fransen der Blütenfarbe entsprechen. Es kann aber auch wie bei der 'Burgundy Lace' eine andere Farbe ins Spiel kommen. Von den Gebrüdern Segers aus Lisse stammt eine der beliebtesten gefransten Tulpen, die zartrosa 'Fancy Frills' mit breiter, elfenbeinweißer Basis und weißen, unregelmäßigen Fransen.

NÄCHSTE SEITE | 'Fancy Frills', auf Deutsch etwa „schicke Rüschen", heißt diese Sorte aus der Gruppe der Gefransten Tulpen.

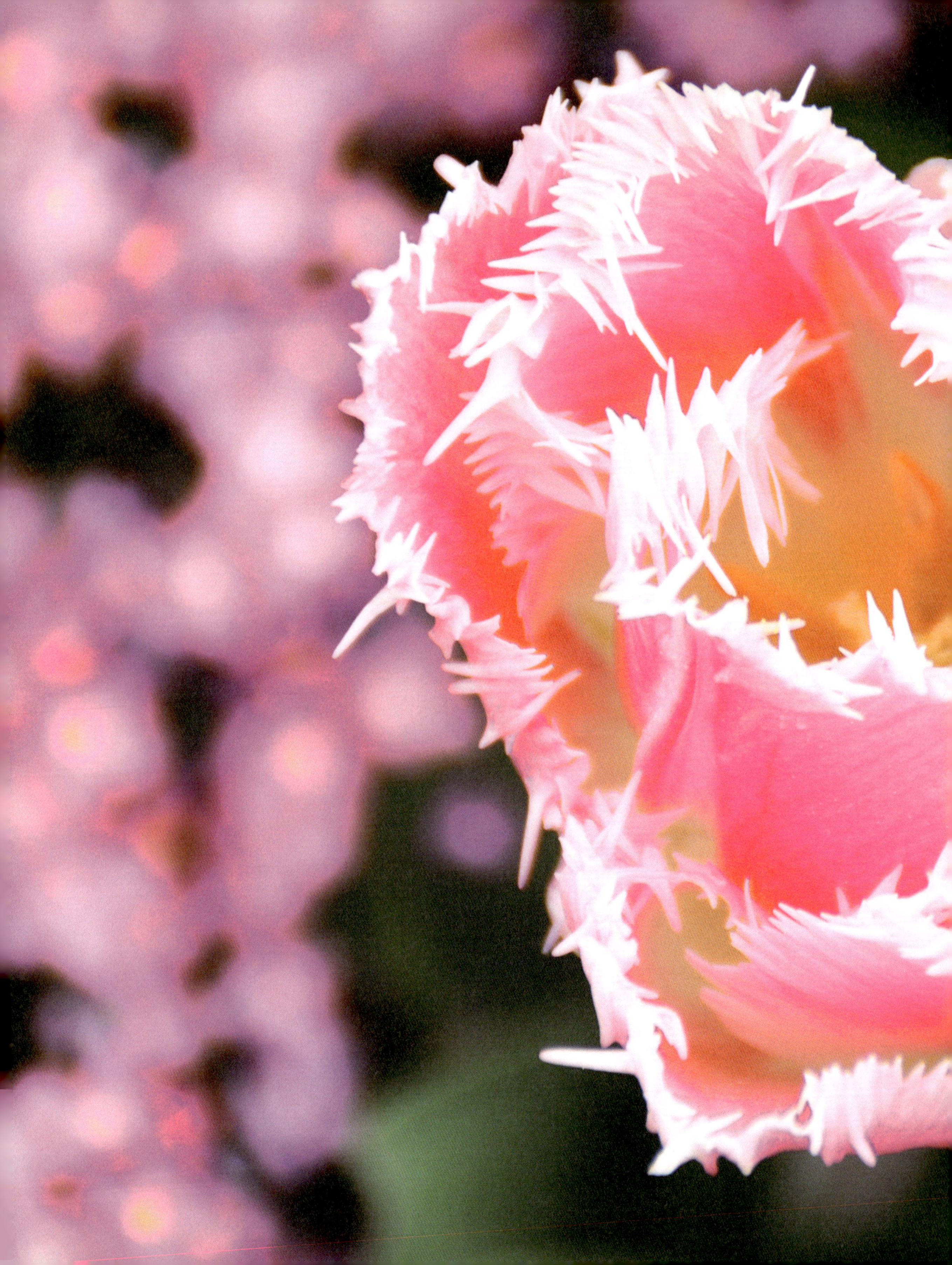

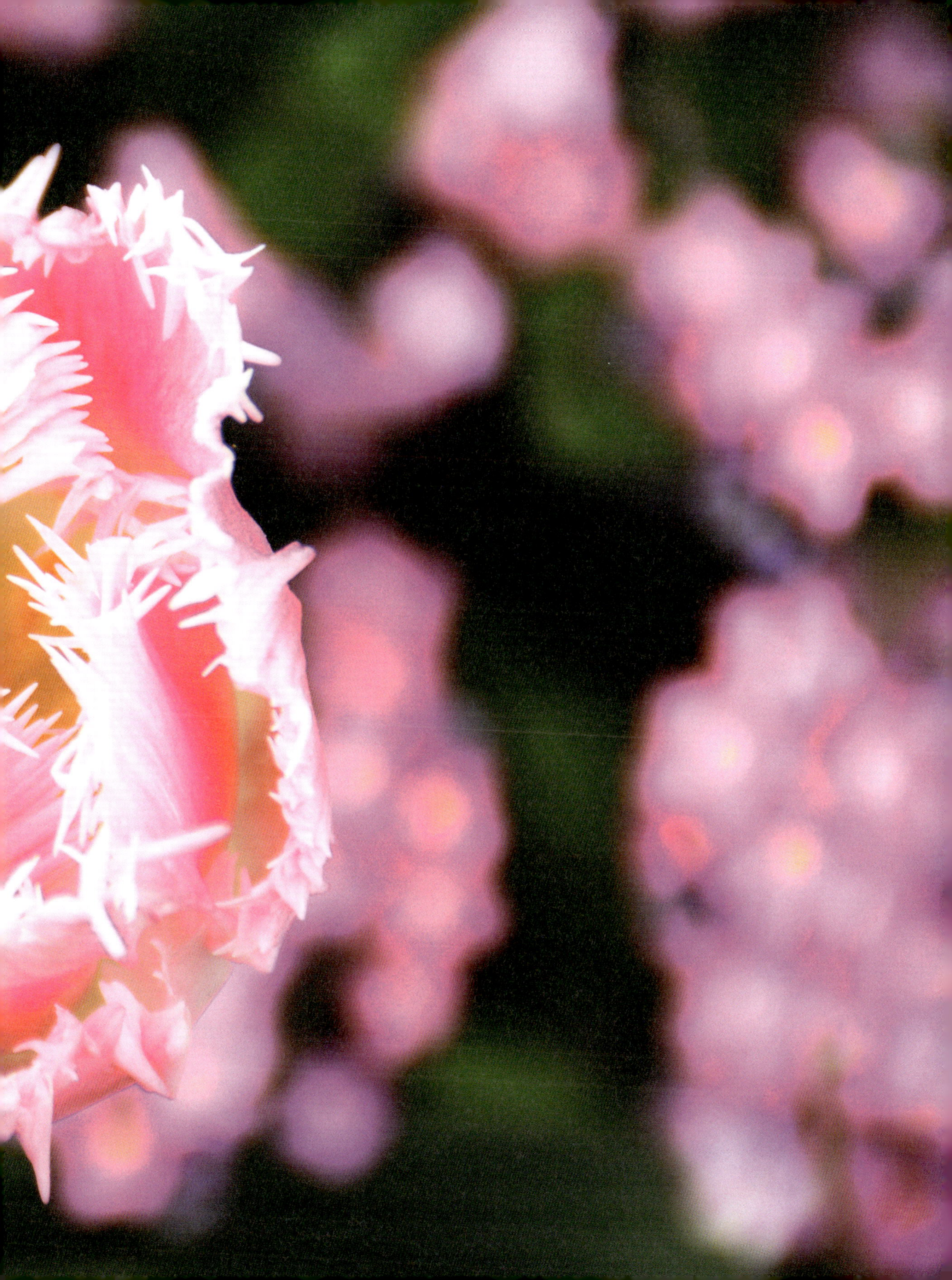

Group 8

VIRIDIFLORA TULIPS

THESE LONG-LASTING FLOWERS ARE PRETTY IN FRESH SPRING GREEN

When thinking of the best color for pretty flower petals, green might not be the first color that springs to mind. However, Viridiflora tulips may change all this. True to their name, these are green flowers—Viridiflora is derived from Latin *viridis* (green) and *flos* (flower, blossom). The tulip varieties in this small group showcase flowers with exceptional coloring: green flames extend from the flower base to the tips of the petals. This green feature, combined with contrasting colors on the more or less broad edges of the petals, such as yellow ('Yellow Spring Green'), cream ('Spring Green'), pale pink ('Groenland'), and purple ('Doll's Minuet'), makes these tulips truly stand out. Thanks to the additional green in the petals, the blooming period of the 11–21 inches high Viridiflora varieties is exceptionally long during May.

NEXT PAGE | Green lines and patterns running through petals are a typical feature in Viridiflora tulips—as pictured here in the 'Groenland' variety (left). A pale trio of green-flamed Viridiflora, rounded Darwin, and delicately fringed Crispa tulips

Gruppe 8

VIRIDIFLORA-TULPEN

FRÜHLINGSFRISCHES GRÜN STEHT DIESEN LANG HALTENDEN BLÜTEN GUT

Beim Gedanken an attraktive Tulpenfarben kommt Ihnen die Farbe Grün vermutlich nicht gerade in den Sinn. Möglicherweise schwenken Sie jedoch um, wenn Sie Viridiflora-Tulpen betrachten. Dem Namen nach sind das grüne Blumen – so lässt sich Viridiflora von lateinisch *viridis* (grün) und *flos* (Blume, Blüte) übersetzen. Die Tulpensorten dieser kleinen Gruppe zeigen Blüten mit einer außerordentlich hübschen Färbung: Grüne Flammen ziehen sich vom Blütenboden bis zur Spitze der Blütenblätter. In Kombination mit kontrastierenden Farben an den mehr oder weniger breiten Rändern der Blütenblätter, beispielsweise mit Gelb ('Yellow Spring Green'), Cremeweiß ('Spring Green'), Zartrosa ('Groenland') bis Purpur ('Doll's Minuet'), ziehen diese Tulpen bewundernde Blicke an. Aufgrund des zusätzlichen Grünanteils in den Blütenblättern ist die Blühdauer der 30–55 cm hohen Viridiflora-Sorten während der Blütezeit im Mai ausgesprochen lang.

NÄCHSTE SEITE | Kennzeichen der Viridiflora-Tulpen sind grüne Linien und Muster, welche die Kronblätter durchziehen – zu bewundern bei der Sorte 'Groenland' (links). Ein weißes Dreierlei aus grün geflammten Viridiflora-, rundlichen Darwin- und filigran gefransten Crispa-Tulpen (rechts)

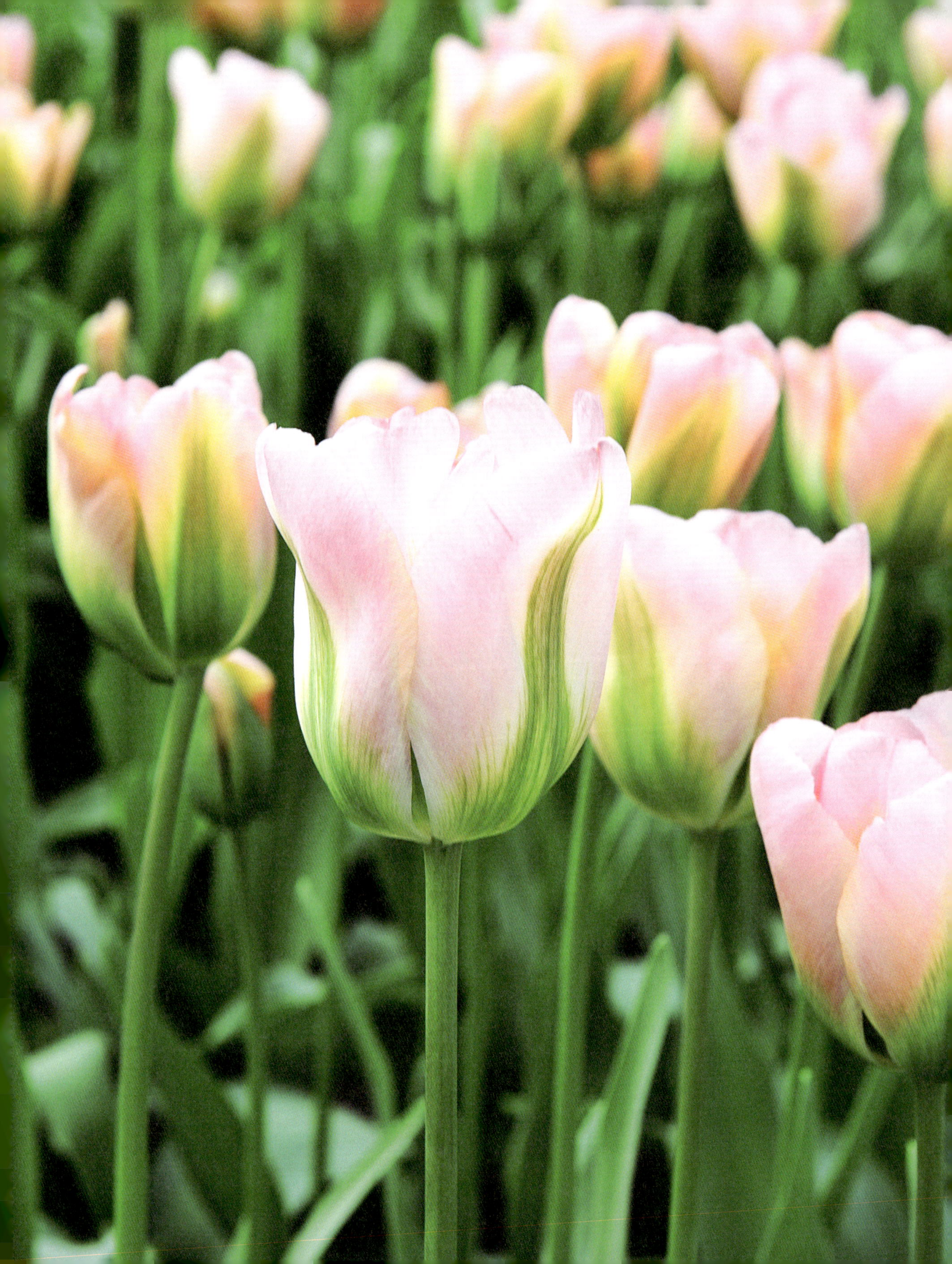

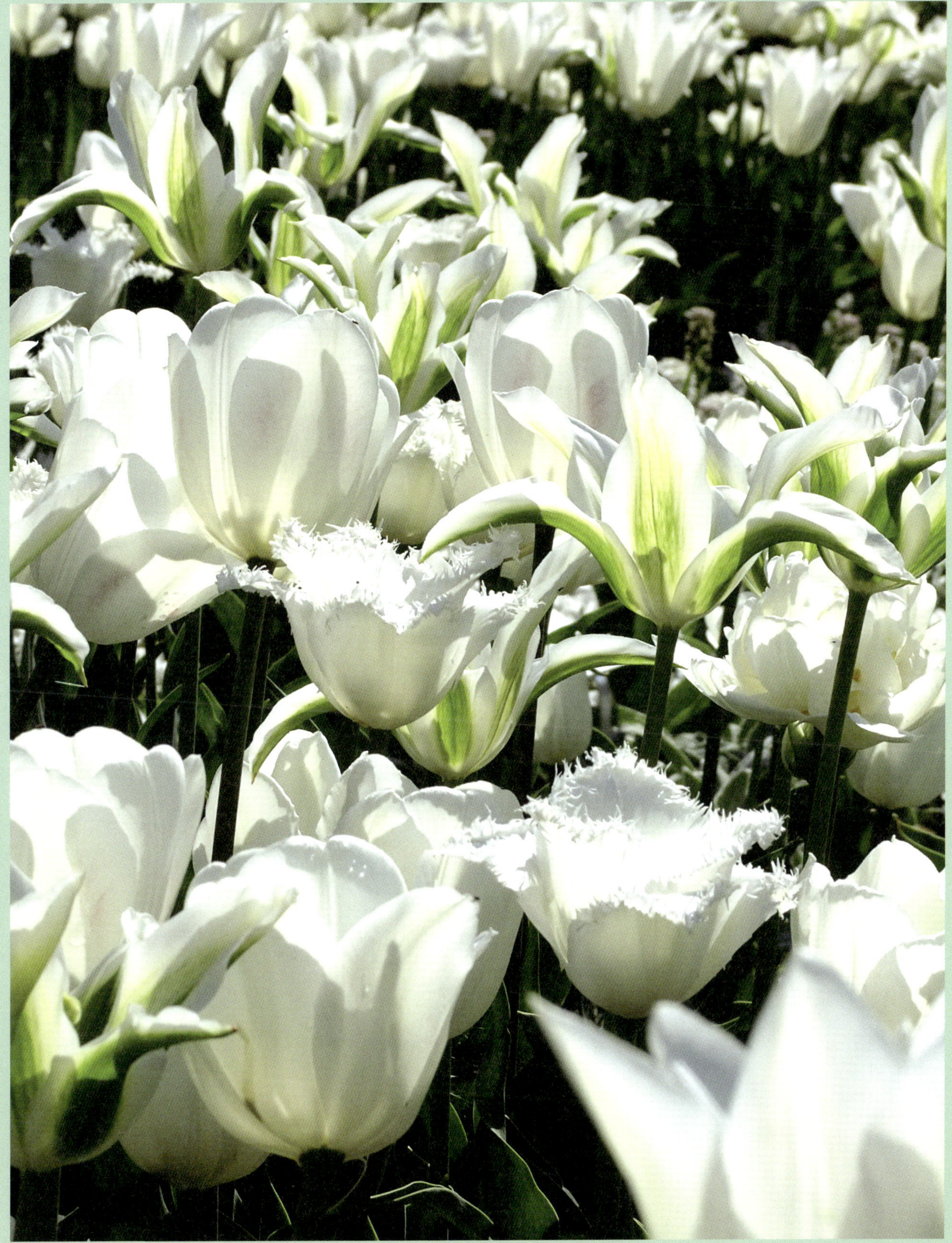

Group 9

REMBRANDT TULIPS

FLORAL ARTISTIC SPLENDOR

This group is named after one of the most famous painters of all time, so it should come as no surprise that the tulips in it all feature petals that are of picturesque beauty. The flowers of Rembrandt tulips are flamed, striped, spotted, or feathered. Highly coveted, the very best varieties in this group, like 'Viceroy' and 'Semper Augustus', triggered the tulip mania (see page 58). Targeted breeding was not possible, as the extraordinary patterns seemed to occur randomly. Some breeders even made highly original yet ultimately unsuccessful attempts to tie the halves of two bulbs producing white and red tulips, respectively, together.

In the 1920s, the mystery of the so-called broken tulips was finally solved: a virus, transmitted by aphids, was responsible for the mosaic-like patterns on the petals. The aforementioned historical varieties have sadly disappeared from the market; now, only individual enthusiasts cultivate them for their own pleasure. The Wakefield and North of England Tulip Society's Annual Main Show conveys the multifaceted charm of the lost treasures; it is held for the 189th time in 2024. Today's flamed tulip varieties, free of viruses and genetically multicolored, are now listed in other tulip groups.

NEXT PAGE | In today's tulips, marbled, striped, or veined flowers are no longer caused by a virus infection.

Gruppe 9

REMBRANDT-TULPEN

EINE BLÜTENPRACHT WIE GEMALT

Benannt nach einem der berühmtesten Maler aller Zeiten, gleicht jedes einzelne Blütenblatt dieser Tulpen tatsächlich einem Gemälde. Geflammt, gestreift, gefleckt oder gefedert sind die Blüten der Rembrandt-Tulpen. Höchst begehrt, waren die allerbesten Sorten wie 'Viceroy' und 'Semper Augustus' Auslöser für den Tulpenrausch (siehe Seite 59). Eine gezielte Zucht war nicht möglich, traten die außergewöhnlichen Muster doch scheinbar willkürlich auf. Originelle Ideen wie das Zusammenbinden von Zwiebelhälften weißer und roter Tulpen führten nicht zum gewünschten Ziel.

In den 1920er-Jahren konnte das Rätsel um die sogenannten gebrochenen Tulpen geknackt werden: Eine Viruserkrankung, von Blattläusen übertragen, ist für die mosaikartigen Zeichnungen auf den Blütenblättern verantwortlich. Die historischen Sorten sind tragischerweise aus dem Handel verschwunden, werden nurmehr privat von einzelnen Liebhabern gezüchtet. Die „Annual Main Show" der Wakefield and North of England Tulip Society vermittelt alljährlich den vielschichtigen Charme der verlorenen Schätze, im Jahr 2024 traditionell zum 189. Mal. Die geflammten Tulpen unserer heutigen Zeit, virusfrei und genetisch mehrfarbig, findet man nun in anderen Tulpen-Klassen.

NÄCHSTE SEITE | Marmorierte, gestreifte, geäderte Blüten beruhen bei modernen Tulpensorten nicht mehr auf einem Virusbefall.

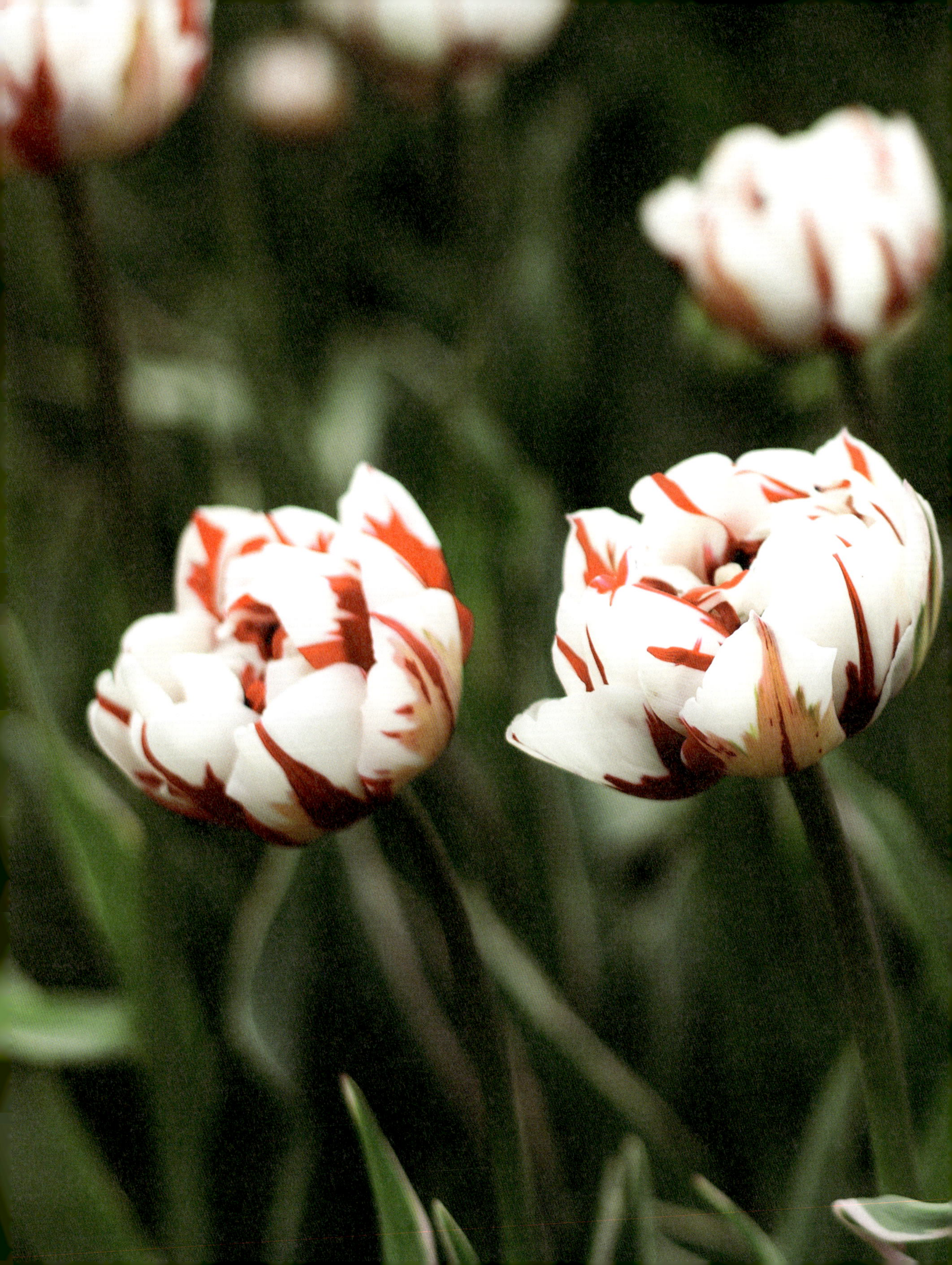

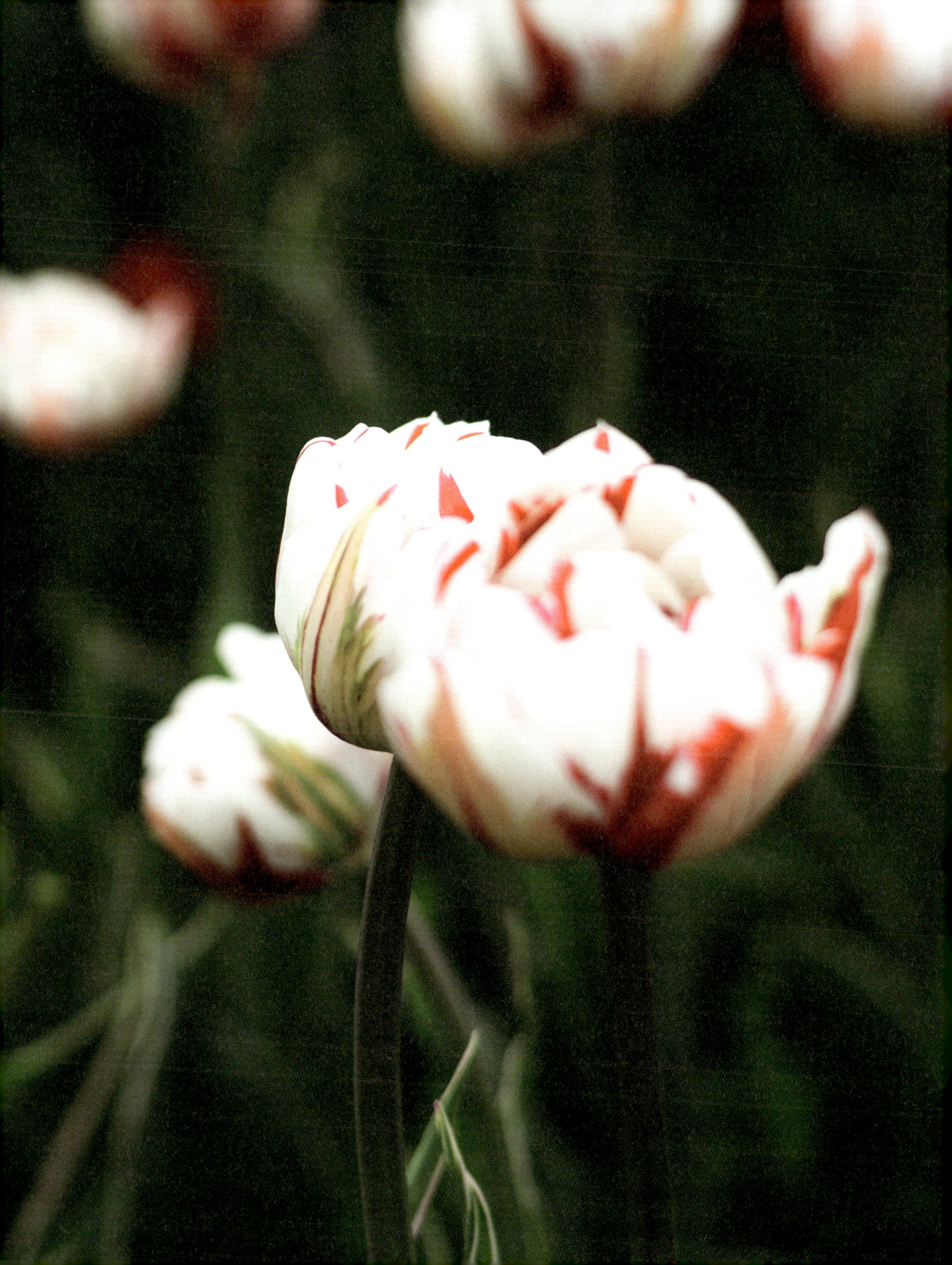

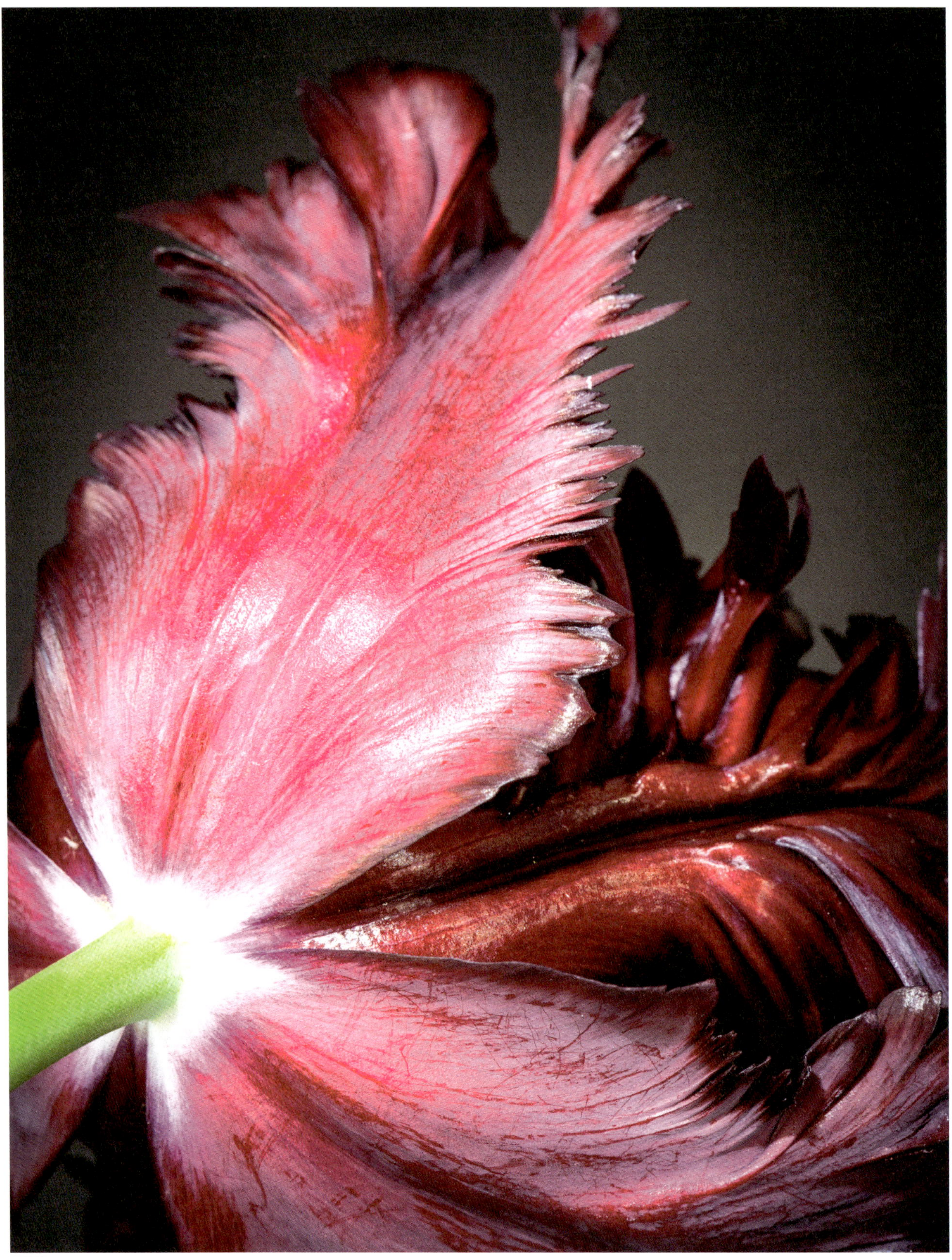

Group 10

PARROT TULIPS

WILLFUL AND ECCENTRIC, BOLD AND EXTRAVAGANT

These mostly multicolored tulip flowers feature feathered, wavy, and twisted petals somewhat reminiscent of colorful plumage. Parrot tulips originated from random mutations in color and flower shape. They were first mentioned in 1620 and subsequently appeared in many Dutch flower still lifes. A very old tulip in this group is the 'Admiral de Constantinople' from 1665. The oldest Parrot tulips still on the market today are the striking red 'Rococo' (1942) and the red-and-white-patterned 'Estella Rijnveld' (1954).

Gruppe 10

PAPAGEIEN-TULPEN

EIGENWILLIG UND EIN STÜCK WEIT SONDERBAR, GEWAGT UND EXTRAVAGANT

Die meist mehrfarbigen Blüten haben eingeschnittene, gewellte und gedrehte Blätter, so dass sie wie ein farbenprächtiges Federkleid aussehen. Entstanden sind die Papageien-Tulpen durch zufällige Mutation in Farbe und Blütenform. Bereits 1620 wurden sie zum ersten Mal erwähnt, in der Folgezeit erschienen sie auf vielen holländischen Blumenstillleben. Eine sehr alte Tulpe dieser Art ist die 'Admiral de Constantinople' aus dem Jahr 1665. Die ältesten Papageien-Tulpen, die man heute noch im Handel erwerben kann, sind die auffällig rote 'Rococo' (1942) und die rot-weiß-gemusterte 'Estella Rijnveld' (1954).

Group 11

DOUBLE LATE TULIPS

LAVISH YET ENCHANTINGLY DELICATE

In addition to Double Early tulips (Group 2, see page 166), some double varieties bloom in late spring, starting in mid-May. Although in the past century, English enthusiasts scorned the flowers in this group for lacking elegance and grace, today most people find their abundance of petals quite charming. They are also called peony-flowered tulips because their plump flower heads resemble peonies.

Susceptible to rain and wind, these 18–23 inches tall tulips are best used as attractive cut flowers or enjoyed as potted plants. Classics include the highly decorated 'Angelique' in delicate pink (1959) and the impressive 'Carnaval de Nice' (1953) with red feathers on a glossy white background.

Allow us to introduce Coronet tulips, the latest addition to the tulip group family. In 2018, the KAVB, or Koninklijke Algemeene Vereeniging voor Bloembollencultuur (Royal General Bulb Growers' Association), added this new group to the classification of tulips. After 'Picture' (1949), 'Witty Picture' (1992), 'Liberstar' (1999), and 'White Liberstar' (2010), more varieties with similar characteristics were registered in the following years at increasingly shorter intervals. They all share petals that are lightly twirled, with outwardly bending tips, making each tulip blossom look like a crown. Truly royal!

NEXT PAGE | Two beauties: 'Carnaval de Nice' (left) from the Double Late tulip group and the Coronet tulip 'White Liberstar' (right)

Gruppe 11

GEFÜLLTE SPÄTE TULPEN

POMPÖS, UND DOCH VON BEZAUBERNDER LEICHTIGKEIT

Neben den Gefüllten Frühen Tulpen (Gruppe 2, siehe Seite 167) gibt es gefüllte Sorten, die erst im späten Frühjahr ab Mitte Mai blühen. Auch wenn englische Liebhaber die Blumen dieser Gruppe im letzten Jahrhundert wegen mangelnder Eleganz als plump abgestempelt haben, bezaubert uns heute die Fülle an Blütenblättern. Päonien-Tulpen heißen sie auch, da die prallen Blütenköpfe an Pfingstrosen erinnern.

Gegenüber Regen und Wind anfällig, nutzt man die 45–60 cm hohen Tulpen besser als attraktive Schnittblumen oder erfreut sich an Topfpflanzungen. Klassiker sind die vielfach preisgekrönte 'Angelique' in Zartrosa (1959) und die eindrückliche 'Carnaval de Nice' (1953) mit roten Federn auf glänzend weißem Grund.

Dürfen wir vorstellen? Kronentulpen sind „die Neuen" unter den Tulpen. Die KAVB, die Koninklijke Algemeene Vereeniging voor Bloembollencultuur, hat die Klassifizierung von Tulpen 2018 um eine neue Sortengruppe, die Coronet Group, ergänzt. Nach 'Picture' (1949), 'Witty Picture' (1992), 'Liberstar' (1999) und 'White Liberstar' (2010) wurden in den Folgejahren immer mehr Sorten in immer kürzeren Zeitabständen mit den gleichen Eigenschaften registriert: Leicht in sich gedrehte und nach außen gebogene Blütenblätter lassen jede Tulpenblüte wie eine Krone aussehen. Wahrlich königlich!

NÄCHSTE SEITE | Zwei Schönheiten: 'Carnaval de Nice' (links) aus der Gruppe der Gefüllten Späten Tulpen und die Coronet-Tulpe 'White Liberstar' (rechts)

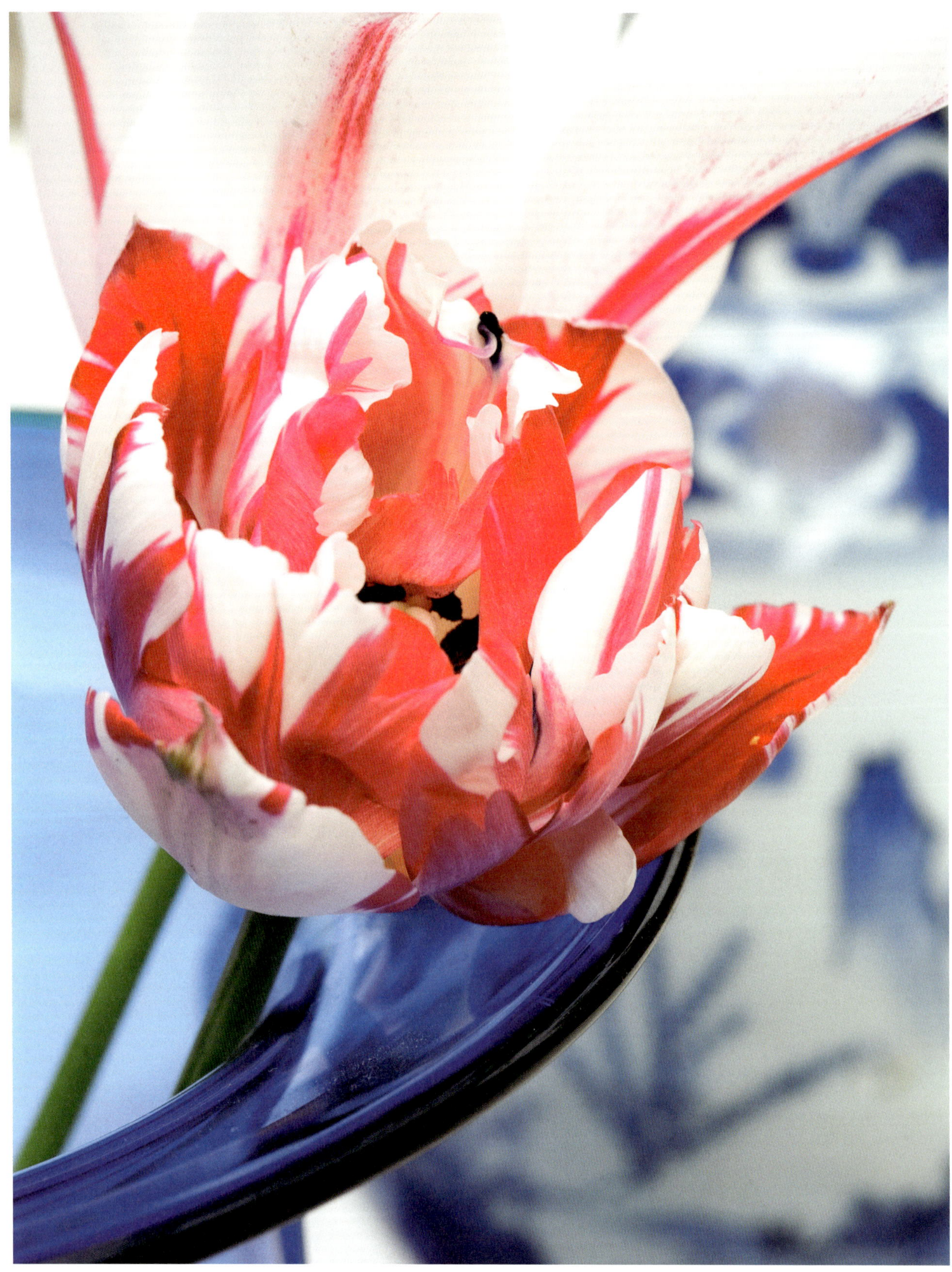

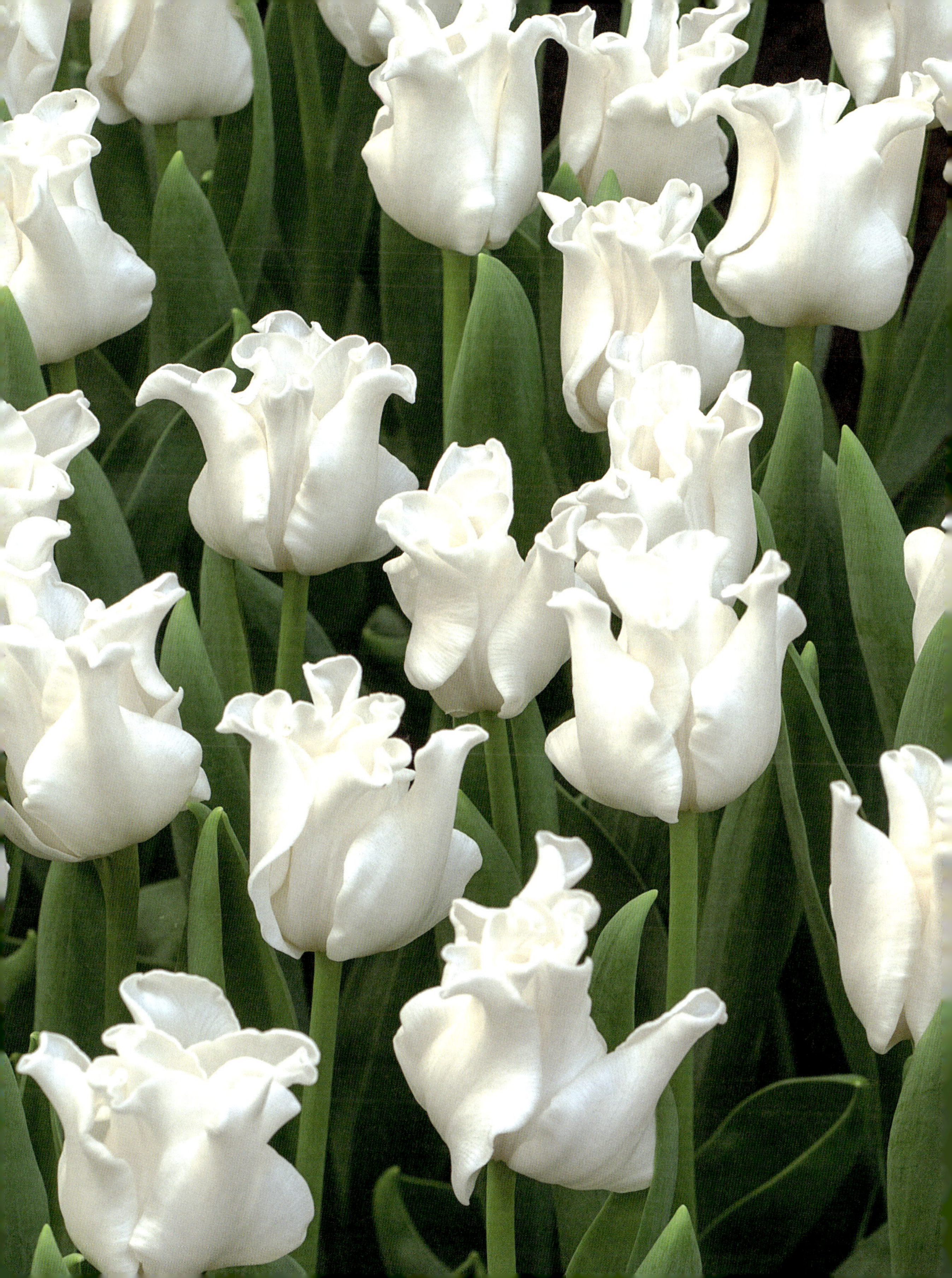

Liriodendron tulipifera, Magnolia × soulangeana & Co.

TULIPS THAT ARE NOT TULIPS

TULIP TREES, MAGNOLIAS, AND CHESSBOARD FLOWERS

Expanding our purview beyond wild and cultivated tulips, we can admire "tulips" that are not really tulips. The tulip tree *(Liriodendron tulipifera)* is native to eastern North America, and the Chinese tulip tree *(Liriodendron chinense)* can be found in East Asia. These majestic trees, planted in Europe in parks as ornamental trees, owe their name to the green-orange flowers in characteristic tulip form.

The magnificent flowers of the saucer magnolia *(Magnolia x soulangeana)* are also quite reminiscent of tulips. Before leafing out, these garden plants provide a spectacular display of colors ranging between white, pink, and violet.

The guinea flower, leper lily, or chess flower is about 12 inches tall. These are all common English names for the snake's head fritillary *(Fritillaria meleagris)*. Its German names translate to "guinea fowl tulip" or "cuckoo tulip". It owes its English nicknames to the checkered petals' perceived resemblance to the plumage of guinea fowl or a chess board, while the shape of its flower head looks like the bell once carried by lepers or a snake rising from the grass. Its German names also reference its appearance as well as the fact that it blooms in spring when the cuckoo calls.

Perhaps you can think of other "tulips" that are not really tulips. The common poppy *(Papaver rhoeas)* comes to mind. Oh, there is even a tulip poppy *(P. glaucum)*, also known as Turkish tulip.

NEXT PAGE | Tulip tree from eastern North America (left), snake's head fritillary (right)

Liriodendron tulipifera, Magnolia × soulangeana & Co.

TULPEN, DIE KEINE SIND

VON TULPENBÄUMEN, MAGNOLIEN UND SCHACHBRETTBLUMEN

Weitet man den Blick über wilde und gezüchtete Tulpen hinaus, kann man „Tulpen" bestaunen, die keine sind:

Der Tulpenbaum *(Liriodendron tulipifera)* ist im östlichen Nordamerika beheimatet, der Chinesische Tulpenbaum *(Liriodendron chinense)* in Ostasien. Die stattlichen Bäume, in Europa als Park- und Zierbäume angepflanzt, verdanken ihren Namen den grün-orangen Blüten in charakteristischer Tulpenform.

Ebenfalls tulpenähnlich sind die prächtigen Blüten der Tulpen-Magnolie *(Magnolia × soulangeana)*. Vor dem Laubaustrieb bieten diese Gartenpflanzen ein fulminantes Farbenspiel, das zwischen Weiß, Rosa und Violett changiert.

Etwa 30 cm wird sie hoch, die Tulpe von Goudebas, Perlhuhntulpe oder Kuckuckstulpe. Alles regionale Bezeichnungen für die Schachbrettblume *(Fritillaria meleagris)*. Warum? Weil die Blume an eine Tulpe mit gesenktem Kopf erinnert und der Großteil des Schweizer Vorkommens im Flachmoor Les Goudebas gedeiht. Und weil die schachbrettartig gemusterten Blütenblätter dem Federkleid eines Perlhuhns ähneln und die Liliengewächse erblühen, wenn der Ruf des Kuckucks durch die Lande schallt.

Vielleicht fallen Ihnen noch weitere „Tulpen" ein, die keine sind. Möglicherweise der Klatschmohn *(Papaver rhoeas)*. Ach, es gibt sogar einen Tulpenmohn *(P. glaucum)*, auch Türkische Tulpe genannt.

NÄCHSTE SEITE | Tulpenbaum aus dem östlichen Nordamerika (links), Schachbrettblume (rechts)

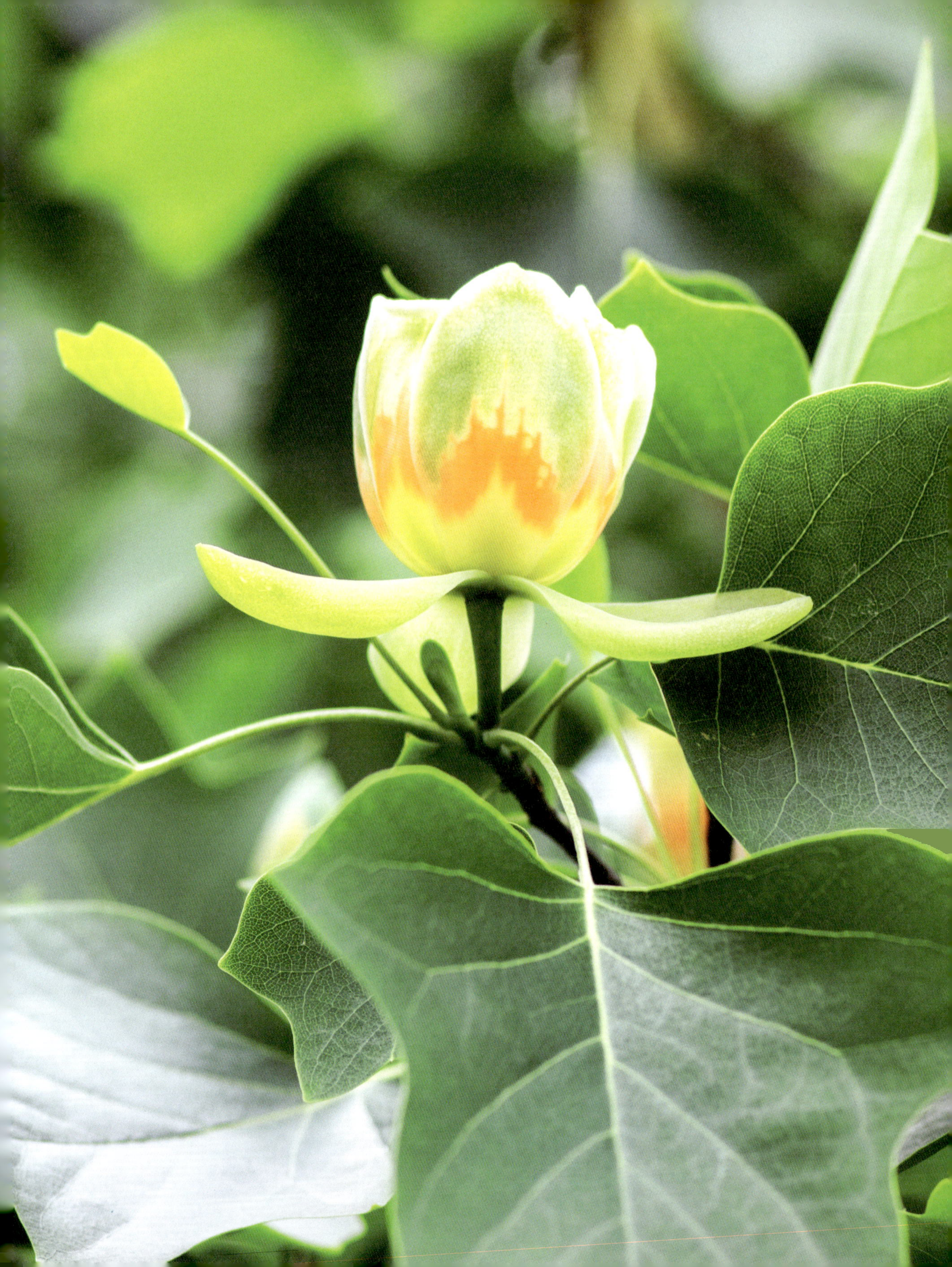

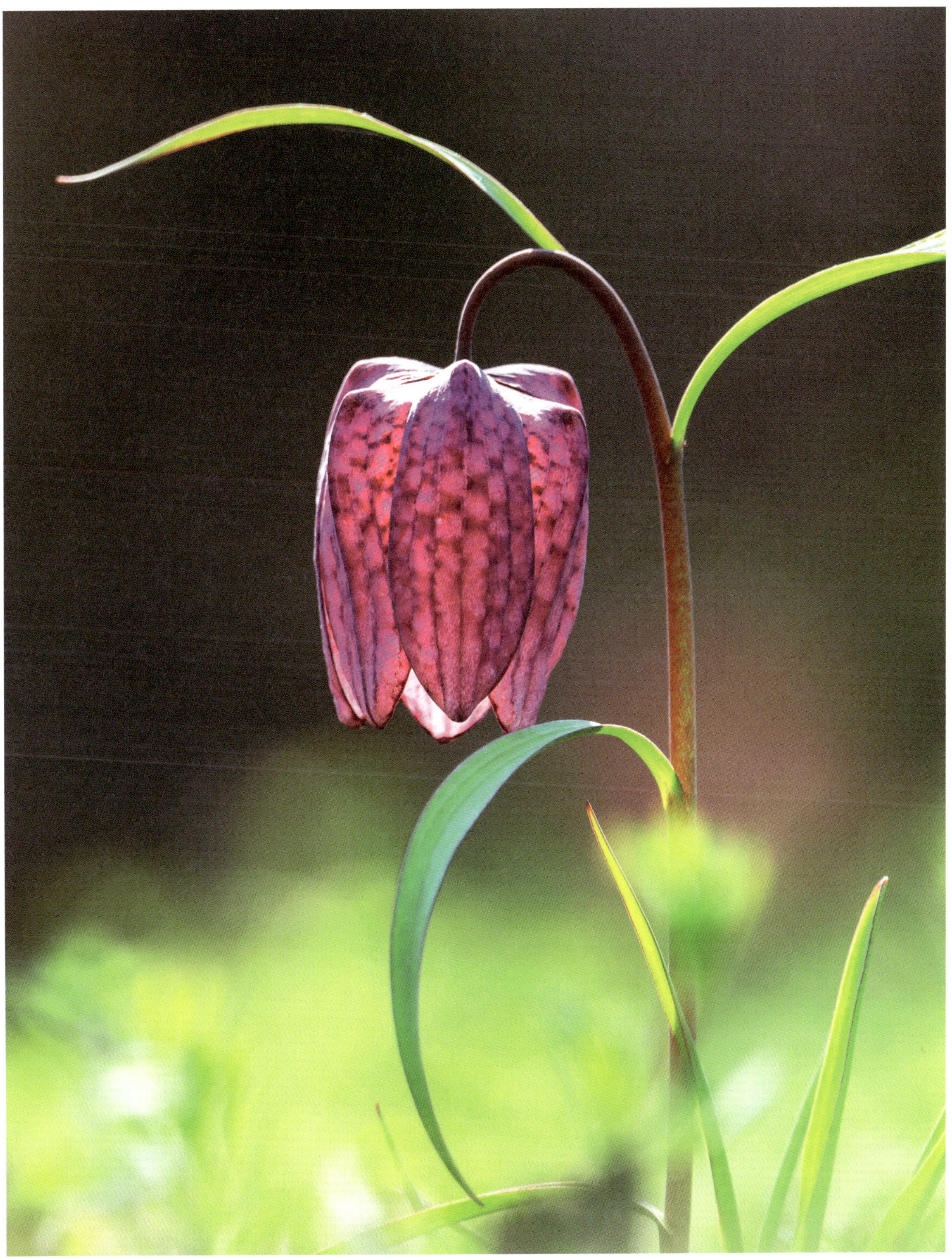

PICTURE CREDITS | BILDNACHWEIS

Cover: Illustration: Eva Stadler | Endpapers: Illustration: Eva Stadler

p. 2 illustration: Eva Stadler, p. 8 Simone Braun, p. 10 hcast/Adobe Stock, p. 11 Eyewave/ Adobe Stock, p. 12 Matthias Gotzke/unsplash, p. 14 iIllustration: Eva Stadler, p. 18 Boudewijn Huysmans, p. 22 Florapix/Alamy Stock Photos/mauritius images, p. 25 Florilegius/Alamy Stock Photos/mauritius images, p. 26 Ayhan Altun/Alamy Stock Photos/mauritius images, p. 28, 29 Duncan Andison/Adobe Stock, p. 31 World Book Inc./mauritius images, p. 35 Hortus_floridus-ULB-1-27.png via Wikimedia Commons, p. 37 Kristine Tanne/unsplash, p. 40 Charles Mahaux/AGF/mauritius images, p. 43 CuboImages/Paroli Galperti/mauritius images, p. 46 Historic Illustrations/Alamy Stock Photos/mauritius images, p. 47 Old Visuals/mauritius images, p. 50 Noppasin Wong-chum/Alamy Stock Photos/mauritius images, p. 52 Fortgens Photography/Adobe Stock, p. 54 Iva/Adobe Stock, p. 56, 57 _Vilor/Adobe Stock, p. 60 Heritage Images/IMAGO, p. 61 Pictorial Press Ltd/Alamy Stock Photos/mauritius images, p. 64 ARTGEN/Alamy Stock Photos/mauritius images, p. 66 illustration: Eva Stadler, p. 68 Wim Wiskerke/Alamy Stock Photos/mauritius images, p. 71, 72 Simone Braun, p. 75 Maris_K/Alamy Stock Photos/mauritius images, p. 76 Derek Harris/Florapress, p. 79 Alexandra/Adobe Stock, p. 80 Simone Braun, p. 84 Getty Images, p. 85 Sandra Baker/Alamy Stock Photos/ mauritius images, p. 88 Alfons Taekema/unsplash, p. 89 Getty Images/unsplash premium, p. 92, 94 Simone Braun, p. 96 tunedin/Adobe Stock, p. 99 Nordwood Themes/unsplash, p. 100 Adriana Stampfl/Alamy Stock Photos/mauritius images, p. 104 Tatyana Sidyukova/Adobe Stock, p. 106 illustration: Eva Stadler, p. 108 Paul Martindale/ Alamy Stock Photos/mauritius images, p. 110 Coprid/Adobe Stock, p. 112, 115 Simone Braun, p. 116 Karin Greiner, p. 118 hhelene/Adobe Stock, p. 121, 122 Simone Braun, p. 126 Olesya/Adobe Stock, p. 128 артем яр/Adobe Stock, p. 130, 131 Екатерина Литвинова/ Adobe Stock, p. 132 illustration: Eva Stadler, p. 138 Simone Braun, p. 140 Brigita/Adobe Stock, p. 144, 148, 150, 154 Simone Braun, p. 157 Julia Gavin/Alamy Stock Photos/ mauritius images, p. 158 Karin Greiner, p. 161 Ellen McKnight/Alamy Stock Photos/ mauritius images, p. 162 Dominic Steinmann/Alamy Stock Photos/mauritius images, p. 164 Olesia Sarycheva/Adobe Stock, p. 168 Walter Erhardt/shutterstock, p. 169 Trevor Sims/Garden World Images/mauritius images, p. 171 Sergey V Kalyakin/shutterstock, p. 172 Markus Spiske/unsplash, p. 176 Alexandra/Adobe Stock, p. 177 AY Images/Alamy Stock Photos/mauritius images, p. 180 Pranee PhotoSpace/Adobe Stock, p. 182 Yan/ Adobe Stock, p. 186 Calandra/Adobe Stock, p. 190 Sergey V Kalyakin/shutterstock, p. 191 Karin Greiner, p. 194 Андрей Жерновой/Adobe Stock, p. 196 Larkspur/Adobe Stock, p. 200 Modeste Herwig/Garden World Images/mauritius images, p. 201 Oscar D'Arcy/Garden World Images/mauritius images, p. 204 Iva/Adobe Stock, p. 205 Kozma/ Adobe Stock

Karin Greiner is a biologist and lecturer with a passion for sharing her knowledge about gardens, trees, flowers, herbs, and nature in books and magazines, as well as in courses and seminars. She is known as a plant expert on the German radio station *Bayern 1*. In 2008, she started her blog, *Pflanzenlust* (Passion for Plants), where she shares her passion for native flora with a large audience.

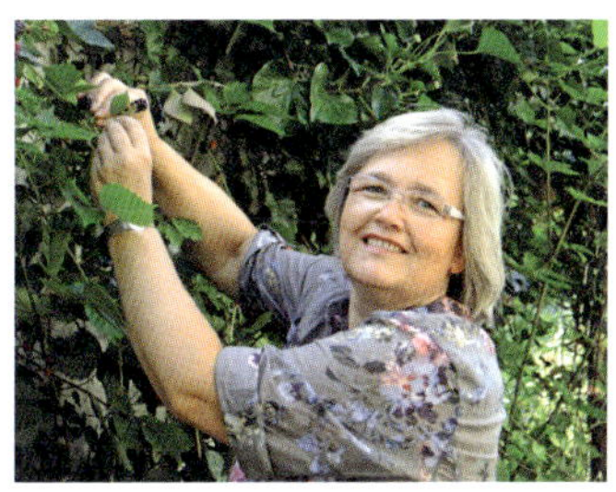
Karin Greiner

Als Diplom-Biologin und Dozentin gibt **Karin Greiner** ihr Wissen rund um Garten, Bäume, Blumen, Kräuter und Natur in Büchern und Zeitschriften, in Lehrgängen und Seminaren weiter, zudem ist sie als langjährige Pflanzenexpertin beim Rundfunksender *Bayern 1* bekannt. Seit 2008 führt sie den *Pflanzenlust*-Blog, in dem sie ihre Leidenschaft für die heimische Flora mit einem großen Publikum teilt.

Simone Braun is a high school teacher who explores the secrets of mathematics and physics with her students. In addition, the trained herbalism teacher and amateur photographer loves to discover the small and large wonders of nature along the roadside. She aims to encourage people to be curious about the complex world of botany and to take inspiration from the beauty and diversity of plants through walking tours and articles for a plant magazine.

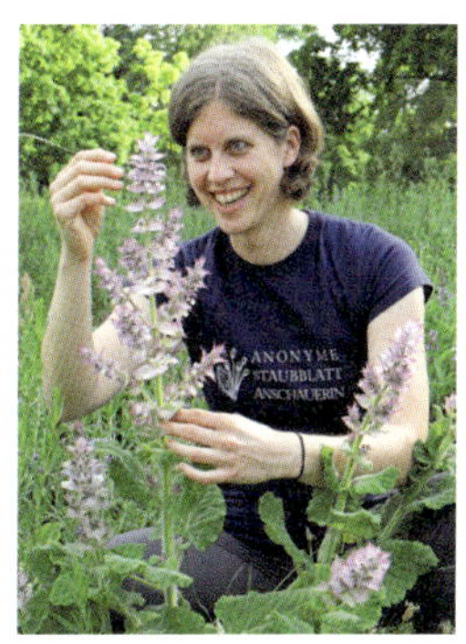
Simone Braun

Als Gymnasiallehrerin erforscht **Simone Braun** mit ihren Schülerinnen und Schülern die Geheimnisse der Mathematik und Physik. Darüber hinaus liebt es die ausgebildete Kräuterpädagogin und Hobbyfotografin, die kleinen und großen Wunder der Natur am Wegesrand zu entdecken. In Führungen und Artikeln für ein Pflanzenmagazin ermuntert sie Menschen, neugierig auf die Details und Zusammenhänge der Botanik zu blicken und sich von der Schönheit und Vielfalt der Pflanzenwelt begeistern zu lassen.

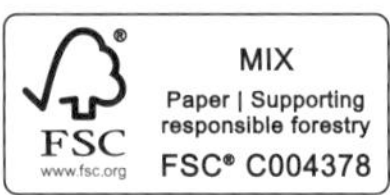

Published by teNeues Publishing Group

teNeues Verlag GmbH
Ohmstraße 8a
86199 Augsburg, Germany

Düsseldorf Office
Waldenburger Straße 13
41564 Kaarst, Germany
e-mail: books@teneues.com

Augsburg/München Office
Ohmstraße 8a
86199 Augsburg, Germany
e-mail: books@teneues.com

Press Department
e-mail: presse@teneues.com

teNeues Publishing Company
350 Seventh Avenue, Suite 301
New York, NY 10001, USA
Phone: +1-212-627-9090
Fax: +1-212-627-9511

www.teneues.com

teNeues Publishing Group
Augsburg / München
Berlin
Düsseldorf
London
New York

teNeues

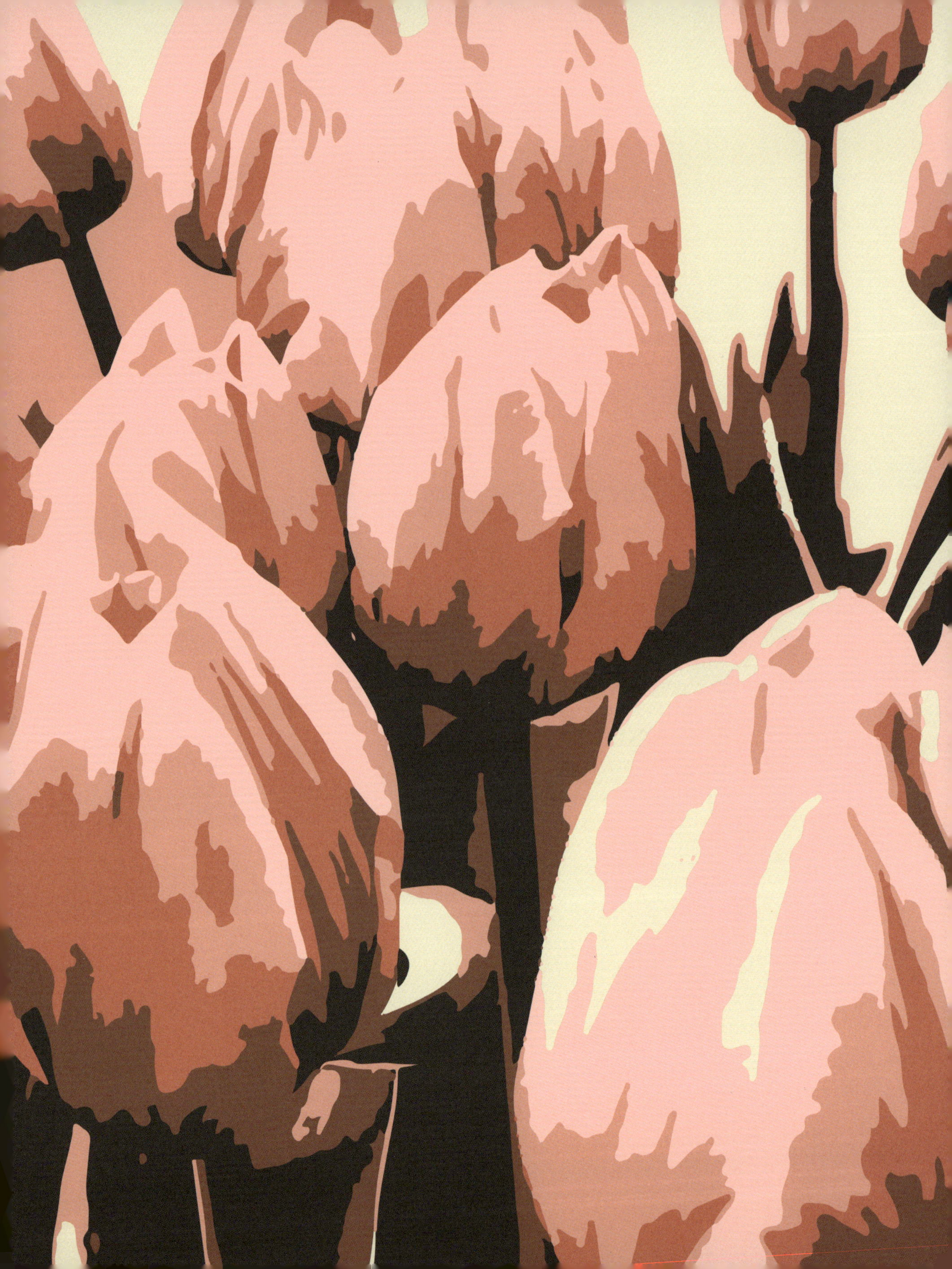